THE WIZARDS

THE WIZARDS

Millionaire Magicians
of the
Vancouver Stock Market

Michael Caldwell

Creative Classics Publications, Inc.

Creative Classics
8571 Ansell Place,
West Vancouver, B.C.
Canada, V7W 2W3

ISBN: 0-9692129-1-7
Caldwell, Michael, 1946–

THE WIZARDS . . . Millionaire magicians of the Vancouver stock market.

Graphics: Hartley and Marks
Printing: Hemlock Printers Ltd.
Edited by: Kathleen Caldwell
Photograph: "Gold bars/coins" provided by Ron Slenzak/Image Finders

Acknowledgement

*To my mother, Kathleen, who painstakingly tore down the structure
within and rebuilt it from the ground up . . . thank you.*

Contents

Foreword

While the remarkable figures in Vancouver's securities community provided the main inspiration for writing this book, their story would be less outstanding perhaps were it not for the Vancouver Stock Exchange, the unique marketplace in which they work. Now in its eighty-first year of operation, the Exchange has served as an important source of venture financing since its inception, and today plays a key role in the funding of new enterprise, both domestically and abroad.

As anyone who has ever watched the market knows, new businesses are highly speculative, making the market more volatile—and more controversial, as media coverage of Exchange activities amply demonstrates. Over the years Vancouver has been both praised and roundly criticized for its venture-capital focus, and for its approach to the regulatory challenges this kind of market presents. Yet the Exchange continues to grow and diversify, fired by the continuing need for venture capital and by the interest of small investors.

At no time has this interest been greater than during the past decade. Since 1978, the volume of shares traded annually on the Exchange has quadrupled, as has their value. Transactions have risen by fifty per cent. And most significantly, financings— the actual investment dollars raised from the public at large—have increased by almost eight times. This increase follows a general trend toward greater market participation on the part of Canadians country wide. But it also underlines the Exchange's accessibility to new-investor interests.

In fact its accessibility is precisely what makes Vancouver unique. As one of North America's largest and most diversified venture-capital markets, it gives small investors a chance to "play the market" by investing in promising new companies—at an average cost per share of less than two dollars, compared to $15 or more for blue-chip stocks. The risk involved in this type of investment is much higher, of course, but so are the potential rewards. Obviously, all successful companies have gone through such an initial start-up period also.

Through the years Vancouver has been associated with a number of such success stories, from Royalite Oil, Craigmont, Afton and Bethlehem Copper to Breakwater and, more recently, Glamis and International Corona. In virtually all cases the firms have been resource-based, starting as small exploration companies with nothing more than a promising property and the skills and aspirations of their principals and staff.

The drive for resource development was actually the original reason for establishing the Exchange in 1907. At that time European immigrants were swarming to western Canada by the thousands, and the area's abundant natural resources were serving as a dual source of employment and economic growth. As a means of stimulating this economic activity (and benefitting from it as well) twelve prominent members of the Vancouver business community petitioned the British Columbia Government to form a stock exchange and "prayed for its incorporation," according to the original act authorizing the Exchange's establishment.

At least one previous attempt had already been made to establish a Vancouver market, and competing exchanges in Victoria, Seattle and Portland also flourished briefly. Yet none survived save Vancouver—and it only barely during its first year of operation. In fact, days and even weeks went by between transactions during that first year. Coeur d'Alene, Dominion Trust and B.C. Permanent were among the primary stocks traded, along with Rex and Wonders, at one and two cents a share.

Early by-laws limited the number of Exchange members to thirty, and set the price of a seat at $250. Members also paid an annual subscription fee of $25, and a further monthly assessment based on the cost of keeping the Exchange open.

Trading in 1908 totalled $291,000 at year-end, more than double the 1907 figure, and continued to increase over the next several years, to such an extent that the Exchange was obliged to move to larger quarters (158 Hastings Street) in 1910. By that time, VSE seats were selling for $1,750 and membership had risen to thirty-five.

Four years later the discovery of petroleum in Alberta's Turner Valley put the Exchange on the map as an oil and gas trading centre, and, until the onset of the Great Depression in 1929, trading activity boomed. In response to this new growth, the Exchange moved again, three times in fact—first to Homer Street in 1918, then to 553 Granville Street in 1924, and finally to 475 Howe.

About this time a little publication called *Ticker Tape* was being prepared and distributed on a monthly basis to securities personnel in several cities across North America. It contained anecdotes, news about local staff, and short articles. The following article, regarding the wire services of the period, was written by C.H. Drake of the Miller, Court & Co. wire department and printed in the August 1929 issue:

"The Miller, Court & Co. wire department began a little over eighteen months ago with a "drop" on another broker's leased wire. Several months later, a private wire was installed, linking Winnipeg, Calgary, and Vancouver; almost exactly a year ago, a second circuit, connecting Victoria with the head office, and operated by keyboard telegraph machines, was placed in operation. This was the first teletype-operated circuit in Vancouver. Today the wire system comprises approximately six thousand miles of wire, and serves sixteen cities. And the wire companies are busy building more wires to be placed at our service when completed."

. . . . A telling commentary, is it not, on the extent of the electronic evolution the securities industry has since undergone, particularly during the past decade.

The stock market crash of 1929 saw trading values on the Exchange plummet from an all-time high of $133 million to a low of $2 million, and drop even further to $1.2 million a decade later with Canada's entry into World War II. In fact, trading on the Exchange was not to regain its original pre-crash momentum until the early 1960s, some thirty-five years after the event. Seat prices also vacillated during this period, of course, with seats selling at about $2,500 during the war.

The postwar years saw prosperity return to Vancouver with a steady rise in trading volumes and values. Seat prices increased gradually to $6,000 in 1960, then, with the advent of a mining boom, jumped to a record $65,000 in 1969. The Exchange also moved again, twice in fact—next door, to 540 Howe Street, in 1947 and down the block to 536 Howe Street in 1965. This growth continued at an accelerated pace during the 1970s, permitting Vancouver to establish MARS, its quotations service, and the VSE Service Corporation, its clearing and settlement facility. By 1980, it had forty-eight members, 1137 listed issues, and monthly trading volumes of just under 143.2 million shares on average, for an average monthly value of $368.3 million.

The historic crash of 1987 may well cause a significant slowdown of VSE activities. But it is far too early to make an assessment of its effect, as Vancouver and other markets worldwide strive to recoup their index percentage losses and return to normal trading.

Much of Vancouver's recent success can be attributed to its flexibility in adapting to several major trends across the securities industry. Like virtually all international businesses, the securities field has been considerably affected in recent years by the growth in electronic technology and the corresponding trend to globalization. These have influenced, and been influenced in turn by, the demand for venture capital worldwide, and subsequent competition among exchanges to capture this demand. Let us look now at each of these influences and the effect they have had on VSE operations.

Trend to Electronic Technology—The Exchange has long recognized the importance of computerization and telecommunications in its continued growth and, at the beginning of the 1980s, established technological change as a major Exchange priority. Since then it has computerized most of its internal operations and now plans to introduce automated trading to its Trade Floor.

VSE Board members and staff first became aware of the need to be updated in this area in the early 1980s. By that time trading at most major exchanges was at least partially computerized, and securities officials were talking about the eventual globalization of the industry through electronics. Vancouver had no desire to be left behind in this general industry trend, and in March 1985 the Board approved the allocation of half a million dollars to investigate the feasibility of automating the VSE Floor. Eighteen months later, in November 1986, it approved a further expenditure of $6 million to complete the project.

The Exchange now has installed its own unique computerized trading system, called Vancouver Computerized Trading or VCT. Scheduled for implementation in early 1988, it features a multi-functional or "smart" terminal which allows traders to conduct trades right into Vancouver's mainframe computer.

VCT's chief advantages are its speed and its ability to provide complete and timely depth-of-market information and quotations. This puts the Exchange on an equal footing with North America's other major markets, provides the basis for future global trading links, and enhances the VSE's credibility with the international investment community.

Trend to Internationalization—While investor interest from the United States and Europe has traditionally been a factor on the VSE, foreign investment was not significant until the early

1980s when American-based companies began to list in number on the Exchange, drawn by its less-stringent listing requirements and low listing costs. Today this U.S. group has so increased as to represent an estimated twenty per cent of the VSE's total listings base and the majority of international companies.

The rapid growth in American listings led Vancouver to establish a trading and settlement link with the Midwest Securities Trust Company/Midwest Clearing Corporation of Chicago in 1983. Called ACCESS (acronym for American and Canadian Connection for Efficient Securities Settlement) it joined the VSE's own clearing and settlement facility with a network of major clearing corporations and depositors across the U.S., ensuring settlement of all trans-border trades within the normal five-day period. ACCESS's popularity has grown steadily since its introduction, with more than thirty VSE member brokerages now participating in the service.

Also on the increase are the number of Asian-directed companies on the Exchange, part of a new international trend evidenced first in 1985 and of sufficient importance to Vancouver's growth that VSE representatives recently made a marketing trip to Hong Kong, expected to be the first of several such missions to Pacific Rim business centres.

A major impetus in the general movement toward internationalization has been the recent deregulation of markets across Canada. In British Columbia this took the form of a policy on deregulation published by the B.C. Securities Commission in February 1987, providing for the entry of foreign investment dealers as well as non-industry firms into the local securities market.

Demand for Venture Capital—Since 1980 the number of VSE listings has increased by more than 400 to 2,115, as small or beginning companies with properties in British Columbia, eastern Canada, the United States, Central America, Australia, Great Britain and southeast Asia have listed in increasing numbers on the Exchange. Most of these firms are involved in precious metals exploration and development, although several also have interests in oil, gas, and base metals exploration.

As its traditional resource listings base has continued to expand, the Exchange has also experienced an increase in its non-resource listings. Current non-resource companies total approximately seven hundred, and generally fall into the advanced technology or junior industrial category, with interest ranging from clothing and food production to computer software and hardware, medical research, and communications technology. Many of the firms are American-based or have American interests, and an increasing number have interests in the Pacific Rim.

Vancouver's long experience in junior resource financings has been a major factor in attracting non-resource companies to the Exchange. Through eighty years of operation, the VSE has accumulated considerable knowledge of small or emerging ventures and has fostered a general understanding and acceptance of small financings (those of $5 million or less) among investment professionals in the local community.

Increasing Competition—As demand for venture capital has continued worldwide, competition for venture business has increased, with several exchanges establishing second markets for junior firms. Technological innovation has only intensified this trend, as has deregulation, prompting the Exchange to establish a small options market and make services such as quotations a key priority.

VSE quotations are now available virtually worldwide, as a result of the Exchange's current involvement in the Consolidated Canadian Data Feed (CCDF). CCDF, developed jointly in 1984 by Toronto, Montreal, and Vancouver, combines the raw trading data from all three exchanges (plus Alberta) and transmits it within seconds through Toronto to New York, where it is accessed by major American and European quotations vendors and marketed abroad. Currently all seventeen of the world's major vendors carry CCDF. This includes Reuters, which picked up the feed in January 1987 and now sends it to an estimated 20,000 terminals in the United States, Europe and Asia.

Vancouver diversified into options in 1982 as a means of broadening its business base. Currently it is a member of two options networks, Trans Canada Options (TCO) for trading equity options and the International Options Clearing Corporation (IOCC) for trading commodity options in gold, silver, Canadian dollar currency and platinum.

The VSE joined TCO in 1983 as a full partner with the Toronto and Montreal Exchanges. Today it lists fourteen equity options classes, all exclusive to Vancouver. It joined IOCC in 1982. The IOCC network, one of a growing number of international trading systems, links Vancouver with the Montreal Exchange, the European Options Exchange in Amsterdam, and the Australian Exchange (Sydney) operation on a virtual 24-hour basis.

As the Vancouver Exchange moves ahead to the next decade and the next century, it plans to maintain its leading position in venture-capital markets and enhance its role in the global marketplace. In doing so the Exchange acknowledges its responsibility to uphold and, where possible, improve its regulation of listed companies, working with the B.C. Securities Commission and other regulatory bodies to ensure a fair marketplace.

New ventures, while their size and inexperience make them more volatile, are a critical component of both the domestic and international economies, spawning vitality, growth, and new direction. Nothing demonstrates this better than Vancouver's own history, and the experiences of some of the financial wizards who have contributed significantly to the growth of the Exchange over the past few decades.

These are their stories.

CHAPTER 1

Egil Lorntzsen

The rewards of persistence

If you have ever thought that all the golden opportunities have been taken; if you have ever felt that you can never hope to hit paydirt when the experts, with all their advantages, have failed, stop for a moment and consider the story of Egil Lorntzsen, and the piece of scrub timber and rock in B.C.'s wild interior that became Canada's biggest copper mine.

The feisty Lorntzsen has always been a maverick in the mining industry, a reputation he still maintains by offering his opinion, requested or otherwise, to anyone within earshot. His sometimes irascible manner and his lack of respect for conventional wisdom may have kept him from winning popularity contests among his peers, but no one can dispute the fact that his personal style has brought results.

Egil Lorntzsen and his wife Iris live in a more than comfortable home in the University of British Columbia area of Vancouver, purchased from Norman Keevil, Sr. His study is lined with mining manuals and survey records, the resource centre of a self-sufficient, self-educated man. This is as quiet and comfortable as Lorntzsen ever gets. A strapping Norwegian, well into his eighties and strong and healthy as a horse, Lorntzsen has always been more at home with a pack on his back out in the wilds than in a three-piece suit talking with the big-money boys.

His "nose" for mines is instinctive, a sense honed in his early days as a prospector tramping over every inch of countless claims. The single-mindedness and energy with which he tackles mine-finding projects have not diminished, even though he could certainly afford never to look at another core sample. He married the first pretty young woman to share a campfire with him, expecting her to fall into step with his breakneck pace, and this she has done with grace and wit. Typically, he had some ups (Tungsten King Mine) and some downs (a rough prospecting stint amid piranhas and bush snakes in Dutch Guiana) before hitting the big one. And he has been involved with some good properties since. But for Egil Lorntzsen there is only one mine and one story. He settles into the wing-back chair in front of the fireplace in his study and embarks on the story he has told so many times before, the story of Lornex.

When Lorntzsen returned to B.C. from his disappointing jungle experience in the late forties the economy was pretty tough, but interest in copper exploration in the Highland Valley area was running high. He headed for the hills again and staked his claim on the area that is now Lornex. "At that time," he explains, "several mining companies came in around that area. ASARCO (American Smelting & Refining Co.) was the first company that had an option on property around there. ASARCO was up drilling Bethlehem, and after spending one million dollars they backed out and left everything."

Lorntzsen knew the overburden on the Highland Valley claim necessitated the expensive drilling that only a larger, more experienced company could afford, so he went looking for a partner.

"Kennecott Copper spent a year in exploration and backed out—so I just kept on digging. The following year I got Noranda interested."

He was so confident about the Noranda team that he went home and told Iris, "I haven't been away from the hills now for so many years, how about us taking a trip to Europe?" As they toured, starting with a visit to Egil's homeland of Norway that he hadn't seen for thirty years and continuing to Sweden, Denmark, Austria, and Italy, they checked back on Noranda's progress. No news yet, but Lorntzsen's monthly cheque kept coming, so they extended their travels to Greece and the British Isles. On their return to B.C., Noranda told him, "It's a nice place to spend a summer, but we haven't come up with anything."

Another major firm, Anaconda, had an option on a nearby property and its chief geologist, Dr. Glen Waterman, agreed to study the documentation of the previous exploration teams.

"One day I got a call from Glen. He said, 'I want to meet with you at the Georgia Hotel.' I went rushing down to the hotel and he came in with a big brown envelope, the same one I had given him, with all the maps and information. He walked over to me and said, 'Egil, you've had three of the world's best exploration groups looking at your property. I think you must come to the conclusion that there's nothing there.' So I said to myself, 'it's about time I got off my fat ass and did something for myself.'"

The summer of 1964 saw Egil and Iris poking around on the property themselves. Egil was convinced the other mining companies had not done any "honest to God prospecting" and had missed the clues.

"On one area of the slope there was a long grade where they had done some soil sampling, but I saw a melt-water channel on the south side and a steep hill," he says. "Usually when you're tracking through the country you take the easiest going, which in this case was along the Skeena road to a plateau." Because of the difficulty of access, the ravine had probably not been covered by the previous teams. "This time I cut across the plateau so I was halfway up the hill, and I look across and see a lot of alteration. It didn't make sense. What's all that alteration doing in the moraine? I look down and notice a lot of broken granite that had no damn business in the moraine. So I cross the little creek and there was broken granite for almost 400 feet. I noticed that there wasn't any copper stain and there wasn't a single rock that had been broken.

"The other companies had taken samples everywhere, but they had a bunch of young students with no experience. They did exactly what they were told, took soil samples every hundred feet or so and went then back. They didn't notice that there weren't any copper stains. So I broke one rock and it was loaded with malachite, chalcopyrite, and specks of bornite. I showed Iris and she said, 'Well, they're pretty colours.'"

On the basis of these preliminary findings Egil set up a company which Iris named Lornex, after the first four letters of their name. "I looked around and found a fellow named Dave Ross who was interested in helping me raise some financing in trade for some stock." The two men found it tough going, however, because the majors had all given up on the area.

With the first $5,000 he was able to get his hands on, Lorntzsen acquired a bulldozer and brought it to the ravine where he had found the broken granite. They quickly uncovered what appeared to be a porphyry copper deposit. Lorntzsen hired geologists Gus Skerl and Bill White to examine the property, but again refused the advice of the experts when they suggested that he drill a couple of wire line holes on the site.

"I told Skerl, 'I'm going to take the cat and start trenching. If I can find by trenching that I have widespread mineralization here and that this is the beginning of a big porphyry deposit, then nobody will be afraid to put in a lot of drill holes. But putting in just two holes can break this property, especially after three major companies have already walked away from it.'"

Lorntzsen continued trenching and peeling away the fifty to one hundred feet of overburden along what would prove to be the Lornex Fault. He tested out the new overburden drill that Chester Millar was using in Kamloops and bought one to use at Lornex. With the drill results, financing started to come more easily.

Still skeptical that any major company could manage the exploration of Lornex as well as he could, Egil stipulated that only sixty per cent of the company was available to a major investor and that he was to have control of how the first $500,000 was to be spent. His associates scoffed at the idea, since the majors were used to getting seventy-five to eighty per cent. However, after some shrewd bargaining with Rio Algom, he got the deal he wanted, with Yukon Consolidated taking twenty-four per cent to Rio Algom's thirty-six per cent. Egil continued as president for two years, during which time work on the property progressed rapidly. In its heyday, the mine has processed up to 90,000 tons per day.

"It was no picnic being president of Lornex then," he once confided to financial writer Frank Keane. "A guy from the campfire rubbing elbows with some of the cleverest guys in the mining and financial business. Rio Algom was nothing but big lawyers. . . . They were very kind to me until they had invested enough money; then I was out, and was just a director." But Egil Lorntzsen had achieved what every prospector hopes for — he had found the big one and been rewarded very handsomely for it. Lornex shares have traded up to $80, and Egil and Iris have done well.

"Lornex was a fantastic experience but it shows how mines are lost due to lack of effort. They get cold feet too damn soon. I was talking about this over dinner with a mining engineer and his wife recently. Just for fun I pulled out some old records and found instances where the experts had passed up five of the most outstanding mines. It's fine to have these highly educated people and geniuses but they have to have persistence."

Persistence and the direct approach are the only ways Egil Lorntzsen knows. He was born in Norway, 240 miles north of the Arctic Circle, in a land where half-measures just don't exist. Winters are understandably cold and ice-bound, but, "In the summertime you have twenty-four hours of beautiful sunshine. It gets too damn hot, usually in the 70s."

The sea had been his family's way of life for generations, so after he had completed his education in commerce his father told him, "You go to sea and show me how you can save money and I'll help you start in business." After two seasons as a merchant seaman Egil decided the world had more to offer than a family business.

"So I jumped ship around St. Lucia," he recalls. "We had about a mile to swim to get to shore. My friend said, 'It's a long way. Are you a good swimmer?' I had never even swam around the ship. I said, 'I can't swim but salt water is buoyant. When I get tired, I'll just relax and keep on paddling.'" They made it to shore, but not to New Orleans where they had planned to go. Egil drifted north to Montreal, and then to B.C. where he crewed on salmon-fishing vessels. In the off-season, he took mining work.

In one of these jobs a fellow Scandinavian talked of heading out prospecting. It was an idea that immediately appealed to Lorntzsen's adventurous spirit, and changed the course of his life.

His first mine-finding success was Tungsten King, a small tungsten mine near Bridge River. With the passage of time, however, it became evident to Egil that the day-to-day management of a small labour-intensive operation was not for him. He sold his shares to his partner and returned to the prospecting that had become an absorbing interest.

One afternoon Egil returned to his camp to find visitors. Three hikers, two sisters and a male friend, asked if they could camp there for the night. The lively nature and irresistible smile of one of the young women did not go unnoticed by Egil.

The next time Egil went to Vancouver for supplies, his shopping list included "one wife"—if not in words, then certainly in thought. He took "a pretty little nurse" to the movies one night and there encountered one of the sisters he had met camping.

"Iris is back from school now. Why don't you drop in and see us?" she said. He accepted the invitation with alacrity—and Iris and Egil have been partners since 1945.

He heard of promising gold mining activities in South America and bought concessions in Dutch Guiana (now Surinam) and British Guiana (now Guyana). But the meagre amount of gold he found did not compensate for the hardships and expense and he returned to B.C.

With the success of Lornex a few years later Egil could have retired, but he has continued to work and to educate himself through books and travel. He and Iris have travelled the world, although, to Iris's dismay, these travels have inevitably included tours of the local mines. And he has continued to prospect and Iris has gone along every step of the way, albeit reluctantly at times. "Once she was camping with me, sleeping on an air mattress in this little pup tent. The air mattress was hard and cold and every time she rolled over it made a hell of a noise. She said, 'You've always tried to make an outdoor girl out of me, and I hate it!'"

His latest project is Plumbago Mine in Sierra County, California, a gold mine operated by his own company, Norsemont Mining Corporation. When sending out their Christmas cards for 1986, Egil included a picture of Plumbago and a short message he penned himself that summed up his feelings about his life's vocation—and avocation:

> "A mine is a precious lady endowed with the
> riches of nature. Believe and have faith in
> her—give her some attention and time and she
> will reward your efforts with the bountiful
> harvest of the earth."

"A mine is a precious lady... humph!" Iris commented scornfully when she read it. "A mine is a hole in the ground with a bunch of liars on top."

CHAPTER 2

Bern Brynelsen

Never a dull moment

Bern Brynelsen is not about to stop yet. At seventy-five he looks sixty and his Scandinavian ruggedness and vigour pour forth in a booming laugh that sets the china rattling. That Noranda has been called "after Canadian Pacific, the greatest company in Canada," that the Vancouver Stock Exchange has grown to its present stature on the strength of its early mining successes, these incontrovertible facts are largely due to the ground-breaking efforts of men like Bern. He calls himself re-tired, but in truth he has just backed off a step or two. His only concession to advancing age is that he now hosts, by telephone from the kitchen table, board meetings of some of the twenty-five or so companies in which he holds directorships.

"What else is there to do?" he asks. "I have fun. I'm on that telephone from six o'clock every morning. Something's always going on somewhere. People phone me and they've got a new project or property. I can't help it—I've got to go and take a look at it."

Bern's simple tastes have stayed resolutely constant through his dynamic rise in business fortune; he still lives in the same modest home he bought early in his career. Many of his memberships in the exclusive local clubs have ripened to honorary lifetime status, but he insists he hates long luncheons and that one game of golf per year is all he can stand. "I can't relax too long. Honest to God, I can't," he says somewhat apologetically. "I couldn't stay around here for a week and do nothing. It would drive me nuts."

After this cup of coffee he is driving to Seattle. This compulsive pace that he still so willingly thrives on demonstrates that it's the hunt and not the prize that has kept him hard at work for six decades.

Ever the company man, Bern still keeps Noranda apprised of opportunities that he comes across in his travels. Noranda has always had first refusal and always will.

Today mining explorations depend on well-informed sleuthing, a scrupulous digging through old records for clues that may have evaded previous investigations or for abandoned projects that now have potential, due to improved technology. For Bern exploration was always guided by a gut feeling that was developed over years of criss-crossing wilderness country, where a gravel road was considered downright luxury.

Bern Brynelsen *was* Noranda in the West, from the company's initial acquisition of Quebec Gold Mining in 1948 until his retirement in 1975. When Noranda took over Quebec Gold it took over Bern as well. "That's how it started. I was alone out west here for many years as explorations engineer. I looked after the western United States, too. Anywhere. They sent me all over the world."

A tough pioneering spirit has helped Bern outlive most of his contemporaries. "I guess we're one of the very few old families left in Vancouver," he surmises.

Bernard Orlande Brynelsen was born in the family house on Prior Street that his grandfather built shortly after coming to Vancouver in 1886. Grandfather Brynelsen had the first tugboat in Vancouver. "He also had a little fishboat and he used to bring it right up to the house on Prior Street," Bern recalls. "I think the house is a heritage building of some sort now. I notice it's all painted."

Bern's father worked for B.C. Electric, tending the city's early street-lamp system. As soon as Bern was old enough, he

went out fishing in the summers to earn money for his own education. And even as a fifteen-year-old rookie, he commanded a
respect that would later put him in positions of authority over
older and more experienced men.

Bern started out as a cook. Since his first three near-lethal
weeks, working in a tiny galley continually filled with fumes
from the old Scott gas engine, he has never again felt a twinge
of seasickness.

On one of his first trips halibut fishing out of Barclay Sound,
the boat was in Port Alberni for a twenty-four hour layover on a
Saturday night. The skipper sent young Bern to round up the
rest of the crew and bring them back. As Bern looked over the
swinging doors of the saloon he could see his crew-mates sitting
with some other fishermen, evidently there for the duration.

"You're supposed to come back to the boat now," he announced to them. "Skipper wants to make an early start tomorrow."

"You're not going to take orders from a kid, are you?" one of
their friends taunted and, towering over young Bern, he helped
himself to a couple of hammy handfuls of Bern's shirt.

"Now I was a good size, even at fifteen," he recalls. "I didn't
have this," patting his spare tire, "but I was still a solid 210 or
220 pounds. So I thought I might as well give him one while I
had the chance."

A neat, quick uppercut from nowhere sent the man sailing
right over the table and out cold on the floor. His buddies threw
beer on him but Bern saw no reason to wait for his recovery. He
departed from the saloon forthwith and fled back to the boat,
his crew-mates close behind.

A couple of weeks later the same scene was waiting for Bern
as he looked over the saloon doors to round up the crew again.
Feeling certain he was now going to get his comeuppance, he
summoned all his courage to stride in and deliver the skipper's
orders. Then, looking over at his nemesis, he added, "And what
are you going to do about it?"

The man didn't budge from his chair.

Bern fished his way through his first couple of years of university, switching over to stints up north in placer mining de-

velopments in the Dawson and Atlin areas as he gained scholastic credentials in engineering. "In '35 I graduated and then took a year's extra work in geology. That's the year I was president of the student body. Got my mining degree; never did get my geology degree. It was more fun being president."

In 1985 his class held their fiftieth anniversary reunion. As he toured the campus for the first time since he was a student, and reminisced with his classmates, memories came back to him, of being dubbed the "Golden Blond," and of immersing himself in fundraising activities to build the Students' Union Building. "I think that's where I started being a promoter," he concludes.

After graduating, he spent the next four years in the isolation of the Yukon Territories, running the Polaris Taku mine. "That was the first property that I actually put into production. Grassroots right through. It was good experience."

More than good experience, it taught many aspects of mining that the university texts had not: being cut off from the outside world for weeks at a time during the stormy winters; sending concentrates down the river on the old *Princess Louise* in the summer months; lengthening the airstrip and setting up an extra wireless in readiness for war; rounding up the drunken miners from the red-light district of Juneau, Alaska, escorting them back to camp and going back to Juneau for more; and filling in on every odd job, from cook's helper to anaesthesiologist.

Bern tried to run a booze-free camp, and had the miners' private stock confiscated at the Customs office seven miles down river. Bill Wilson, the Customs official, would put the bottles on a shelf with the owners' names on them and the men were free to walk down and have a drink anytime. Seven miles down for one drink (all they were allowed) and seven miles back. Such was the social life at Polaris Taku.

Arbitrating squabbles among the 350 men in camp was all part of a day's job, and often the desperation of such a bleak existence erupted with the full force of pent-up frustration and misguided energy. One Christmas morning the foreman showed up at Bern's door saying, "You've got to come down, there's havoc down at the bunkhouse."

"The only liquor that would come in, the Indians would have smuggled up," Bern explains. "But this one shaft crew, they had everything: alcohol, shaving lotion, vanilla extract, the whole works. They had saved all this stuff up for Christmas, in one big barrel. The most awful stuff you ever saw. I hadn't known about it because they were very careful.

"Christmas was the one day we had off in 365 days and when I got down there all the crews were outside."

"There's a gang of them upstairs and they have axes. They're killing each other," the men told Bern.

"I grabbed a club and went up to the third floor. I was scared as hell but I had to do this. Nobody else would do it. I got up there and there wasn't a soul around. Everything was quiet. I started down the hall quietly.

"Then all of a sudden, a guy came out. It was Bill McInnes — I'll never forget as long as I live. He came around the corner and he had this great big axe raised. I was really scared, but I roared like a bull, 'Bill McInnes drop that damn axe!'

"He stood there and then, by God, he dropped the axe. I said, 'All right, the rest of you, come out now,' And they all came out like little lambs. Then I saw this stuff they were drinking. . . . Do you know, they damn near died? They broke out in rashes later and everything."

Bern settles back and chuckles. "It's been an exciting life. It really has."

When the *Princess Louise* came up for sale on her retirement from coastal duties, Bern and a young promoter named Ted Turton bought her and turned her into a restaurant in Los Angeles.

"We lost a lot of money on her but I had travelled so many years on her all through my university days, going up to Alaska and the Yukon Territories, and all those years that I ran the mines. Every ten days regular, taking concentrates and stuff."

Bern married his university sweetheart and took her with him to Polaris Taku for the last year he was there. They started married life in a tent, until a house could be arranged for. Later that year Bern was sent to operate a tungsten property. (Tungsten was in new demand for the war effort.)

The war was heavily on the men's minds at that time. Most of the miners went into the Paratroopers and Bern wanted very much to follow, but a chip in his spine kept him home. Instead he served in the Royal Officers Training Corps, and later oversaw the blasting for all gun emplacements on the west coast.

Here again, Bern showed a knack for getting his way. His jolly, easy-going demeanour often belied a serious intent. During his blasting assignments he occasionally had to ask that vehicles be moved. He asked only once; then he blasted.

"I'll never forget when I first started blasting this big underground tunnel in Victoria. There was a small dry-dock that was opposite it. I had put up all my breaks and things to keep the debris from scattering all over. Then I went up and told the commander I was going to blast and to move the people away from there. And be damned if he would listen. Never did a darned thing about it. So I had my own men move them and I let my blast off. Well, do you know, it set off the alarm on the whole coast. They thought they were being bombarded!" It's the kind of story Bern loves to tell.

Then it was back to mining, first with Quebec Gold and later with Noranda. It was originally planned that Bern would go back to Toronto but he dug in his heels. Noranda relented and soon found that this lone wolf did his best work when left to his own devices. "So I headed the whole operation out here. Archie Bell looked after the East. Together, we put a lot of companies, a few major mines, into production. And one of them was Brenda. Still operating."

Brenda is an oft-recurring name in Bern's conversation, a happy testament to the Bern Brynelsen style. Bern took Brenda on originally on his own initiative.

"I used to go and do everything and then tell them about it afterwards. I don't think I ever wrote a report in my life," he says with a flash of pride.

Bern had visited and laid claims on many of the open-pit properties in B.C. over the years but could not get Noranda interested. They were more at home with the underground-mining techniques that had worked so well for them in the east.

"One day Mr. Bradfield called me. He and Dick Urquhart

were both engineers. They were the old-style boys; that's why they used to tolerate me, you see."

According to Bern, John Bradfield, Noranda's president, told him, "On that Brenda thing, please don't spend any more of our money. It will never make a mine. How can you work such a low-grade mine?"

"Can I have it?" Bern asked.

"Do what you want with it," was the reply.

"So I formed Brenda Mines, a little public company. I think I mortgaged my house or something to put some money into it. I got the Japanese to put money in. Nippon Mining Company put some funds in and we raised some money on the Stock Exchange and went public. I think our original shares were twenty cents a share. Ted Turton and Peter Brown were involved in those days.

"We drilled, and put a 100-ton-a-day mill in for big bulk sand. Meantime Noranda watched it like a hawk. They didn't put up any money at all.

"And we did it. I guess it's the lowest-grade open-pit mine in the world. Thirty thousand tons a day out of there. The grade is low but I think it was just well operated."

It was not long before all the major companies became interested in Brenda: Placer, Power Corporation and, of course, Noranda.

A deal was eventually made with Noranda but, "They had to buy their way into it. They only bought 51 per cent but it cost them about $8 a share at that time to get into position. They had to put a lot of money into it. We had built the whole thing and spent about $75 million, I think.

"I remember our stock on the market," Bern says happily. "It's funny how markets are. That damn stock was going up about a dollar a day. You know, everyday you'd become a millionaire again. It's the funniest thing in the world." He roars with laughter and then grows serious again.

"But it's all paper. I found that out in life. You know, with all the money I've made and lost I've never changed my method of living."

That method of living was one of being on the road constantly, visiting operations and scouting new properties, of travelling fifty to sixty thousand miles a year, driving all night and working all day, then—on to the next site. His marriage could not survive this peripatetic life, although his only daughter, Karen, has inherited Bern's wanderlust. As the only female jet pilot in British Columbia's emergency air service, she has logged over six thousand flying hours.

On some of these trips Bern had the brass from back east along for a tour of the western operations. J.Y. Murdoch, vice president, and Dick Urquhart, senior director, came through often and always sent a case of their favourite Scotch on ahead to sustain them on their rounds. Bern would meet them in Prince George, load the case of whisky in his rumble seat and off they'd go.

Murdoch and Urquhart soon discovered one of life's purest pleasures was good Scotch mixed with branch water from a fresh stream.

"We'd come to a point where there was a creek down below, and they'd want a little drink. I'd have to climb down and get them branch water. They'd want to stop half a dozen times before we reached Quesnel.

"Eventually, I thought, to hell with this noise, so I got a Thermos bottle. You want water. Here's water."

But no, bottled water just did not measure up to the superior flavour of fresh branch water that had just minutes before been racing along on its way to the sea.

"This went on for all the years that I had to take them through. And they wouldn't accept the Thermos flask. I found out that the devils were timing me to see how fast I could go down and come back up again with the water. They were laughing over it."

It was on one of those trips that Bern encountered two out-of-work miners in Williams Lake. "They were drunk as dogs, but boy, I sure needed miners. So, I remember, I had these two get in at the gas station. I had the Scotch in the rumble seat—and the two miners. Then I picked up Mr. Urquhart and Mr. Murdoch and they sat in the front with me.

"Urquhart asked me what these two unkempt individuals

were doing in the car with them, and I said, 'Well, they're miners. I'm taking them with us.'"

This threatened to upset the symmetry and comfortable flow of the whole routine. Besides, they would have to share their whisky.

"I don't want these men going out with us," Murdoch announced, and suggested other arrangements be made for them.

"I was a little bit hostile and I said, 'Mr. Murdoch, they're more valuable to me at the mine than you are. I have to get them. If I don't, we can't operate.'

"Murdoch laughed like hell. Sure enough, he cracked a bottle of Scotch and they drank it all the way to the mine. When he went back to Toronto, he told all the directors that story. I think my prestige went up a lot with that.

"They were wonderful people. You couldn't work for finer people in your whole life than the old-style board of directors."

Bern maintains that things have changed dramatically; an organization couldn't run today as Noranda was run in his day. He was able to pick up the phone and get Bradfield's decision on an issue at any time. He never worked to a budget and indeed wouldn't have known what to do with one, he says.

Bern then thunders, "All I knew was that when you want to do something, you do it. Go after it. To hell with it. It's all run by lawyers and accountants today."

This typifies Brynelsen's philosophy that "mining people are different." He was known for hiring men early in their careers and molding them into an intensely loyal and dedicated team. Though Bern waxes nostalgic about lost magic, the Noranda of his day is not unlike the small, ambitious companies leading today's market.

Bern and Ted Turton, who is now the flamboyant chairman of Canarim Investment Corporation, were also involved in a small company called Bermuda Resources, which had taken an option on a coal deposit near the rail line in Chetwynd.

Bern recalls: "I had hired two chaps from Pennsylvania, coal experts, university types. They took a sabbatical of three months to come out and tell us all about coal, I guess. I'm not a coal man. I'm a geologist, but not a coal man."

It was only a matter of two or three days before the learned opinion came back from these gentlemen that the coal deposit was worthless.

"I'd paid them for three months' work and I didn't know what the hell to do with them, so I said, 'Why don't you just look around the country. Size it all up. See if there's a big coal basin or something.' They did. They poled around in that whole area."

The coal experts later came back and reported on a particular site in the same general region. "You know," they said, "you've got the earmarks of a major coal basin here. We really should drill a hole."

The spot that was suggested was not accessible by road, and on the basis of the previous bad news Bern was not about to incur the costs of road-building on speculation. "So I got an old logging map and found where all the old logging roads were. I picked one spot and said, 'Here. Let's drill here.'

"We drilled down about a thousand feet, I guess. Jesus, we had some of the nicest coal seams in the country. Top quality coal. So we staked a hundred square miles in square-mile blocks. That was Bermuda Resources."

Eventually Teck Corporation bought out Bermuda Resources and when Bern found himself on the Teck board of directors, he got out. "I could never work for anybody other than Noranda. I was more like a partner, I guess."

That Noranda loyalty shines through again . . . a loyalty that goes beyond corner offices and brass nameplates. In fact, Bern cannot recall what his exact title was ("Western Manager or something . . . instead of giving you a raise, they'd name a mine after you"). He worked for Noranda as if it were his own company, and went the distance when it came to venturing into new territories. It was Bern who put Noranda into forestry; now, with major holdings like MacMillan Bloedel, Noranda's forest-products arm is just as important as its mining strength.

Bern had had his eye on the potentials of the forest industry for some time and had taken as a green light a comment by John Bradfield that "someday we're going to have to diversify into other natural resources." He heard that National Forest Products, which owned Fraser Mills in Prince George and some other interior mills, was having a tough struggle. When Fraser Mills closed down, Bern started investigating their forest and timber lands. "I went to Victoria and got all the data I could on all the forest lands. I really went to bat on it because I had always wanted the company to get into that business."

Ray Williston was B.C. Minister of Resources at that time and his riding was Prince George, so he was happy to cooperate with Bern in getting something going for the troubled sawmill. "I designed a whole program and had it pretty well lined up to present to the Board of Directors. I was in Williston's office when Alf Powis called me from Toronto. I was just about to go back east."

Powis, then secretary to the president, said, "Bern, don't bother coming back. The Board of Directors aren't going to go for this forestry thing. It's three million dollars. The directors feel we just don't know enough about logging."

"I hopped a plane and went straight to Toronto," Bern recounts. The next morning, after travelling through the night, unshaven and wearing the same clothes he had started out in back in Victoria, he delivered his pitch to the directors.

An old fishing contact helped him out here. Bern had been close friends with Gordon Gibson and his family since his fishing days and the connection had come in handy when Noranda was mining near Gibson's logging operation at Jeune Landing. At this point the venerable "Bull of the Woods" had just sold Tahsis Logging for $20 million and was doing his best to keep the legislature lively in his capacity as Liberal M.L.A., but he was bored. Gordon was happy to help Bern hammer out a proposal for National Forest Products. Gordon had sensed its potential and offered to invest in the deal. Bern asked Gordon for a letter of intent, mainly to keep him temporarily at bay.

"I knew damn well I would never use the letter. If I mentioned his name to Williston they would never let me in because they were mad as hell at Gordon, and if they thought he was part of it we'd never get our timber licenses."

But Bern happened to have the letter in his briefcase when he faced the Noranda directors. And he played it like a trump card, saying casually, "By the way, Gordon Gibson wants it, too. I've got a letter here that says he wants to buy fifty per cent. See for yourself."

Noranda was in the forestry business.

Later, in 1983, when Noranda's diversification helped it survive some serious recessionary losses, current president Adam Zimmerman commented, "That's the principal virtue of this company— we have a number of different legs."

When Bern joined Noranda it was a localized Ontario mining operation. When he retired it was international in scope, and had expanded into forest products, natural gas, oil, and manufacturing. He saw young hotshots like Adam Zimmerman and Alf Powis come in and work their way up to president and chairman, respectively. He helped create the corporate culture that has identified Noranda as "an athletic company—lean, fleet and daring... whose secret to success has been its sportive, risk-taking cockiness."

Bern and his eastern counterpart, Archie Bell, retired at the same time, in 1975. Noranda formed a company called B & B which stands for Bell and Brynelsen. "We call it the two B.S. Boys," Bern jokes. In this way, Noranda ensured that the two men would remain committed through their retirement. But Noranda need not have worried.

"They said, 'We can't afford to have you go and consult for anybody else. You two go where you want, do what you want. You can have all the money you want, anything you want. Just go and find more mines!' So we had some fun years."

Due to the financial difficulties of 1981–82, Noranda was not always able to act on the proposals that Bell and Brynelsen brought forward. One example is Viceroy, one of the biggest open-pit gold mines in the United States, which trades on the Vancouver Stock Exchange. When Noranda could not take advantage of it, B & B went public with it themselves.

Bern is now simplifying his life by putting his diverse holdings into what he claims is his last company, Bryndon. One of the properties, Rossland Mines, had been gathering dust since Bern's Quebec Gold days. "We did some work but the price of silver and lead fell down. Copper, too. Alex Fisher, the lawyer, and I kind of forgot about it in a way. But recently, I was collecting everything I had together. Alex said, 'Well, you'd better do something with this.' So I put it in with Bryndon. Now we're working up here in Rossland Camp. That's on the Alberta Exchange."

Bryndon also owns some gas properties that have a built-in customer in Noranda. "I guess Bryndon is the first company I know of that goes on the Exchange with a cash flow. So it's a beautiful little company in that sense. But that's the connection. The Noranda connections are very loyal."

Bern looks back on a full, active life, ticking off major mines like Yreka, Bell Copper, Brenda and Boss Mountain as his personal successes. He was also involved in the founding stages of Simon Fraser University, the Bank of British Columbia, Alaska Airlines and a rock-wool industry for the province. He's "proud as hell" that his daughter has pursued her own highly challenging path in a career where his influence would not have opened any doors even if it had been wanted. He and his daughter try to talk on the phone everyday, an occasionally tricky undertaking considering their high-mileage lifestyles.

He only looks at the projects that interest him and moves on when they get bogged down in detail and stop being fun. He's only home as long as it takes to repack a suitcase and catch up on the news. For Bern, the creative process of work is life's main joy and he isn't about to stop yet.

———

CHAPTER 3

Jack McLallen and Pat Reynolds

Two for the money

"This book may in part commemorate the great mining men of the past," said the writer, "such as Spud Huestis and Morris Menzies. But what it's really about is the live ones."

"Don't be too sure," said Pat Reynolds, "until you've talked to us."

———

Although this story is really about Jack McLallen and Pat Reynolds, in a more basic sense it is about Spud Huestis, a grass-roots prospector, a real mule-and-pickaxe original who had an unusual vision.

To paraphrase Robert Kennedy, where others looked at tough metal prices and asked "Why?," Huestis looked at low-grade open-pit copper and said "Why not?"

Early in the fifties when copper was selling at marketable levels, Huestis recognized the economic potential that could usher in a record period of B.C. mining development during the sixties and seventies. And that did come to pass—to a greater extent even than he had envisaged. Then world base-metal prices moved downward again, against the trend, and shifted the hunt by big companies and small alike once more to precious metals. . . .

It was Pat Reynolds who worked with Huestis to stake much of the Bethlehem Copper property, and Jack McLallen who worked in the background. With his brothers, McLallen supplied the initial financing for the mammoth Bethlehem project and for many that followed.

But to speak of the Bethlehem saga is to leap-frog the story of two men who literally grew up with modern mining in B.C. If Spud Huestis was a prospector with a vision, Reynolds and McLallen were entrepreneurs who made that vision happen—not just once, but many times over.

Pat Reynolds was a Vancouver native who never dreamed, in his position as controller of Ferguson Trucking on Vancouver's Main Street during the late forties, that he would ever be involved in anything as exotic as the mining business, and certainly he did not dream that he would one day become president of a huge low-grade copper operation.

But in 1951, at the age of thirty-eight, Reynolds made his first formative move when he resigned from the trucking company in order to open his own chartered accountancy practice. That turned out to have been a wise decision. Things began to happen almost immediately, notably with clients beginning to appear in numbers from the mining industry. Jack McLallen walked in one day and gave him some work to do. Shortly afterward Reynolds met Spud Huestis, and a relationship began that ultimately led to their staking properties together on many occasions.

McLallen, a native of Illinois, had arrived in Vancouver much earlier, in 1927, and was by this time deeply entrenched in the timber and lumber industry. In fact, by the time of his meeting with Reynolds he had already become a reasonably wealthy man (a circumstance which enabled him later to invest heavily in mining projects). He had acquired Capilano Timber, a logging and sawmill operation that employed over five hundred men, and he managed it for many years.

It was many years in fact before McLallen found himself

with time for the mining business. In the forties, he took over a shingle mill near Hastings Park, and then another, the Brunette Mill, which was a big step toward achieving a dominant position in the Lower Mainland shingle industry. (Later events illustrate that this was just one of the situations where McLallen knew when to get in, and more important, when to get out.)

McBride Lumber, a sizable company that occupied an entire city block close to where the PNE grounds are today, was then acquired for the princely sum of $60,000. In pre-war Vancouver, in fact, that was a king's ransom.

In the early fifties McLallen, teaming up with his brothers, diversified into construction projects in the eastern States: the first Howard Johnston Motel, a shopping centre in Nashville, a large plaza in Memphis. It may have been the death of his older brother in 1954 that caused him to pull back into the familiar B.C. businesses in which he had been involved.

.O. Henry's three wise guys of Bethlehem, Pennsylvania, were dummies compared with the three wise entrepreneurs who floated B.C.'s Bethlehem Copper. Huestis, McLallen and Reynolds came together in the early fifties and created the collective energy that produced the unprecedented open-pit operation.

The huge ore body had taken shape many years before—200 million years before, as a matter of fact—when a deep molten mass of the metal burst through the earth's crust, cooled and became a mineral deposit.

It was not until 1899 that humans first detected signs of this mineralization. Prospectors who continually expected the rich traces they turned up sporadically to lead to a mother lode were just as continually disappointed. It remained for a certain prospector more than fifty years later to reason that low-grade copper, if there were enough of it, could be economic, and that prospector was Spud Huestis.

The fact that Huestis had taken on Pat Reynolds as his accountant and financial adviser proved fortunate for both. Just as Reynolds introduced Huestis to the intricacies of finance, Reynolds was introduced through this relationship to mining, an unknown world for him up until this point.

So the initial partnership was born that was to develop Bethlehem Copper. The only other ingredients necessary—entrepreneurial experience and financial backing—were put in place when the two were joined by Jack McLallen, the successful lumber and construction executive.

A novel characteristic of this partnership was the complete mutual confidence and trust shown by each to the other two, as if they had been close friends all their lives. If one or two members of the group, usually Huestis and Reynolds, staked a given property, it was done with absolute equality, usually in five names, giving equal holdings to the trio and McLallen's two brothers. Although from widely-varied backgrounds, the partners were all men of the old school, honest first, ambitious second.

Pat Reynolds sums it up in his own way. "Jack and I have been friends for thirty-five years. I can't remember even a word of disagreement."

The partnership came into being in 1954, with the Bethlehem project as its focal point. The enthusiasm might not have run as high as it did had they known that there were eight years of tough, frustrating work ahead before the big mine would reach the production phase.

First there was the matter of feasibility. They made an intensive study of other successful open-pit operations in the southwestern States, Chile, and Peru—other mines that had utilized the principle that sheer volume could overcome the problem of low-grade ore.

When the decision was made to follow the open-pit route, the "Catch 22" was that the highly-automated, sophisticated equipment necessary to make it successful was extremely expensive. And the partnership found that Canadian investors were hesitant because it was the first project of its kind in Canada utilizing a low-grade, high-volume open pit. As new technology, open-pit copper mining in the fifties was as rare as the heap leaching of gold was to be at the beginning of the eighties.

So sponsorship, hesitant at home, was sought elsewhere. Initially ASARCO, the huge American natural resource conglomerate, showed some interest and discussed a tentative agreement. But the deal never came to fruition.

It was 1958 when that plan fell through, and it was two more blood-sweat-and-tears years, following another abortive attempt to interest Canadian institutions, before the Sunimoto Group of Japan after extensive investigation committed sufficient funds to take Bethlehem into production. Sunimoto's eventual equity position amounted to twenty-five per cent of Bethlehem's total share capital.

The first shipment of copper concentrate from the Bethlehem project left the Highland Valley in the winter of 1962. It was a new kind of mining operation for the Canadian economy, and set a pattern that others were to follow for the next two decades.

Bethlehem's process, which reduced low-grade copper ore to an economic concentrate, was a two-phase operation, with huge trucks loading out both ore and waste rock. The latter was carried to a tailings dam, where it was joined by additional waste material from the concentrator's flotation cells. The ore was transported to a series of crushers, passed on to grinding mills, subjected to flotation and filtering, dried, and passed to a storage bin, from which it was trucked, trained and shipped to Bethlehem's offshore customers, largely, at least in the beginning, in Japan.

At first a curiosity in the Canadian industry, Bethlehem became a model for other low-grade copper operations such as Lornex and Brameda. Average grade ran about 0.5%, which meant about 10 pounds of copper from every ton of ore mined. It is evident why it was necessary to develop a highly-mechanized process that would process huge volumes of ore.

Open-pit technology, the partners discovered, is extremely intricate, requiring a very careful, involved mine design. Briefly, the open pit is developed according to the heaviest concentrations of mineralization, and from the top down. A series of levels is created, with benches being uncovered in gradually decreasing circumference as the pit is excavated. At each level, ore and waste rock are broken up and trucked away.

From the beginning the Bethlehem mine consisted of two pits, the Huestis pit and the Jersey pit, separated by about 500 feet of non-mineralized rock. The Jersey Mine, the oldest and largest, began at the top with a diameter of approximately 3,000 feet. It went down for 1,000 feet and yielded about 60 million tons of ore. Even at 60 cents a pound, the copper price level that drove many copper mines out of business, that volume of production represents a huge total cash flow.

Other substantial shareholders subsequently invested in the Bethlehem mine. Granges, the subsidiary in Canada for the Swedish company of the same name, acquired twenty-five per cent, and Newmont Mining came on for twenty-three per cent. Credibility seemed to follow success.

The secret of profitability for a low-grade copper operation lay in the ease of separating the light incidence of metal within the volume of host rock. "Flotation" was the magic word.

In this process, a small quantity of organic chemical is introduced to the solution that has been created out of the ore. This chemical coats the small particles of copper, creating an affinity for an air surface. A mass of small air bubbles is injected into the solution and the copper particles are literally floated out. Four repeated stages of this flotation are necessary to produce the required concentrate, which can then be dried and shipped.

It was much later that McLallen, Reynolds, and Huestis gave up their position in Bethlehem. McLallen had been at first president and then chairman of the board. Pat Reynolds, at first secretary of the company, succeeded McLallen as president. Spud Huestis, the visionary prospector who had staked most of the ground on which Bethlehem realized its success, lived to see the big mine a huge financial triumph before his untimely death from cancer in 1980.

The partners remained at the helm until 1980, at which time they sold their shareholdings to Cominco. "It was a good offer," recalls Reynolds. "They paid us $17 when the stock was trading at $12."

In the timing of this sale Reynolds and McLallen showed judgment as keen as that shown in the original decision to take Bethlehem to production. In short, their getting out was as well-timed as had been their getting in. Shortly thereafter, in the early eighties, the world price of copper began to drop, eventually rendering most copper mines around the world uneconomic.

In the meantime, however, the partners had not been letting any grass grow under their feet. Even while Bethlehem had commanded most of their attention they had been deeply involved with another project, Western Mines.

It is always rewarding—perhaps because it has a certain Horatio Alger tinge to it—when prospectors and grubstakers hang right in through exploration, discovery, development and production, especially with one of the big ones such as Bethlehem Copper. Often, though, at some point they sell it off, sometimes for cash, sometimes retaining stock as they let professional management run with it. One such case was Reynolds's and McLallen's participation in the Western Mines property at Buttle Lake.

Some years ago, Pat Reynolds wrote Jack McLallen a long memo on the subject, solely to fix for both of them (and posterity) the chronology of the Buttle Lake project. Even then, Reynolds admitted, he could not be definite as to the actual dates involved. The period commenced in the late fifties, however, precisely when the group was totally preoccupied with the financing of Bethlehem, which may in part explain the lack of exact dates or close attention to other details.

In the opening scene an experienced geologist named Art Hall, who had worked with Reynolds and McLallen on the Boss Mountain development earlier, approached Reynolds with the suggestion that the partnership should acquire certain Crown grants at Buttle Lake on Vancouver Island. The main grants, Hall said, were held in an estate with the National Trust in Toronto.

Reynolds and Huestis happened to be going to Toronto at that time, and they had ample opportunity to think about the Crown grants as their Vickers Viscount did its milk-run across the country. Reynolds had wisely taken the initiative and obtained a letter of introduction from the senior National Trust officer in Vancouver.

Whatever the strategy devised while they were airborne, it worked. An agreement was made with National Trust for the Crown-granted mineral claims for a total of $75,000, $7,500 in cash and the balance to be paid in easy instalments.

Considering that this financial commitment pre-dated the capital financing of Bethlehem, Reynolds could not have found it easy. "I wrote my personal cheque for $7,500," he says in his memo, "and brought back a brief Letter of Agreement."

For the veteran prospector Spud Huestis, the episode must have been a revelation of the speed with which claims could change hands, given a congenial Toronto trust company officer and a ready cheque book.

Incidentally, the nickname that attended H.H. Huestis all his adult life had nothing to do with the spudding in of oil wells, an activity with which he had as little to do as with ballrooms and wheat fields. The truth is revealed by Dan Reynolds, son of Patrick.

According to Dan, on an early occasion when Huestis emerged from the wilds of Northern B.C., exhausted mentally, physically, and financially, he staggered into a small town and the first restaurant he saw, demanding the best the house could provide.

Since it was after hours the best the house could provide was severely limited, but it did include a huge pot of potatoes, which Spud dispatched with considerable gusto, thereby saddling himself for all time with that monosyllabic nickname. As is not unusual in the mining industry, there may be other versions or elaborations of that story, since Huestis is no longer around to clarify it.

"Those who dwell within this business," Frank Keane puts it in his book *The New Gold Rush*, "tend to be given to embellishment."

As adroit a way of calling an industry a pack of liars as one can imagine.

But we digress.

Later, back in Vancouver, Reynolds and Huestis made certain they had taken all the steps necessary to mop up further Crown grants at Buttle Lake. A prospector in Victoria who had worked with Hall earlier was in possession of further Crown grants, and was persuaded to part with them for a total consideration of $50,000, with a 10 per cent down payment out of Reynolds's cheque book as before.

The process was repeated yet again with an individual in Vancouver for $25,000, $2,500 down, courtesy of Mr. Reynolds in the usual fashion.

Reynolds's complete confidence that McLallen would go along with this venture financially is typical of this highly unusual relationship.

"I now had an outlay of $15,000," Reynolds writes, [not to mention a future commitment for $135,000] "and I approached J.A. and W.H. McLallen with the proposal that they each reimburse me the sum of $5,000 and that we each contribute an equal amount for staking of additional claims and an exploration program."

They agreed, of course, and the ultimate partnership consisted of Reynolds, McLallen and his brother, Art Hall, and Huestis, according to Reynolds's memo, which adds, ". . . . who would each share equally in any benefits derived from the venture." This clause is again a clear indication of what a partnership it was, with the contributions not always strictly monetary.

The late 1950s were bizarre but wonderful years in which to do business in B.C. The advertising agency that coined the phrase "Super, Natural British Columbia," was at least thirty years late. Anyone who believes John Diefenbaker was "The Chief" in the late fifties and early sixties was never in Victoria when W.A.C. Bennett was in action.

It has often been said that during the Bennett years nothing moved in the province without the Old Man's benediction. If it was a monarchy, it was a benevolent one. If Bennett was everything everyone, even his detractors, said about him, his enormous capacity for getting things done is the salient fact to remember about his regime. It often took the form of consensus decisions and telephone legislation, as well as those unilateral judgments that periodically issued from the Premier's office.

Once Reynolds and McLallen struck their partnership over the Buttle Lake property, two prospectors were hired and Hall immediately directed them in the process of in-fill staking.

But then a consideration of immediate importance arose—the fact that Buttle Lake was on provincial park land, where at that time not even exploration could proceed without a rash of permits from the government. (Actually, later it became worse. Close by, a property known as Cream Silver developed by Dick Hughes and Frank Lang was stalled for fifteen years because of a provincial law declaring that mining could not take place on park land, period.)

Reynolds and Huestis went to Victoria, armed with a strong report on the Buttle Lake project that had been written by Hall, and presented their case to the Minister of Mines, Kenneth Kiernan. Hall's report unequivocally stated that the Buttle Lake prospect deserved to be developed, with the flat assertion that a mine could result.

"And," said Hall as he handed the report to Reynolds, "they'll have to spend a hell of lot of money to prove me wrong."

Needless to say "they" never did.

"Hall even went so far," adds Reynolds, "as to say in his report that the property could produce a gross value in excess of $100 million in minerals."

All of W.A.C. Bennett's cabinets, despite their limitations, loved to hear, and had a weakness for, potential success stories. Following an impressive presentation by Huestis and Reynolds, there followed several phone calls, and the pair were on their way back to Vancouver. Not far behind them came the necessary permits.

With the two McLallens and Reynolds grubstaking the operation, Hall acquired and directed a diamond drill crew. It did not take long to come up with indications that the property hosted ore that was clearly of mining grade. For the necessary development drilling, however, the costs would escalate.

Reynolds says, "It happened to be a time when interest in

mining ventures was at a low ebb because of low mining prices."

Overtures were made to several majors in the East, accompanied by Hall's report and the most recent drilling results from the property, but the big companies, concerned over their own properties, metal prices, and their own budget priorities were not in an expansionist mood. Some displayed academic interest, but declined any financial participation.

The breakthrough came in an unusual way. During one of the group's frequent strategy meetings, Hall suggested they abandon the idea of acquiring major financing and going for a large mill. Instead, he said, why not erect a small 50 to 100 ton-per-day mill and commence mining immediately?

"It may not make a lot of money," Hall acknowledged, "but there's also no way it can lose money."

The group liked the idea, reasoning that it might even attract enough attention from major companies that one of them would take a position in spite of the poor economy. That is what almost happened.

Before they had a chance to work on the small mill idea, Reynolds was walking down Hastings Street one day when he ran into an investment-dealer friend.

"I asked him," writes Reynolds, "if he knew where we could beg, borrow, or steal (or even trade for an interest in the property) a 50 or 100 ton mill. He answered that he was involved with a small company called Western Mines, which had a 100-ton mill at Greenwood, B.C. that was not in operation."

Two days later, Reynolds was sitting in his office shooting the breeze with Spud when a Western Mines director walked in. He displayed a lot of interest in the details concerning Buttle Lake as Huestis and Reynolds laid them out for him. The Western Mines director missed nothing.

A few days later he telephoned Reynolds. The gist of that conversation was that Western Mines's management thought it would be a shame to erect a small mill on a property of such obviously vast potential. Reynolds of course could only agree. In brief, Western Mines wanted a piece of the deal, and a major part at that. When the agreement was finalized, Western

Mines had agreed to pay out the $135,000 commitment Reynolds and the McLallens had made, give them $20,000 in cash and issue them 250,000 shares of Western Mines stock.

In mining deals, sometimes a great notion should be pursued doggedly to the end; on other occasions, it may be more prudent at a given point to bail out—if the price is right. If Bethlehem was an early example of the former case, Buttle Lake represented the other extreme. One can second-guess these decisions *ad nauseam*; given McLallen's and Reynolds's visible box score over three decades it is safe to say they called it right on almost every occasion.

Since resigning from active management with Bethlehem Copper, McLallen and Reynolds seem to have taken a new lease on life. Selling out to Cominco for a sizable fortune would have been enough to send most of us trotting happily off to the paddock. Rather than simply taking the money and running, Reynolds and McLallen seem to have converted the event into an opportunity to enter the contemporary mining scene, where gold is king, small operations are *de rigueur* and base metals are, well—base.

"Our golf is better than ever, too," says Reynolds, as an indication that they don't commit the time or stress to as many mining projects today as they did twenty years ago. As an extension of their long friendship they play a frequent round together, their relative years (McLallen's eighty-two and Reynolds's seventy-four) not necessarily reflecting their golf scores.

According to Dan Reynolds, from the time he was a teenager it was simply assumed that his father would be playing golf on the weekend with McLallen. McLallen always arranged the foursome, the only variables week after week being who the other two players were and how much McLallen won on each particular weekend.

"We still play golf," says McLallen, "but the energy we used to have is hard to imagine now. While we were staking Bethlehem, for example, Spud Huestis made fifty separate trips into the property."

But even today both Reynolds and McLallen are recognized as men of unusual energy who—"supposed to be retired," as

Dan Reynolds describes their status—still put in long days. Their timetable would weary many younger men. Until recently both of them served on the board of Mascot Resources, a highly successful gold-mining company; they show up at their joint office on Hastings Street, albeit for only part of the day; and they concern themselves for the most part with their current pride and joy, Queenstake Resources.

In 1977, when Queenstake was launched, base-metal prices were still economic, but some far-sighted individuals, notably the senior management in companies such as Placer Development, had already foreseen the necessity of turning to precious metals, wherever they could be found.

For Placer that meant Australia and Papua, New Guinea. For Reynolds, McLallen, and Queenstake it meant initially a project in the Yukon, although Queenstake eventually became the holder of a well-diversified portfolio of properties deployed all over the western side of North America.

The Queenstake team comprised, in addition to the two partners, a geologist, Gordon Gutrath, Lauch Farris, a businessman, and Ted Turton, a senior western Canadian broker.

Queenstake's first major project, a tungsten-gold property in the Yukon, had all the elements of fortunate timing that attended most of the McLallen-Reynolds scenarios. In 1978 both tungsten and gold were strong, and the project attracted the attention of Canada Tungsten Mining Corporation Limited. To begin with, Canada Tungsten took a twenty-three per cent equity position in Queenstake, later raising it to forty-four per cent.

The next move by the partnership was to divert the cash flow generated by the public financing and later private placements into a second phase of operations focussing on placer mining in the Klondike. Gold reserves were built up in much the same fashion as a company might develop cash balances.

Placer operations, or gold dredging, had at one time been the favoured method of gold-mining in the Yukon mining. The practice had sunk out of sight economically, with pegged gold prices no match for constantly rising costs.

Now Queenstake staged a one-company renaissance, launching eventually four separate bucketline dredge operations. It offered a parallel of sorts to the heap-leaching technology that had taken hold in the western States and western Canada. That too had developed out of the basic equation that higher gold price combined with volume production could more than offset increased overhead and low grades.

Act III for Queenstake was to employ the placer revenues to acquire and develop more conventional gold-mining properties. Some were limited in size—although with promising grades—specifically to avoid competing with the majors. Heap-leaching properties were well-represented in the half-dozen sites identified, especially in California and Nevada.

Queenstake's endeavours in the first few years of operation were crowned with the acquisition of the Chichagof Mine, historically one of the richest locations in Alaska from its discovery in 1905 to its wartime closing in 1942. Development work indicated a near-ideal mining situation—good grade, low costs, close access to a sheltered harbour, and much of the necessary infrastructure, particularly underground, already in place.

In many respects, Chichagof, as perhaps the partnership's last big play, is diametrically opposite to Bethlehem Copper, where mining fortunes began for McLallen and Reynolds. But in terms of excitement, commitment, and reward, both of the partners would agree that a mine is a mine.

"Mostly what they like to talk about," says Dan Reynolds, "is the way things used to be and the ways in which mining has changed. And of course they have changed too. I remember going up there to Bethlehem as a kid in the back of a jeep—how it took forever. Today, it's a three or four-hour car trip."

Times have indeed changed since the fifties. And so have the relative prices of copper and gold. But, like most professionals, McLallen and Reynolds have managed to create successful careers with their impeccable timing, knowing when to get in and—when to get out.

———

CHAPTER 4

Gus MacPhail

A labour of love

The phones in the chairman's office appear to be jumping. Lights flash, and as soon as one goes out another lights up. The slim, greying chairman picks up one phone, then another, gives a terse direction and moves on. "How much? Sell," he says firmly to one. "Fine," he agrees with another. The office cannot be said to resemble that of a V.I.P. Amidst the clutter of paper, computer, coffee cups, and prospectuses, there are two other persons working. MacPhail fairly crackles with energy as he moves from one crisis to another.

"I've spent most of my life on the floor of the Stock Exchange and I like to be in the centre of action," he explains cheerfully. "I don't like being isolated. I'm not happy unless I have a phone in my hand. I find that even when I'm at home the phone is ringing constantly and I don't get away from business." He pauses. "My whole life is the Stock Exchange. And I love it. I've tried to have other interests but it always comes back to business."

Gus MacPhail's blue eyes light up when he mentions the Vancouver Stock Exchange. As he talks he takes off his glasses and twirls them, or holds them like a telephone, almost as though he misses the feel of one in his hand. MacPhail's love of the stock market and his ability to cool-headedly take risks in a very emotional business are both reasons why he is one of the key players in the Vancouver Stock Exchange, and has been since the fifties. As the former president and current chairman of Continental Carlisle Douglas, MacPhail is responsible for millions of dollars in such billion-dollar deals as Bethlehem Copper and Afton Mines.

"We're basically stockbrokers," says MacPhail. "We're Vancouver-oriented. We do predominantly Vancouver venture-capital deals; general broking business; some investment banking. We're underwriters and we have a research department. We do some options in business, not big." Continental Carlisle Douglas has wire connections with all the major stock markets and it is currently buying a seat on the Toronto Stock Exchange. "We're already members of the Montreal exchange," says MacPhail, "so we'll be members of all the major exchanges in Canada. We also have a branch office in London, England."

Continental Carlisle Douglas and Canarim Investment Corporation are Vancouver's biggest junior-stock traders and when Continental sought London regulatory approval to open its office in London the Vancouver Sun called it a "costly gamble." It is now the first Canadian brokerage firm to specialize in VSE-listed stocks in the United Kingdom. MacPhail seems convinced it is a good move. He says the future of British Columbia doesn't necessarily lie in the Pacific Rim region. "I think it's going to be in London and Europe," he says. "It's going to be the world," he adds as an afterthought. "Communication. The world is getting smaller."

During his decades on the VSE, MacPhail has watched the world get smaller. "I remember when making a trip back to Toronto to make a deal was something special. Now they make deals over the telephone," he says. "Or the Toronto people come out here. It's changing. I've seen the changes in the business," he adds, "I've been in it for thirty-five years."

Gus MacPhail started "in the business" at age seventeen in 1950, and when he says he worked his way from the ground up he is quite serious. "I wanted to leave school," he explains. "I got restless and wanted to do something exciting. My homeroom teacher at that time was a fellow called Tom Alsbury. [Alsbury later was mayor of Vancouver from 1959 to 1962.] He'd heard of this chap John McGraw, who was virtually the kingpin of the Stock Exchange, and he told me I should take this great opportunity to go into the Stock Exchange. I went down to see McGraw and all I knew about stocks was these numbers in the newspapers—pages of numbers. I went down, and I was interviewed right on the floor of the Stock Exchange. There was yelling and screaming going on. Mind you, there were only twenty or thirty people in the Exchange those days, mostly members, but it seemed pretty exciting to me."

He gestures with his glasses. "And I just fell in love with it. I didn't know what a stock or a bond was. . . ." But he did realize that this exciting place was where he wanted to be. He became John McGraw's protegé, McGraw his mentor. McGraw's firm was called Continental Securities, and in February 1950 Mac-Phail joined it as office boy. "I left Vancouver Technical School where I was taking grades 11 and 12 together," he says. Bob Stewart, the current chief of police, was in the same course, he recalls. MacPhail left halfway through the course to join McGraw at Continental, and he has never looked back.

"I used to come in at seven o'clock in the morning; in those days we opened at seven. I started on the floor of the exchange and later I did the deliveries. We never had any salesmen," he explains. "McGraw and I had three or four traders, and we did a big brokerage business until he passed away." MacPhail obviously loved and revered McGraw. "He was a 'one-man band,'" he says. "He was a very powerful man in the Vancouver stock market. I respected him. He was tough." McGraw also knew a potential business partner when he met him. "I guess I did a hell of a job for him," says MacPhail modestly.

Nothing in MacPhail's background indicated that he would become one of the wizards of the Vancouver Stock Exchange. His father was a seaman from the Hebrides Islands, off the west coast of Scotland. At age twenty-three, while on an English fishing vessel, MacPhail the elder jumped ship. "There was no work in the Hebrides," says MacPhail. "My father came to Vancouver and while he was passing a park or something they were playing music and passing out oranges and he said, 'Jeez, this is a helluva place. We're staying here!.'" MacPhail's mother came from the Prairies. Her father had been a home-steader who in the 1880s settled in the Red River region, and pioneered there.

It is possible that MacPhail's respect for money and his ability to stay cool while trading in the millions derive from his prudent, down-to-earth family. "You had to be sensible with money because you didn't have much," he points out. "My parents were just ordinary people. We didn't have a lot but we always thought it was a lot and it was all I wanted. I had a great time growing up."

At one time MacPhail thought he might become a fisherman and go to sea like his father. "My father was a sea captain on the coast here," he says. "He was a sort of senior man on the coast with Northern Navigation—coast boats and whalers. At one time I thought of going fishing. There was big money being made there in the fifties and I had a couple of friends that went and did very well. I think I did just as well as they did, though."

MacPhail was born and raised in Vancouver, "right by Hast-ings Park, down by Boundary Road." He may have considered becoming a fisherman but even as a youngster he always had some sort of deal or business under way. He sold peanuts at ball games. He sold programmes at soccer games. "I always had something going," he says. During World War II MacPhail was just a child, but he remembers that his father was in the navy; he was away for a good part of the war, transporting the troops to Hong Kong on a ship called the *Prince Robert*.

John McGraw, MacPhail's other father figure, also did his bit for the war effort. He volunteered for service, and became the manager of Boeing's Canadian operation. "He closed Con-tinental in 1939, 1940," says MacPhail. After the war, C.D. Howe ("I was a great admirer of C.D. Howe," says MacPhail, "McGraw used to tell me about him and the things he did dur-ing the war") offered McGraw the presidency of Air Canada, then known as Trans Canada Airlines, but he refused. Instead he re-opened Continental and ran it as a virtually one-man op-eration until 1950, when MacPhail joined him.

"Before I started with Continental it consisted of one man and two girls," recalls MacPhail. "We had two or three traders on the floor that we used to trade with, but McGraw and I were the two people that handled the main players in the market." Over the years MacPhail has been involved with almost every major name in the Vancouver stock market, from Murray Pezim to Bruce McDonald. During that time the VSE was much smaller that it is today and the volume of trading was minimal. "One day," says MacPhail, "I crossed 20,000 shares of Canam Copper at 16½ cents and I got so excited that I phoned John McGraw at the Vancouver Club (the Exchange used to close for lunch in those days from noon to 1:30) and I said to him: 'I just doubled the volume on the Exchange today!'"

Doubling the volume on the Exchange was not MacPhail's only source of amusement. He says that in his younger years he was what was known as "wild." "Brokers were hard-drinking, hard-playing types," he says. "I think they still are to some extent, although moderation seems to be the order of the day. There's more interest in the health kick. There was no 'fitness program' in those days, except bending the elbow." He laughs. "The occasional broker played golf, which led to the nineteenth hole of course. . . ." MacPhail himself never really took to golfing. In his younger years he was too busy partying, and later he preferred to do things with his family.

In 1957 MacPhail was married, at the age of twenty-four, and he now has a son and a daughter. His son, who is twenty-five, is working with him at present, and his daughter, twenty-one, attends Capilano College in North Vancouver. MacPhail does not care to go into any more detail regarding his home life. "I'm very happily married," he says. "I have a wonderful home life — I enjoy it — and I know that that's helped me in my business. I'm positive that without my home life I wouldn't be where I am today. . . . I was lucky."

He has been lucky in more ways than one. MacPhail was told he had cancer in April 1986. "It's all cleared up now, knock wood," he says devoutly. "I had an operation and I'm on this macrobiotic diet. . . ." He grins. "I'm a great believer in mind over matter. If you want to do something you can." He had the operation on 28 April 1986, and at the end of September was given a clean bill of health. "It was all gone," he says with relief.

He is trying to slow down a little. "I'm an avid fisherman," he says, "and I spend weekends during the summer on my boat. I go to fitness class. I run the seawall in West Vancouver. I find it easier to run the track, though, where I can do three miles in about twenty-eight minutes," he finishes proudly. "For me that's not bad. I haven't been to the track for awhile but I go to aerobics class with my wife. I love skiing too." MacPhail started skiing when he was a teenager. "We used to walk up Seymour," he recalls. "We used to get the bus to Deep Cove on Friday afternoons and then walk up from Deep Cove right to the top of the mountain. There were no chair-lifts in those days." This was in that "wild" period. "We partied a lot," he says. "I was a very wild one when I was younger." He is wild no longer, and prefers to engage in activities he can share with his family. This is why he took up boating rather than golf, although like his father he feels a strong affinity with the sea.

MacPhail's stay in hospital made him a bit of an egalitarian. "It sounds corny," he says, "but it's true that everybody puts their pants on one leg at a time. We're all working people; some of us just get a little more money than others. But we're all basically the same. I found when I was in the hospital that it didn't matter if you had money, everybody gets treated the same way. There was an old pensioner across the hall from me. He had the same room, the same problem, the same treatment. Except that he got out faster than I did!"

It made him think. "What's the difference?" he asks. "There's no 'them' and 'us.' We're all people, working people, with the same likes and dislikes. We all want our nice clothes and our nice homes and surroundings. It's just that some people are willing to take risks. Some people don't want to do that, they're happy doing one particular thing. I've got people here at the office who want to work at a certain steady pace. Fine and dandy. But they don't slow down the people who want to work harder."

MacPhail is one of those people willing to take risks. He acquired some of these gambler's instincts from John McGraw. MacPhail remembers clearly the day John F. Kennedy was assassinated. "It was one of the most fantastic things that ever happened," he relates. "I was standing on the floor of the Exchange in 1963 when Kennedy was assassinated, and the market was all gloom . . . gloom. The stocks had plunged and they closed Toronto and New York. In Vancouver, old McGraw said, 'This is just crazy. Keep Vancouver open. People should be selling.' And he told me to buy. He started at one end and I started at the other and we just bought all the good things we could afford: B.C. Telephone, M & R, all leading stocks at that time. They were all plunging.

"He must have bought two or three million worth of stock. That was a lot of money in '63. I bet he almost doubled his money by Monday, Tuesday morning. That was the greatest opportunity. We couldn't buy enough! Because, you see, there were all sorts of rumours. Rumours that Kennedy had been shot by a coloured person and there would be race riots. . . . But McGraw was a very astute market man, and he said, 'You'll see. Life will go on. One man doesn't make the United States or the world.'"

After that frenetic day of trading MacPhail went home. "I saw people going into and out of Woodwards," he says, "as though nothing had happened. . . . most people hadn't even heard about it. When I got home my wife had the television on and they were swearing Johnson in, and within a matter of hours Johnson was president and Kennedy was history. Life went on."

This was when MacPhail learned the lesson that is hardest to absorb when one is involved in the stock market: "Buy when they don't want them, sell when they do." He concedes that is more easily said than done. "It's emotional," he admits. "You've got to have a little bit of a cool head when there's mass hysteria." That was one of the most important lessons to learn. McGraw taught his protegé well, and when he died in 1970 MacPhail bought the firm from the estate. "I bought Continental Securities from his family and I operated it with a couple of other partners until November 1974. Then we merged with

Carlisle Douglas, which was another small regional firm, and we became Continental Carlisle Douglas and here we are today."

That period, particularly during the sixties and early seventies, was not quite as smooth as MacPhail makes it sound. "We have had some bad times," he admits. They have also had some very good ones, when risks have paid off handsomely. Until the late 1970s, Continental did most of the Vancouver underwritings, backing many big-time winners.

Bethlehem Copper led to a major open-pit porphyry copper industry in British Columbia, later taken over by established companies. The original money was raised by Continental, and Continental also did the public financing at seventy-five cents a share. At one point, after ASARCO (American Smelting and Refining) pulled out and just before Sunimoto of Japan came in, they actually put money in from their own pockets in order to keep the venture going. Bethlehem ended up a major winner, with production eventually over 3000 tons of copper daily.

The Afton Mines deal was another big one for Continental although it started slowly, as had Bethlehem. In 1971 a large American mining company drilled some holes in the Afton area. Some of them were good, others useless. MacPhail and others at Continental met with mining engineer Dr. Bill Patmore and Chester Millar, trying to determine what to do. They decided to go with it, but it was a tense decision. As it turned out, Afton became a hot seller, with Teck Mining and Placer Development fighting for control of the mine. The stock sky-rocketed and a good time was had by all. This, says MacPhail, proves "that there is more money made by accident in the venture-capital market than there ever is by sound investment practices."

But by far the biggest deal, and the one that put Vancouver on the world's financial map, was Pyramid Mining. The late Jack Wasserman, columnist for the Vancouver Sun, wrote: "In case you were wondering what all the shouting was about here's the Pyramid story in words of one syllable and six figures. The mooches made more than $10 million on paper Monday alone. Little old ladies in tennis shoes, bartenders and bootblacks, rogues and remittance men, cabbies and call girls, sewer diggers and socialites shared in a bonanza that outdid the Irish Sweepstakes. . . ." (2 November 1965). The Pyramid Pine Point market found lead-zinc ore, rumours were flying, and the market went into a frenzy.

"Pyramid Pine Point market was one of the biggest markets we ever had," recalls MacPhail. The pace of the trading made anything else done on the Vancouver Stock Exchange seem tame by comparison; the average trading during that time was nearly a million shares *per hour* for the seven-hour session on 3 November 1965.

"We've been involved in nearly all the major mines that came into production in British Columbia," says MacPhail proudly. "One way or another we have helped finance everything from the Highland Valley deal to Dynasty." Dynasty was another billion-dollar deal that started small. Dynasty found the Anvil Mine in the Yukon, originally discovered by the legendary "mountain man" and geological engineer, Dr. Aar Aho. The original exploration went vastly over budget, but eventually they found ore.

It is obvious that the venture-capital market is not for the faint-hearted or the weak-kneed. MacPhail agrees, but adds that he finds it perpetually exciting. "It's exciting to create something, to start something, to see it get off," he says enthusiastically. "Every day is interesting. You do different things. And then there's that thrill of winning." Sometimes there's also the misery of losing—or thinking you might lose. "It's a hard business to be in," says MacPhail. "One day you're on Cloud Nine, the next day you're down. Sky's the limit, then something happens—market, politics, prices, commodities. It doesn't go smoothly. It's very hectic. There have been times I've thought 'Why did I ever get into the stock market? Maybe I should have become a fisherman.' But that's all part of the game."

The main part of the game, says MacPhail, is the people. He says the only trick, if there is one, to successful investment in the venture-capital market is knowing your people. "It's the people and the story they tell," he says of how he decides whether or not to go into a venture. "This is basically a people-business although there's no real set criterion." There are the promoters, the technical ones and those who can raise money. "The technical people are varied and the tools they have are fantastic," says MacPhail, "but it still takes a diamond drill. If you're drilling for oil you still need that hole in the ground that tells you whether you've got it or not. If you've got the technical people, and if you've got people that can raise money and attract a following. . . . I mean, you can have the greatest thing in the world, but if you can't sell it what the hell good is it? Chrysler was going nowhere before Iacocca, and I don't think they've really changed anything about the Chrysler cars; he just convinced everybody they have." He adds, "That's why, when these promoters team up with real technical people, there's no stopping them." Politics is another part of the game, and one which can have a greater effect than any other. "We've had some bad periods," says MacPhail. "They came in cycles. We had a gas-and-oil pipeline crisis in '57 with the Suez crisis, and that was a helluva big pipeline market. And then the Conservatives got in — Diefenbaker — and we had tight money. The early sixties were pretty slow too." One of the worst times was the early seventies when the NDP were in government in B.C., according to MacPhail. "We just couldn't get through the '71 to '75 period with the NDP government. It was just disaster for the markets and everybody fled the province. We had quite a copper market going at the time and everything just went into the tank, the sewer."

Then the inherent optimist in him comes to the fore again. "As it turned out, it was a great blessing in disguise. A lot of people started to go into the different areas of the world and it's made the Exchange stronger in the long run."

MacPhail does not affiliate himself with any political ideology. He considers himself an independent, although in many of his stated views he sounds fairly conservative in the textbook sense. "We have this thing in Canada," he says a little incoherently, groping for words. "How do I put this? Usually, when something is going well the government taxes it or something. They won't leave well enough alone," he goes on with a tinge of bitterness. "Things have been going well for whatever reason, like the oil business, then all of a sudden they had to put in this oil-policy thing. They start taxing, shutting them in. We couldn't do this, and we couldn't do that. Then, all of a sudden, there's no market for oil stocks."

This goes against all of MacPhail's views and market expertise. "If people want blue ties you've got to sell them blue ties," he points out. "Too many things in Canada are manipulated." MacPhail's policy has always been flexibility. "Although markets have been quiet, I've always been fortunate with Continental," he says, "and we've always had something going. Oil markets went, we were into gold; gold went and we were into something else. We were very flexible—you have to be. We made it a policy to be flexible. If the public doesn't want blue ties you can't sell your blue ties."

He briefly and uncharacteristically gives some advice. "I think people should be buying oil stocks right now, but they're not in vogue. Usually that's when we buy. As I said before— buy when they don't want them and sell when they do. You've got to 'go with the flow', but there's still a lot of bargains around." He learned his lessons on the market and from McGraw well. "Nothing's really changed," he says sagely. "It goes down and then it comes back up."

McGraw taught MacPhail more than market dealings; he also instilled in his pupil a real love for the Vancouver Stock Exchange. McGraw had devoted most of his life to the VSE, even making sure that such mundane tasks as doors being opened on time and floors being swept were accomplished. McGraw began to slow down after the Pyramid market in 1966 and MacPhail took on more and more responsibilities at Continental. He took it over completely when McGraw died in 1970, with partners Bob Faye and Grant McDonald, who are now president and chief executive officer respectively.

MacPhail is proud of his contribution to the Vancouver Stock Exchange. He is also proud of the fact that he has been one of its key players for so long. He is on the Board of Governors of the VSE, and "I've got a lot of pleasure out of that," he says warmly, "working out problems, being a part of it. It's been a fantastic experience, accomplishment, to be considered—without bragging—as having been one of the key players. From a small exchange I think we've come a long way, and we're going further."

How can he be so sure? "The one thing that Vancouver grew from is that we had the venture-capital start-up companies," he explains. "Toronto wanted to be the more established, conservative stock exchange. They wanted to be the New York, the London, of Canada. For different reasons. They had scandals down there and so forth. So they figured they'd give the venture-capital business to the orangutans in the west. And we took it. We said, 'Sure, what's wrong with it?' Well, we are the venture-capital market of the world right now." He looks pleased. "We're doing more than an adequate job. We've got the experience, the people, here."

MacPhail repeatedly comes back to the notion of "people." He believes very strongly that in business it is people that make the difference. "It annoys me very much when certain groups say we're not people-oriented," he says with the first touch of rancour he has shown. "We never laid any staff off, even when things were tough here in 1982." He is convinced that the secret to success is to treat people well, and fairly. Even in McGraw's time, he recalls, "although he was very frugal and tough and that, we never saved on the pencils. Or wages. And we've carried that through. We know the industry average and in terms of salary we're at the top."

Just as important, says MacPhail, is treating employees equally. "It's results we're after," he says flatly. "If someone calls in and they're a great salesperson it doesn't matter if they're male or female. Or handicapped." MacPhail considers himself a team player, one who works well in a group. "I like to be in charge, naturally. Who doesn't? But I think I'm a good group worker," he says.

Working hard and getting things started have always been MacPhail's passion. He is a little concerned that government and our "Canadian inferiority complex" will eventually hold things back. "There's so much east-west controversy here," he says. "Part of it is because of the language, and the way the power structure is. They overwhelm us. We have a more natural north-south relationship than we have east-west. But I think that will change to a certain degree over the years if we become more of a financial center here."

MacPhail is hopeful. "I think Canada will always be a resource base," he says, "because we don't have a large population and we never will. We were so advanced in the fifties and sixties. Everybody came to us, wanting things. Now I think we've got to go out and sell ourselves. We had it pretty easy. Everybody wanted our wheat, our lumber, now they don't want it so much. Things are changing. Look at Argentina, they're producing more wheat, as much as we've got. And in Britain now they're producing more wheat per acre than we do in Canada. Not in tonnage, but more per acre. The world doesn't need Canada, Canada needs the world." The grin appears again. "But I'm very optimistic."

He has a right to be. He is fifty-two, and involved in a business he loves and knows. Work is his life. Unlike many others in his field, MacPhail is not really interested in the social perks that go with the position. "I don't do any of that stuff," he confesses. "Peter Brown and all that. I take my hat off to Peter. He's a hard-working boy. Terrific public speaker, he's on the board of the university, and does a lot of things for the community. I think it's fantastic that we have people like that." MacPhail tends to be more of a loner. "I do what I do and don't bother with what other people do," he says simply. He works hard, spends time with his family, tries to take time out to relax with his various supporting activities and to see a few close friends. "I feel comfortable with what I am," he says.

Comfortable enough to help the less fortunate. "Every Christmas I take a trip down to the missions in the east end," he says. He used to work in that area, at American Can. "There's a Union Gospel mission down there by what used to be called the Hadden Hotel," he chuckles. "We used to go and cash our cheques there and party it up. There were no clubs in those days, you see, and pubs closed at eleven. . . ." So MacPhail tries to do something good for the people in that area who are hard up.

He also started a trend recently: he donated one hundred

shares of some stock to Junior Achievement. The day he did this, "one of the fellows who was going to speak at the Junior Achievement convention in Los Angeles was sitting in my office." MacPhail looks pleased. "And he said, 'When we're at the convention we'll get the fellows in New York to do this too.' That's how these things get started."

There's a knock at the door; there's a telephone call for Gus. He has to head off. Back to the stock market that is his life; back to venture-capital deals that he wants to get started with. "Hard work," he says. "That's what it takes to succeed. A love of the business. . . . a love of challenge." He's off again to the centre of things where he belongs. And watching his brisk departure you know that no matter what challenges await him he is bound to emerge a winner in the end.

———————

CHAPTER 5

Murray Pezim

Needing another mountain to climb. . . .

On Murray Pezim's wall a framed etching reads; "I saw a man chasing the horizon. I shouted to him, 'You'll never reach it.' He replied, 'You lie.' And rushed on." Words which aptly personify Pezim, also known as The Pez: a man of humble origins who has rushed on regardless of nay-sayers; a man who has scrapped, fought, shouted, cajoled, joked, and worked himself from the ghetto into becoming one of the major business figures in Canada; a man who has been called "The Godfather of the Vancouver Stock Exchange." He has been called many other names, some of them downright vicious. Stuck right in the middle of all those superlatives, epithets, and expletives is a large, loud, extravagant, flamboyant, generous, enthusiastic figure. The adjectives are huge, because The Pez himself is larger than life, both in girth and in spirit.

"I don't worry about money," he brags, "I can make it any time." "I'm a reformed whore," he soberly insists on another occasion. His public persona is one of a man who has fought the establishment, often to win, but when he is taxed with it he says, "I'm a *member* of the establishment. Peter Newman has written me up in his book." Then he does an about-face. "But I wouldn't consider myself that. I consider myself a damn good citizen."

He is, but he also has an ego that "belongs in the Smithsonian, where they keep the stuffed whales and other huge things," according to *Vancouver Sun* columnist, Denny Boyd. It's that enormous ego that has made The Pez one of the most talked-about, carped-about, and loved promoters in town. He has been the subject of endless magazine and newspaper articles and chapters of books like this one. What other man would buy out all four hundred seats for a Joey Bishop concert—Bishop is a personal friend of Pezim's—and get all his friends to open newspapers and read as Bishop walked on stage? (Bishop is reported to have quipped: "Just keep reading everybody, and when you get to the want ads let me know. 'Cause tomorrow I'll be looking for another job.") Who else would buy all Swensen's outlets because he didn't have ice-cream at his bar mitzvah, then re-stage that event all over again, with ice-cream this time? On the other hand, who else would put on an opulent charity dinner that raised $1 million for the Vancouver General Hospital Foundation, or would raise $200,000 for children at Camp Miriam?

Nothing that Pezim does is half-hearted. He wins big or loses his shirt and goes bankrupt; he says nothing, or says something that stirs everyone up. The entire business community reeled as he fought for control of BCRIC, going on record with comments like: "There are 118,000 shareholders in that company, not counting the people who have three shares. And I care about those people. The management has not acted responsibly. They couldn't care less about the shareholders. And, win or lose, they are going to have to toe the line from now on." Not a statement guaranteed to win friends and influence influential people. Pezim lost that fight, but he has won others. He lost his shirt in 1972 with two major miscalculations; he bounced back in 1977 with BX Developments. The RCMP took him to court over BX and he won.

The Pez never actually fades into obscurity; when he lost over $7 million and went to Scottsdale, Arizona, to recoup his forces, Denny Boyd devoted an entire column to Pezim, tracing his history and concernedly outlining his ups and downs. He made headlines with his attempted take-over of BCRIC, and made the world papers with Hemlo, the Ontario gold mine he originally financed, the largest gold find in North America. "You must never quit," says Pezim firmly. "I wouldn't quit. The easiest thing to do in life is to quit. Anybody can do it. I've climbed mountains that people will tell you are impossible, but I've done it just by persevering, suffering—whatever it takes."

Pezim learned young about suffering, and that made him tough. His introduction to the stock market would have made an even slightly nervous person scurry away, never to return. But not the Pez. That was in 1950, when he was twenty-nine. He worked in a butcher shop in Toronto. "I worked hard," he says now. "I was a good boy, hard-working. But it was terrible work. Cold, right in the slums, the worst of slums, right by the packing houses on Roger's Road." One day, in walked a smartly-dressed man, asking to buy some centre-cut pork chops. "Now up there," emphasizes Pezim, "*nobody* buys centre-cut pork chops. Total poverty. So I was impressed. I was impressed by him and I listened to him."

Pezim had saved $13,000; he had worked hard to earn it. The pork-chop man, Max Guthrie, who is still a promoter, told Pezim about Duvay Gold Mines. It was going for 5¾ cents, but the literature asked, "Can this be a $10 stock?" Pezim gambled that it was. "My buying put it up to 12 cents," he chuckles, "but when I stopped, it stopped. I lost $13,000—every cent I had. I'd worked ninety to one hundred hours a week for that money, and I lost every goddam cent. In six weeks I'd lost it." A different sort of person might have sworn off the stock market, but not the Pez. "I thought, 'if I lost it, somebody made it. It took me four years to earn this money and I lost it in six weeks. I've got to learn this business.'"

It was not just the money. For Pezim, the thrill of the game was just as important. "Money means nothing to me," he once said. "Money's just a way of keeping score." This is not to say he hasn't made money, the "odd buck" as he calls it, versus the "serious money" he has helped other people make. But what of all those stories claiming that every few years he manages to lose it all? "People say 'you're broke,'" he laughs. "If I'm worth less than $10 million I'm broke, O.K.? That's about it. I let them talk because they just don't know."

Pezim currently has the substantial look of a man who knows about money. His office has a practical look, rather than an opulent one. Two large desks arranged in an L-shape are dominated by five computer terminals, all spewing out numbers. The two phones ring, and at intervals well-dressed people wander in with important-sounding questions dealing with large sums of money. An enormous TV screen silently prints out the latest stock-market figures, hieroglyphics to anyone not in the know but obviously meaningful to Pezim. Mementos of Pezim's chequered career are scattered around the office: a ceramic squirrel given to him by Peter Brown (who calls Pezim, for some unknown reason, The Squirrel), a stuffed bull, an original print of the 1972 Mohammed Ali-Chuvalo fight, in which Pezim lost his quarter million. In the print Pezim is a small, tuxedoed figure anxiously looking at the ring.

The walls are covered with awards and citations from various organizations and city groups for his charitable work. His ego may be large, but so is his capacity for giving. "I love doing charity work," he says, lighting another king-size filter-tipped cigarette. "You have to learn how to give in this life. It's not a one-way ticket. It really isn't," he concludes earnestly, then starts to chuckle. "Maybe I'm a socialist at heart. I don't know. But I have a very deep feeling for my fellow human beings." He chortles again at the thought that he might be a socialist, then finishes more seriously, "I was poor myself. I know what it's like."

Perhaps the story has been exaggerated in the re-telling, but Pezim's roots really were poor. His father was a Romanian Jew who came to Canada to make his fortune. He opened a drugstore in Toronto, and did so well during Prohibition selling "medicinal" alcohol that he opened another drugstore and moved his family into a flashy house near Bloor Street. But then the Depression hit, and they ended up in a butcher shop in the slums. "We didn't have anything to eat," says Pezim flatly. "We didn't have anything, period." So he made the odd quarter parking cars near Windsor, then dominated by gambling clubs. "As kids we used to go up and be car jockeys," explains Pezim, "hoping that somebody wanted to throw us a quarter. That quarter meant you ate the next day. That's how it was. Ninety-nine per cent of the kids I hung around with drifted down to Vegas and into the gambling clubs." That is why Pezim knows so many of the club-owners down there—he grew up with them.

During World War II Pezim went into the army—"in order to *eat*"—and he wound up in Jamaica. "We had a big POW camp down there," he says. "Those were happy years for me. . . . Then I came back and worked in the butcher shop up to around 1950." That was when he lost his life's savings, and resolved to learn about this risky business where you could make or lose what it took an honest wage-earner years to make.

"Being a bit of a gambler (from my past associations) I went downtown, spoke to somebody I knew there and asked him if I could hang around. He said they couldn't pay me, but they'd teach me everything they could. So I spent about three hours a day there for four months—I still had to work. Then one day he called me in and said, 'Murray, there's no more to teach you here, but, if you want my advice, before you get into the business you should move to New York.' So I went to New York; worked in a firm just for room and board." Pezim stops at this point to reflect on his younger self's enthusiasm. "I've had *great* jobs," he interjects ironically. His last job there was working on the floor of the New York Stock Exchange; six months later he returned to Toronto and went to work.

He joined Jenkins, Evans and Company, which no longer exists but was then a dealer in penny mining stocks. "I got lucky right away," Pezim relates. "The first deal I really worked on was Dennison Mines, which turned out to be a phenomenal success. It started at 40 cents and went up to about $85 a share. And my history carries on from there," he concludes. "A series of ups and downs, struggles, fights, and then Hemlo came along."

Hemlo is certainly the shining star in Pezim's crown, but long before Hemlo was even a glimmer in a prospector's eye

Pezim left Toronto to move to Vancouver. It was 1963 and the Windfall Mines scandal had rocked the Toronto Stock Exchange. The Tory provincial government stepped in. "There was a big scandal," says Pezim. "Viola MacMillan was the head of a prospectus putting out phony assays. So Toronto decided to stop financing junior companies. Because this business was my life, naturally I wasn't going to quit, and Vancouver was still open. So I came to Vancouver. When I got here they were only trading with 200,000 shares a day. *That's* why they call me the Godfather of the Vancouver Stock Exchange, because I literally taught everybody here what the business should be—what it's all about."

This is not an idle boast. Frank Keane, author of *The Vancouver Stock Exchange*, writes in his book that "for any follower of the VSE scene, to think of Murray Pezim is to get the adrenalin flowing. It is a fair statement, as anyone who has known Pezim over the years will agree, to say that The Pez almost single-handedly kept the Vancouver Stock Exchange alive during the dog days of bear markets and the reign in British Columbia of the New Democratic Party government."

Being from Toronto gives Pezim a broader perspective on Canadian affairs, but it also makes him mad. "I do know Toronto. I know it very well," he says, "and so I'm aware of the *attitude* of the eastern people towards us out west. No, they can say what they want, that they love us and all that, but that is not the case at all. The West is always taking it on the chin. It's *wrong*. We're as good as they are and we're just as smart, O.K.?" He looks belligerent. "So the heck with it. I'm a fighter and they don't like me. But they're going to have to put up with me." He laughs and the laughter has more than a touch of malice. "Hemlo was discovered in their own back yard. I did it and it killed them. It was all financed from the West—it was all western money. Largest gold discovery in North America, right in their own back yard; right on the highway!" He sounds positively gleeful now.

It's hard not to join in his mirth, knowing that Hemlo, currently valued at $880 million, is the largest gold mine to be found in all of North America; that no less an authority than

the Ontario Supreme Court has castigated a large Ontario mining firm for trying to defraud Corona, Pezim's company, which
originally financed the Hemlo claim; and that the bullish promoter from out west actually challenged the entire moneyed
and established Lac Minerals Ltd. (1980 assets $108 million)
for the $3 billion he claimed the mine was worth—and *won*, in
what *Canadian Business* magazine describes as a lawsuit "not
only about money but about honour."

The Hemlo gold mine story is a complicated one. It began
with a prospector named Don McKinnon shaking hands with
another grizzled prospector, John Larche. The two men, having
similar claims, agreed to split whatever they found in the 680-
odd acres of land in southern Ontario, the sort of honourable
pact frequently made among people in the prospecting and mining business. They realized the odds were slim, but they knew
that the minimal drilling done before 1945 indicated that there
was gold. The question was, how much? Enter The Pez. He
bought the two men's story and set out to raise $1.2 million,
enough to begin drilling by January 1981. "If anyone but Pezim
had been promoting Corona (the company that Pezim formed to
finance the Hemlo drilling) geologist Bell probably would have
drilled a couple of dozen holes and given up," writes *Canadian
Business*. "But Pezim has a habit of falling in love with his
deals. Encouraged by the initial results, which showed gold but
not yet in high enough concentrations to warrant a mine, he
bought more than a million shares (at about $2 apiece) himself.
In June 1981 he became president of Corona and kept the
money coming in (another $719,000 in warrant issues) to keep
Bell in the bush for another eleven months."

Pezim was convinced they would strike gold. The only real
concern was whether the gold would be on their 680 acres, or if
it would spill onto the adjoining land, in what is known as a
"puddle."

This is where the story really starts to get tortuous. Toronto-
based Lac Minerals, which owned some land close by, became
interested in the activity. Some investment letters published
data on Bell's encouraging results, and Lac's vice-president arranged a meeting with Bell and Nell Dragovan, the woman who

had originally lent money to Pezim for Corona. Prior to the meeting, Lac inspected the property, and immediately started to consider the possibility of buying the land adjoining Hemlo—the same land that Pezim and others had thought might hold the "puddle" of gold. (That land belonged to a widow, and McKinnon, the prospector, had already approached her with a view to acquiring the land for Corona.)

The Lac vice-president then ambled on down to meet with Bell and Dragovan, who showed him all the data on Hemlo. Lac thereupon made the widow an offer, doubling the amount offered by McKinnon and Corona. (Lac's royalty payment was not as attractive as Corona's, although the cash payment was more. Given the current value of Hemlo, a mere 1.5 % difference in royalty payments could work out to close to $60 million.) In the end, the widow accepted Lac's offer. Lac then contacted Pezim, who reportedly shouted the man out of his office. "Give me back what you stole from me!" he is said to have roared.

The upshot was a court case before the Supreme Court of Ontario, with Corona and Pezim charging that a larger firm with more assets had victimized a potential partner, abusing all rules of confidentiality and "honour."

"You should have heard what people had to say," Pezim says. "My friends would come to me and say, 'Murray, you're nuts. Quit.' And they were my *friends*. You should have heard the others. I had to put up with two years of abuse. Hemlo didn't just happen overnight, like I just got lucky. For two years the East, the establishment, the whole country pooh-poohed Hemlo. They said 'there's nothing there. Nothing. Who's Pezim? He's a promoter.' Now they wish they had listened. Hemlo vindicated me."

The courts agreed with Pezim. He eventually sold out to a Toronto friend, but continues to benefit through holding companies and through the 40,000 or so shares of Corona he still owns.

Hemlo vindicated Pezim, and it also proved that he had not lost his touch. "For me, finding a mine is like having a baby," he says. "And I'm good at it. I think I have a great nose for it. But I do know how to work at it." Hundreds of reports can cross his desk in a day. "You look at the report. You get a feel for it. You look at the area, where it is, get the past history of the area," he says. "Call your engineers in. We might look at one thousand properties and might not accept any. You believe or you don't believe, because essentially what you are buying is people."

Sometimes, of course, buying people can be dangerous and— because Pezim is the sort of captain who goes down with his ship— costly. "I put my money where my mouth is," he says. "I tell people to buy it; I'm buying it too. Simple. Sure, I'm an enthusiastic guy. I can't help myself. I'm a believer. But they know me. And there's nothing wrong with being enthusiastic. If we weren't it'd be a dull life."

Pezim's enthusiasm has landed him in the occasional spot of trouble, however. In 1977 Pezim bought a company for $2.5 million which he says "was a clean company, a producer of lime." The company was BX Developments, and it precipitated him into the biggest scandal of his career. "An alleged kickback and cover-up in the purchase of an Arizona lime plant will be the basis of the crown's case against Vancouver stock promoter Murray Pezim," one newspaper reported. Pezim, his partner Arthur Clemmis, and several business associates were charged with conspiring to defraud and commit theft from BX Developments Ltd.

"They made a terrible mistake," says Pezim now, "and we were awarded our money back, over $700,000. I think the investigation was instigated by the NDP." The RCMP taped Pezim's phone calls. "Five thousand phone calls!" exclaims Pezim. "Five thousand. I mean this is unheard of. Now if you can't convict anyone after listening to that many phone calls, boy, God help you . . . We were innocent," he finishes. "We didn't do anything wrong. The only thing I did wrong was put up with their abuse. We created a company that we bought for $2.5 million; worked at it and sold it for $45 million. Now if that's doing something wrong then I'm guilty."

The Crown agreed. In November 1979 a judge ruled as follows: "While wiretap conversations relied upon by the Crown may raise a great deal of suspicion as to the conduct of the accused, they do not provide any direct evidence to support the conspiracy alleged. . . ."

At the time it was Pezim's "darkest hour," according to some. "It was tough for me," said Pezim in 1983. "It was like being charged with rape. That kind of thing never leaves you." Now he is more sanguine. "It had no effect on me. They might have used it as a weapon against me, but I was acquitted. We did nothing wrong."

"I've got very thick skin," he adds. "I've been in this business for thirty five years. A long time. I haven't had a conviction for anything." But is it possible to be totally honest when dealing with risk capital? "Sure, people exaggerate. I can become over-enthusiastic about something, but if I ask somebody to *invest* I've put up my own money. I buy more stock than anybody." He points out that this is *Vancouver*. "Risk capital," he says, "that's what we are. And that's what people are buying. As long as you tell them the truth it's all they care about. People don't mind losing their money, they just want to be told the truth." He nods sagely. "I'll show you some people who have made money —serious money. You do not come to Vancouver to buy Bell Canada stock. The people who come to Vancouver with their money are people who are not happy with twenty per cent. They want 200 per cent, or 300 or 400. And they have to know that there is a lot of risk involved in that. They have got to know that a lot of the time they are going to end up with shares in Moose Pastures Mines!"

It's good for us, he maintains. "Risk capital is more important than investment capital in Canada," he once said. "Always has been. And sure, I'm waving a torch for that; I'm waving a torch for us right here in Vancouver. We've been despised too much and I've been at the forefront of it." Pezim certainly has been in the front line, and not just for the money, or for the joy of play-ing the game. Building, creating, developing a company, he points out, is good for the economy. "This market, if the truth be known, is the fastest-growing industry we have, this finan-cial market," he says. "We should examine how many jobs are here now. We employ 20,000 people. It brings in money from all over the world, not just B.C." He looks fierce again. "They should pay attention to that," he says, "pat us on the back, instead of talking about 'The Casino' and this and that. Sure, there are some bad things, but there are bad things in New York and Toronto too."

Pezim is convinced the future lies in the Pacific Rim. "I predict that you'll see, right here in this exchange, you'll see days this year where we'll trade 30 to 50 million shares a day. Become bigger and better all the time. It will happen." At last count, Pezim had eighty-eight companies listed on the Vancouver board that accounted for some twenty per cent of the total dollar value—up in the tens of millions. He definitely has a stake in this.

Keeping the money working is a priority for Pezim. In 1983, when Hemlo was just starting to take off, he was quoted as saying, "The politicians, they haven't paid enough attention. They talk about creating jobs. Hemlo has 1200 men working right now.... By 1986 it will have created 20,000, maybe 30,000 jobs. Do you realize what this means in foreign exchange? Maybe $30 billion. Maybe $40 billion." [Well, perhaps he did exaggerate a little, but he is an enthusiastic individual.]

The Pez's main enthusiasm has always been work. Two marriages failed because of this, although the first lasted twenty-two years and the second thirteen. "I make a bad husband," he confesses. "I guess my love is business. I can be a great friend to a woman, that's all I want to be." So he's single now. The Pez has three children by his first wife, two girls and one boy. "My son is in Rochester, Minnesota, at the Mayo Clinic," he says proudly. "He's a surgeon. But he's coming back in June, they've made him an associate professor of surgery at UBC. He's not even *interested* in what I do!" His two girls live in Toronto. One is a school-teacher, the other a "wife and mother."

When Pezim talks of his children he sounds like any other doting parent, but he really does seem to feel that in the final analysis his mines are his babies. "I think I've probably found more gold than anyone ever has found in Canada," he says, as proudly as he talks of his son the surgeon, perhaps more so.

One baby Pezim never had was BCRIC. In 1983 Pezim sounded like Superman, flying out to save all B.C. shareholders. "I have a plan for BCRIC and it's dynamite," he announced grandly. "It would blow your mind. I'm talking about a real business plan. I'm going to get BCRIC."

He did not get BCRIC. Now he says, "It's a simple story. I think that had I carried through I would have made the grade. I was asked to back off; I backed off. Don't ask me who asked me to, but you can well imagine." He looks mysterious. "I disagreed with what they were doing. The one thing I objected to deeply was this investment they had in North Sea oil." His voice rises slightly. "BCRIC have $800 million invested in North Sea oil and the money was raised from the people in B.C. to *spend* in B.C., create employment. I said 'what the hell are we doing with that? Let's get rid of that . . . . spend the money here, on housing, whatever.'" Doing well by B.C. is important to The Pez. "They didn't do it," he finishes. "They sold it out for—I think—$110 million. They could have got $800 million. So I just walked away, sold my stock, passed the dice."

He didn't walk away without having made every major headline in every business paper. Trumpeted the 12 June 1983 *Province*: "In a flurry of publicity Vancouver stock promoter Murray Pezim announced last weekend that he had entered the market to buy enough shares of B.C. Resources Investment Corp. to challenge the company's board of directors and management's operating policies. Since then 1,806,420 BCRIC shares have changed hands on the VSE, of which 1,322,505 were traded last Monday. Pezim is believed to have picked up between 750,000 and one million of these shares."

The flurry died down, and Pezim went back to what he does best, promoting mining companies. It is hard work. Pezim is up at five every morning, at his desk by six. Most of his deals now come from large corporations who want him to raise speculative capital for them. "Normally the odds are one in a thousand," he says, "but with something like that I have a one-in-twenty shot." He wheels and deals during the day, often continuing over dinner or drinks. "I dine out a lot," he says. Then the giant ego elbows in: "I'm a lot of fun," he says. "I really am. Frankly, I'm a stand-up comic myself. I'm fun to be around. I don't know what it is, but people love being around me." Perhaps it's all that wheeling, all that excitement, all that money changing hands on paper.

Pezim maintains an office in the U.S., also a home. "When I want some real sunshine I work down there," he says of his home-cum-office in Arizona. The rest of the time he spends with show-business friends like Bob Hope and Joey Bishop, or organizing charity events in Vancouver. It can be argued that you haven't really lived until you've been at one of Pezim's black-tie "do's," where he has persuaded several hundred of Vancouver's glitterati to pay over $500 a plate to eat a prime-rib dinner and listen to, perhaps, Red Buttons—with the profits going to some charity. Pezim often speaks at these dinners, something he does not usually have time for. He speeches are usually colourful and "off the cuff." One engagement he was very proud of was speaking at a conference in New Orleans. "This kid from Vancouver's been asked to speak at the Gold Conference in New Orleans," he crowed to *Equity* magazine in 1983. "With people like Allan Greenspan and Milt Friedman! How do you like that for bananas!? Show me one member of the Toronto Stock Exchange that's been invited to speak down there. It has the biggest financial speakers in the world."

It is easy to sympathize with Pezim's glee. Although now, at sixty-six, he is one of the elder statesmen of finance, he was not accepted into the Brooks-Brothers M.B.A. world of the Toronto (or even Vancouver) elite very kindly. Vancouver has always had a soft spot for eccentrics, which is probably why Pezim is so staunchly pro-West and anti-Toronto. A poor Jewish boy from the slums of Toronto certainly had to fight for recognition from his peers.

Pezim once said he was probably the first Jewish member of the Vancouver Stock Exchange. That could be one of the reasons he now amuses himself with odd fancies, enjoying the fact that now he has enough money to pay for them. He once toyed with the idea of buying a vineyard in Bordeaux because it was called Chateau de Pez. He loves to hang out with the famous, the interesting, the exuberant. But he balances all that with a very serious consideration for those less fortunate.

The Pez learned an important lesson as he was bobbing up

and down in the tricky world of risk-capital finance; he learned to stay out of debt. In the 1981-82 VSE downslide he lost his last $2 million—"but I was able to survive because I didn't have any debt to speak of," he says. "That's what I learned that last time. I learned that you stay out of trouble by staying out of debt. Banks love you when they're lending you money; they can't do enough for you. But when they want the money back they'll kill you."

Perhaps Pezim really has learned how to stay out of trouble this time. So although he may be still pursuing that elusive horizon, he will not lose everything if he fails to reach it.

POSTSCRIPT

October 1987:

An Ontario Court of Appeal upheld a lower court decision giving International Corona the gold-laden Williams property at Hemlo.

Within 24 hours Pezim and several of his companies were $63 million richer as the share price of International Corona Resources Ltd. soared $31.50 to $79 on 772,506 shares.

CHAPTER 6

Ted Turton

Some nice guys finish first

There is a rare kind of individual who is less concerned with accumulating wealth than he is with simply helping people, companies and his community. Ironically, he usually ends up as successful financially as those who singlemindedly pursue money all their working lives.

Such a person isn't unique, but it always comes as a pleasant surprise to find one in *this* industry.

—the late Harry Gassard
former Managing Director,
Investment Dealers' Association
of Canada

The fact that Ted Turton, born and raised in Brandon, left that quiet Manitoba city to follow a financial career is not particularly unusual. That he returned thirty years later at the invitation of a group of businessmen who needed his help is something else. And that his help was timely and successful, and was derived, to begin with, from his own pocket is what this story is all about.

Turton first located in Edmonton, which at that time in the late fifties was a sort of investment wasteland, crouching on the edge of an oil industry that was not yet confident or mature, but was in any event concentrated in Calgary. The town was removed both geographically and in sentiment from Vancouver's fitfully brawling mining industry, and too much of a backwater to count with any significance in the investment grade market emanating from Toronto and Montreal.

But the Morris Fraser organization with which Turton cut his teeth as a broker was able to instill in him enough of the rudiments of the investment game to hook him forever. After Edmonton Turton could never have settled for insurance or haberdashery. He could never, as a matter of fact, have settled for being simply a broker. He was a visionary promoter.

"Ted was a long-ball hitter," says Keith Anderson, a Vancouver broker and long-time friend. "He could always become enthusiastic about a deal, follow through on it and motivate everyone else about it."

Commencing in 1960, Turton had a brief flurry in Dallas, about which he isn't explicit; presumably it gave him an additional grasp of big men and big markets. Then it was off to Vancouver, how or in response to what particular stimulus is not recorded. Perhaps it was a kind of magnetism in the Vancouver of the sixties that simply drew him there.

He organized A.E. Turton & Company, a broker dealer organization which, under the curious securities statutes of the day, enabled him to perform only certain broker and dealer functions; he could underwrite companies, for example, but he could not engage in retail sales or the distribution of the securities he underwrote.

One of the earliest pieces of business Turton was involved in, and perhaps the most famous, came to him as casually as a cup of coffee with a neighbour. One day one of the guys down the hall in his office building, Alex Lenec, brought Turton a deal with the intriguing name of Pyramid. What was shortly to become almost a generic trademark for B.C. bonanzas had its beginning in a modest way. Turton, who has been known to say that he sometimes forgets a face but never a balance sheet, has good cause to remember Pyramid's—there was $7 in the bank.

"A position play," as the old timers used to say, was what Pyramid was all about. The property consisted of three blocks of 50 claims each, staked adjacent to Pine Point. In fact, the claims had Pine Point bracketed.

Turton, naturally, had to mobilize his "selling brokers," but he underwrote the deal, personally putting up some of the front money to complete the claims.

"The geophysical work," says Turton, "had been done by 'Segal out of Toronto', which I recall gave it some sort of prestige. In any event, the first drill hole hit ore, and away it went."

"Away it went," is something of an understatement. The stock went from zero to $23, virtually overnight.

"One of the interesting effects of Pyramid," says Turton, "was not what happened to the company itself, but the shot of adrenalin it provided for the VSE."

In the early sixties, the Vancouver Stock Exchange was still trying to outgrow its legacy as a resource-based shooting gallery, with everything that had ever been said about it still substantially true. Straight promotions by far outnumbered legitimate efforts to find an ore body, only a small proportion of underwriting funds ever found their way into the ground, and many were the company treasuries that seemed to be operated for no more serious pursuits than buying promoters cigars and memberships in the Terminal City Club.

Toronto's righteous disdain for VSE listings was curious, given its own chequered history. The Windfall scandal in the sixties had so aroused the Ontario government that a mandate was issued declaring the penny stock business a thing of the past, forcing most of the dynamiters and scam artists to leave Bay Street. Regrettably, many took up residence in Vancouver.

Now, suddenly, the hick exchange that had inherited all those sharpies had a valid winner, trading in *dollars*, and since many TSE brokers and salesmen were following Pyramid and involving their clients, the TSE had no choice but to take the whole thing seriously. Money has a strange way of homing in on more money, usually jettisoning scruples in the process. It was a heady change for Howe Street, at least for a time, before the honeymoon was over.

And so it came to pass that in 1964, Alfred Turton opened a Vancouver office for Waite Reid & Company, domiciled in Toronto but anxious to partake of more western goodies if Pyramid was a typical example. Alas, as has been demonstrated since, Pyramid was not.

In addition, misfortune fell upon that house, not because of its Vancouver operations but higher in the hierarchy, and Ted Turton suddenly and unceremoniously found himself once again in search of a hatrack. It was at this point that he entered into earnest consultation with Bill Irwin and Jack Van Luven.

It was the era when Bill Irwin reigned supreme in Victoria as Superintendent of Brokers. Irwin was eminently fair but definitely overworked, fleshing out the bones of a non-existent Securities Commission. And at the VSE, Jack Van Luven was the other half of this Gemini-like legislation-regulation partnership. In the slightly primitive (at least by eastern standards) street life that was Vancouver's securities industry, Irwin and Van Luven often wore the hats not only of referees but of coaches.

Both suggested the same course of action. H. H. Hemsworth & Company, a seasoned if not scintillating Vancouver house, was up for grabs. Harold Hemsworth had reached that age of reason when he preferred to be inactive, to take out a little capital and leave his name on the masthead. There was nothing on the Howe Street of the early sixties, as in Shakespeare's peacetime army, that so became a man as modest stillness and humility.

In a deal reminiscent of the bargain-basement purchase of Rollie Miles for $500 by the Edmonton Eskimos, Turton bought control of H.H. Hemsworth for $28,000 in equity plus something less than $200,000 injected into the company's working capital. Hemsworth Turton & Company was born, son of A.E. Turton and father of the future Canarim, which would eventually wow the railbirds as the fastest horse on Howe Street. It would be only a matter of time before Turton would be joined by the Vancouver *wunderkind*, Peter Brown, and then, to put it mildly, the stock certificates would begin to hit the fan.

Brown, a Vancouver native who was graduated from St. George's School, fitfully skirmished with UBC's Faculty of Commerce without success, and then backed off to assess the situation. It was Brown's personal conclusion that making money must be easier than making good grades. On the basis of his track record in the subsequent twenty years it would appear he was right. Whisking off to Montreal, he wisely chose the former Greenshields organization (later merged with James Richardson & Sons) as his training ground.

Greenshields, as it had with other good men and true before him, honed Brown's already keen sense of judgment, gave him the discipline that only a tour of duty on a professional trading desk can impart, and inoculated him with a permanent dislike of bond traders.

When Brown returned to Vancouver, not only was Turton glad to welcome him, the whirlwind force that hit Hemsworth's retail sales department was a logical offset for the ventures Turton was involved with. While Brown was heading for stardom as a salesman, Turton was beginning to lay the groundwork for the underwriting reputation that would later make Canarim the envy of Howe Street.

"I couldn't go at the pace Peter does," Turton said later. "I guess I tend to zero in on one situation at a time."

Turton's business philosophy has been one of intense concentration, while at the same time keeping the rest of the world in perspective. A humorist once said that Brown's idea of work was ninety hours a week while Turton's was getting away early for golf at Shaughnessy.

Peter Brown may be a hard act to follow; presumably, he's an even harder act to coexist with. With a completely different array of talents, Ted Turton played Abbott to Brown's Costello

for two decades. The result was a surprisingly resilient organization that was by no means limited to the apparent sum of its
parts.

The era during which Turton and Brown were building their
new organization was partly a time of "concept" stocks, when
few seemed to ask about earnings. It was a period when the
blue chips were something exclusive to those eastern cities,
while the Big Board in New York was celebrating "go-go" stocks
(the distant ancestors of today's high-technology issues) that
sold at multiples as high as eighty times earnings, and Howe
Street was going public with everything from hamburger stands
to garbage dumps.

It was also, fortunately, on a more realistic plane, an era in
B.C. of the high-tonnage, low-grade, open-pit copper mines.
While it lasted, that is until base-metal prices brought it down,
that market saw some of the big ones launched—Bethlehem
Copper, Lornex and Brenda. Turton was closely associated
with all the entrepreneurs who found those giants and the principals in the hefty companies that were formed to mine them.

"Ted was involved with all of us," says Jack McLallen, former chairman of Bethlehem. "And since we've been out of the
base-metal business, he's financed some of our other ventures."

One of the highly unusual underwritings among all those
open-pit copper operations was Brenda. Turton did the first
financing for a highly speculative mining company which, at
that point in its development, did not seem to be impressing
anybody, including both the market and Noranda, which was
Brenda's nominal godfather.

It was typical of Turton that knowing the two individuals behind Brenda was good enough for him—he could take their
word for what was in the ground. Others could come later and
evaluate grade and tonnage.

Morris Menzies and Bern Brynelsen, two outstanding geologists, for some years had a hard time dividing their attentions
between their employer, Noranda, (Brynelsen was western
manager for Noranda, Menzies was his assistant) and what
they at least believed to be a vast copper property in the Interior, by the endearing name of Brenda.

Noranda was on-again off-again regarding the operation but Menzies never gave up. It was ironic because Morris Menzies, especially when fired with the zeal that only a hot ore body could produce, was exceptionally persuasive. In spite of this, however, he failed to interest Noranda, which pulled off the property and discontinued its backing.

The important thing in this context was that Menzies and Brynelsen managed to interest Ted Turton, and the deal was underwritten. Eventually, Brenda was established as a massive low-grade open-pit copper mine, and when the company reached production Noranda was a sizable participant, having finally given its corporate blessing.

Menzies, until his untimely death, was responsible for more than one mega-mine, such as Boss Mountain and Sukunka Coal. As his own success mushroomed he was better able to express his opinion of large mining companies.

"Major mining companies," Menzies wrote, "are like chartered banks. They tend to avoid risk as much as possible, which places great opportunities in the path of small and medium-sized mines and mining entrepreneurs."

In fact, said Menzies on another occasion, if the company had listened to him instead of to some laboratory technician in Toronto, it could have had Lornex as well. Not that Egil Lorntzen wasn't there first, but there was a time in the fortunes of both entrepreneurs when options could have been available.

Joel Sardone, a Vancouver exporter and close associate of Turton's for many years, insists the following anecdote epitomizes the essential Turton. On one occasion, a group of businessmen at the Terminal City Club had assembled a project involving an oil-and-gas play and mining properties in the Interior. They needed initial financial backing.

Somebody introduced Turton to the group as a potential underwriter and on meeting with them Turton committed Hemsworth Turton to finance the deal which, it turned out, only required an initial $40,000.

The difficulty that then arose was that lean days were upon most of Howe Street and the firm was not able to perform an underwriting of this size. Nor was Turton himself, having stretched his personal capacity to the limit to buy control of his organization.

According to Sardone, Turton simply would not let the matter rest as most would have done, which would have been quite acceptable under the circumstances.

"Ted scratched and scrambled," says Sardone, "until he'd dredged up every bit of cash and security he could find, and personally underwrote the deal—all so that he could live up to the verbal commitment he had given us."

The little company, says Sardone, subsequently became T.C. Explorations, a successful exploration and development company.

"There's only one thing Ted has never been able to tolerate," says Sardone. "Any suggestion of the likelihood that he will go back on his word. I know the principle is important in the securities business, but with Ted he lives it to the letter."

Not all of Ted Turton's underwritings were mining. One day, Turton was sitting in his office, wondering what he would do for an encore, when an old friend from Brandon called him, a friend in fact with whom he had gone to school. The friend had a company called Inventronics that manufactured things like special thermostats and custom metals for name organizations, like 3M.

"It wasn't as if they wanted a lot of money," says Turton, "but I could see immediately that they needed at least $100,000 just for outstanding debts. So I put in $45,000 just to keep them solvent, and then I went down home—I hadn't been there for a long time anyway—to have a look at it."

What he found was an apparently thriving company in Brandon employing 130 persons but suffering from the chronic cash-flow anemia that characterizes start-ups. Turton developed a prospectus for an issue of $150,000 and ran ads in the Winnipeg and Brandon newspapers. They generated 1300 enquiries, and the company's problems were over.

"It worked out well for us too," says Turton. "About that time Peter and I had decided to open an office in Winnipeg. So

I went on in to get the Winnipeg office started, and ended up staying ten years."

Turton was in his element, according to Keith Anderson, the first broker to work with him in the new Winnipeg office. And it was not easy, given the nature of Canarim business, Turton's propensity for start-up deals, and Winnipeg's well-documented conservatism.

It was actually more than "opening a Winnipeg office." Partly to escape the image of a one-shop Howe Street house, they had decided to expand throughout western Canada.

Turton rapidly expanded, with offices in Winnipeg, Regina, and Saskatoon, and then Edmonton and Calgary followed. In Saskatchewan and Manitoba alone, Turton staffed his offices with forty producing brokers, who were soon generating twenty per cent of Canarim's revenue and developing oil and gas underwritings to offset the mining deals being handled in Vancouver.

This early expansionary period emphasized high-production salespeople and an almost complete absorption with Vancouver Stock Exchange business. When the recession arrived, with its resultant faltering markets, VSE business was one of the first to go. So, logically enough, were some of Canarim's far-flung outposts.

During the austerity dictated by the recession, retrenchment for Brown and Turton was accomplished, but with a certain stoicism that succeeded in looking more like a class act than taking a beating.

"The only branches we actually closed," says Turton, "were Regina and Saskatoon. The rest we sold to Davidson & Company." How to convert a loss into a gain. And later expansion was accomplished in a far more sophisticated manner, although it had to wait until 1987.

But before that happened, more mining financing was accomplished in Turton's department. Run-of-the-mill underwriting, of course, seemed to go on almost daily—it was one of Canarim's trademarks. One of the most significant was Turton's involvement with Queenstake.

Queenstake Resources, founded on the Queen's birthday in 1977, had a substantial complement of heavy hitters right from the beginning. They included Jack McLallen and Pat Reynolds (the former management team from Bethlehem Copper), Lauch Farris and Gordon Gutrath, both highly experienced mining executives, and in the financial corner, Alfred Turton.

The company was predicated on the ancient prospector-backer half-and-half formula. When the prospectors, one geologist and one businessman, had done their duty, Queenstake was in business in a Klondike placer mine, operating the Chichagof, at one time the greatest gold producer in Alaska, and a couple of other interests in the Western States just for variety.

To set off against its varied collection of properties, Queenstake has an equally interesting roster of shareholders—including Canada Tungsten, a substantial subsidiary of American Metal Climax.

The gold content in the Klondike operation spelled the magic words in the late seventies, when the price of gold in world markets was beginning to move. As a consequence Canada Tungsten, having been a substantial shareholder, optioned the property and became the operating company.

Early in 1979 Turton's Canarim underwrote an issue of Queenstake stock at $1.25 per share, of which Canada Tungsten subscribed a proportionate amount to maintain its substantial share position (23%). By fall of that year, the stock was trading at $5.75, and Canada Tungsten purchased 350,000 shares, followed by one million shares the following year at $7.75. Those purchases increased Tungsten's position to 44%. Meanwhile the cash infusion enabled Queenstake to enlarge its presence at the Klondike camp, acquiring various properties which ultimately saw production.

One of Queenstake's first moves was to acquire a large bucketline dredge that required some renovation, since it had been sitting in its Klondike location east of Dawson City since the mid-fifties. Once in operation the dredge proved highly profitable, gold prices being a far cry from the days when, no longer able to meet their costs with $30 gold, the previous owners had simply walked away from the bucketline.

In this fashion, Turton and the other Queenstake partners tapped into a bit of Yukon history. The second generation of gold miners, who succeeded the hordes of '98 gold-rushers, had consisted mainly of large-scale gold dredgers, who proliferated for the following six decades and produced millions of ounces of gold.

Inevitably, as production costs, and every other kind of cost, escalated in the fifties and sixties, and the price of gold remained pegged, the dredgers dropped out of business. Queenstake has been the first, and so far the only, gold producer to reactivate a gold dredge.

And as the Queenstake partners pressed their advantage in the ancient dredging game they were also expanding. Through the early eighties, Queenstake brought three additional placer-dredging locations into production, heading for a target of 20,000 ounces per annum of placer gold production.

Not content to rely on placer operations, Queenstake's management utilized their dredging cash flow to make lode-mining acquisitions. They deliberately chose a size of operation that would avoid competition with the major companies (perhaps Reynolds and McLallen knew whereof they spoke) and carefully looked at criteria such as the size of capital requirements and lead time to production.

After considerable time and investment, the Company has acquired a portfolio of properties, including leachable gold projects. Two of these are located in California and one in Nevada.

But the Chichagof Mine in Alaska, perhaps for its historic value as well as further potential, ranks high on the Queenstake partners' list of accomplishments.

According to Vancouver columnist Frank Keane, Chichagof was Alaska's richest between 1905 and 1942. In that period the mine produced 660,000 ounces of gold at an average recovered grade of 1.09 ounces of gold per ton. In a single three year period, 1918–1921, a single ore shoot produced 76,000 ounces of gold annually with head grade of 2.12 ounces of gold per ton. And to think it was all sold at a mere $30 to $35 an ounce!

Subsequently, the U.S. Bureau of Mines reported that the Chichagof Mine had the potential of a further 500,000 tons with an average grade of 0.60 ounces of gold per ton. It is likely such information served to interest the Queenstake takers.

Buoyed by the likelihood of extremely low production costs (under US$150 an ounce)—due to its sheltered harbour, completed underground workings with no necessity for hoisting, and adequate water and space for mill and tailings facilities— Queenstake moved in the early eighties to prove up Chichagof's promise and place the old mine back in production.

Queenstake, for Turton and his partners, embodied more than traditional relationships between prospector and backers. It also was a commentary on how former dredging operations and underground mines alike could be reincarnated as a result of contemporary metal prices and ingenuity.

One of the more recent deals in Ted Turton's lexicon departed from the mining genre, and capitalized on a farming operation he had carried on for some time at Shilo, Manitoba. While some people have difficulty getting serious about it, Turton and Sardone have invested the better part of $1 million in the growing of millet, and processing it in an impressive plant to manufacture birdseed.

"The equivalent," says Sardone, "of being a plumber and going to work in a Rolls-Royce."

But Turton is determined that a giant-sized bite of the Canadian birdseed market can be captured with the right kind of management and marketing. He talks about a total $7 million market, while his best friends call him Tweetie-bird.

As Canarim moved into the second half of the decade of the eighties, it might have been tempting to the casual railbird on Howe Street to suggest that Peter Brown (long since dubbed The Rabbit by his friends) had an unlikely partner in Ted Turton. In fact, again among friends only, the two are occasionally bracketed as The Rabbit and The Turtle.

But all joking aside, such an observer would have been dead wrong. On the contrary, it was the blend of two different personalities and talents that made this firm so successful, as far back as the days when it carried the name and style of Hemsworth Turton.

But two major developments began to take place in the mid-eighties which made a further evolution inevitable.

The first was a world-wide movement of openness and freer competition, nowhere as evident as in the storied London Big Bang. In one dramatic gesture the London financial markets were thrown open to all comers, and previously-guarded specialties were no more. The result—in London as well as Vancouver —was the necessity for all dealers, brokers and banks to increase their capital in order to compete more effectively.

Almost all, that is. For Canarim, the route taken differed from those of most other financial players. Instead of simply growing for growth's sake, the company found opportunities to facilitate the accommodation of larger deals, concurrent with the increasing sophistication of the Vancouver Stock Exchange as the focal point of venture-capital investment on the West Coast.

By comparison, a Vancouver house such as Pemberton Houston Willoughby Bell Gouinlock simply added to its size, mushrooming from $11 million in equity capital to more than $60 million in a year and a half.

The second event that partly determined how Canarim would move was Ted Turton's decision to undertake *de facto* retirement in order to pursue some of his private ventures.

For some time Turton's Canarim had no longer been simply a brokerage firm, albeit a leading one, and a mining underwriter that in a good year figured in perhaps three quarters of all VSE underwritings. It had broadened its scope to include the private placements market, and the increased European sourcing of capital to match with U.S.-based mining companies seeking funding.

In addition, early in 1986 Canarim created the Multiple Opportunities Fund, a mutual fund wholly devoted to investment in junior resource companies, that euphemism for low-priced mining stocks. Funded with an initial issue of $9 million, within one year Multiple Opportunities had grown to a value of

$22 million, and had placed second in performance on a national listing of equity growth funds.

Shortly thereafter Canarim figured as a financial intermediary in the fusing of British financial experts, Hollywood film executives, Charles Loewen, a Toronto dealer, and Bruce McDonald, Vancouver mining impresario. The financial package that resulted purchased for $85 million the huge film library of the Coca Cola organization of Atlanta, under the aegis of Nelson Holdings Limited, a company tentatively issued five months previously on the VSE at 50 cents, which, as the film deal was consummated, traded at $5 a share.

In quick succession, Canarim organized a merchant bank capitalized at $20 million, in order to finance deals of a magnitude too great for Canarim's normal capacity, and then, with the reorganization of Canarim itself, there was the opening of a Toronto office and the acquisition of a Toronto Stock Exchange seat.

In 1986 the Ontario Securities Commission's now-famous ruling concerning the securities markets of that province—and, by implication, all of Canada—allowed admission either by outright acquisition or by the creation of new broker and dealer organizations. This deregulatory move had a huge liberalizing effect on Canadian securities and trading.

In addition, the OSC relaxed its requirements for the incorporation of resource-based companies, in recognition of the fact that, while central Canada still dominated total mining activity in Canada, the stringency imposed since the Windfall Scandal in Ontario in the sixties had created a situation whereby much of mining's grass-roots financing was taking place in the West.

It was these two factors that had moved Brown and Turton to make their presence known in Toronto with the opening of an office and the purchase of a TSE seat for approximately $215,000.

It was a new financial sea into which Turton's house was charting its course, and while most friends and colleagues of Alfred E. Turton would bet on his ability to excel in any financial environment, Turton, to change metaphors, was not about to stay in a game where the goalposts were moving just as he was ready for more time on the bench.

With little hesitation Turton sold all but 5% of his 33% position in Canarim back into the firm, to enable new, younger shareholders to take hold.

"After thirty seven years." says Turton, "the thing I see most clearly is that this business is changing more rapidly than ever. It may be old hat to say it, but this is a young man's business. And while I can see that the opportunities are tremendous, greater than ever before, at the same time I can think of other, and for me personally greater, opportunities that I'm more interested in looking at."

For one thing, says Turton, he has several personal interests he wants to concentrate on—such as his farms and his seed operations.

"And there should be time in there somewhere," says Turton, "for a little more golf than I've ever allowed myself time for in the past. Who knows?"

The retired mining financier may have struck the most valuable paydirt of all.

CHAPTER 7

Chester Millar

Reinventing the mine

If Chester Millar was not the actual inventor of the heap-leaching process for gold recovery he was one of its early pioneers. And if, in fact, heap leaching is likened to the automobile, which also had a plethora of "inventors", Millar can without doubt be considered the Henry Ford of this surprising technology.

Strangely enough, Millar does not consider the heap-leaching technology to be the greatest single triumph in his career, although in slightly over a decade it has become so popular as to figure in almost twenty per cent of all gold produced in North America. He considers his greatest triumph to have been his discovery of the huge Afton copper-gold mine in B.C. And Afton is not even a heap-leach operation.

But in order to appreciate why the name of Afton ranks so high in Millar's personal lexicon, it is necessary to back up and take a run at it.

Millar was born and raised in the up-coast B.C. town of Powell River, and came south to the University of British Columbia just after World War II to earn a degree in geological engineering. As Frank Keane, the Vancouver columnist, has

pointed out Millar was graduated in 1950, which was not exactly a scintillating period for employment, particularly in B.C.
and even more particularly in the mining industry.

So for a time Millar, never one to expect something for nothing, worked at just about everything, whatever he could find,
notably construction. And after years of non-mining activity, he
even succeeded in putting his own construction company together. Just as he landed a sizable northern contract his company, in keeping with the times, managed to go broke.

That failure, ironically, led indirectly to his eventual success. When he lost his own firm he signed on with a large construction company, owned and operated by two brothers who
were hard as nails but had the proverbial heart of gold. Before
long they placed Millar in charge of a penny mining outfit with
a property near Kamloops, in the B.C. interior. That company
in itself was nothing to write to Powell River about but it served
as a catalyst. Its location gave rise to Millar's intense interest in
a nearby property that was eventually to become the Afton
Mine.

Millar tried to persuade his two fraternal employers to take
over this additional property. They refused, but agreed condi-
tionally to do some drilling at the site. Much of the differences
that occurred between Millar and the two brothers centered on
the relative merits of conventional diamond drilling versus percussion drilling, which happened to be an obsession of Millar's.
(In fact, at one point in the sort of moonlighting lifestyle he had
developed, Millar owned no less than three percussion drilling
rigs.)

His two bosses relented briefly, had a drilling flurry at part of
the Afton property, and came up dry. Thereupon they pulled
off the property permanently and went back to the construction
business. As tenacious as most mine-finders, Millar hung in by
himself.

Well, not entirely by himself. But Doug Price, one of the two
partners Millar bamboozled into joining him when he drilled
out the Afton property himself, emphasizes that Millar was the
original "hands-on" type.

"He was never happier than when he was working with some

kind of machinery," says Price. "Whether it was making money or not."

Millar's dedication to hard work was rewarded. The three partners formed a company to take up the claims, invested $2,500 each, and when the vast Afton ore body was found, it was with Chester Millar's percussion drill. He also found, as a result of his patience and persistence, an eventual payout of approximately $10 million, which effectively altered his lifestyle forever. He gave up working at construction and other non-mining endeavours and found himself free to go where he wanted and to look at the kind of mineralization that interested him—which happened to be gold.

Before that, however, the fun and games with the Afton mine were to swirl to a bizarre climax. Millar found himself with the dubious distinction of having two of B.C.'s major mining companies working simultaneously at Afton, each assuming it was in the driver's seat.

Because of the potential size of the Afton mine, Millar had realized that it would be necessary to deal it off to a major. In fact, when word about the mine filtered back to the mining community, the number of suitors circling for position resembled the congress of male canines that usually attends the seasonal coming-out party of a debutante female dog.

"I remember Norm Keevil [of Teck Corporation] calling me," says Millar, " and telling me he'd make me an offer I couldn't refuse."

But since *The Godfather* was popular at the time, Millar thought Keevil was just using the expression that was so much in vogue. It had not yet become common knowledge in Vancouver that when a Norman Keevil (Senior or Junior) was interested in a deal, he did not make a habit of bandying words.

Later there was another phone call from the Teck chief executive that was a little more specific.

"Don't do anything until you hear from us," Millar was told. "We're your new bosses now."

Meanwhile, back at the cabin, a firm deal was being negotiated with Placer Development, one that was extremely favourable to Millar, permitting a 60% retention by Afton while

Placer would finance the development in return for only 40%. The late Ed Scholz, Placer vice-president exploration, figured prominently in the negotiations, and the close relationship was later to be important to Millar because of Scholz's vital interest in the heap-leaching technology.

The Placer deal, in fact, was concluded just as Keevil, in workmanlike fashion, and as suggested by the last phone call, had succeeded in acquiring 51% of Afton's stock.

But in the blink of an eye, the whole *menage à trois* was trundled off to the courts and Millar, who was playing the part of a sort of unlucky Pierre, the man in the middle, was being sued by one side or the other or both for $10 million.

The court's decision did little to clarify the situation. The validity of Placer's contract was upheld, but there was no question that Teck held an ownership position. Fortunately Teck and Placer were able to get together and work out a settlement, which could only mean the transfer of a package of legal tender. And Millar now admits to having been slightly miffed, not knowing when he was well off.

But when the smoke cleared (there's nothing quite as superfluous as the former tenant in a Keevil deal) Millar took his $10 million and headed for warmer climes, looking for gold properties to confirm his percussion-drilling hypothesis.

In the standard fairy tale, the hero does a favour for some old codger beside the road, only to discover that the mendicant he has befriended turns out to be a kindly wizard who grants him three wishes. Millar's scenario followed that pattern fairly closely. It went something like this:

Somewhere alongside Interstate 5, an old stranger named Mel Rogers conned him into drilling his property. Millar agreed to do it for nothing (not a common practice in California) provided that he would have first refusal on any paydirt. As it happened there was none, so they both lost. This, however, is not the end of the fairy tale.

The old man in this picture, just like all the closet wizards you've heard about, had contacts, and tipped Millar off to a property owned by the Voit Rubber family of Newport Beach.

Before you could say "what are the other two wishes?", Millar was on for ten per cent.

But all fairy tales come to an end, and a disagreement with the Voit family caused Millar to depart with little more than a single gold brick to call his own. Shrewdly, as soon as gold prices firmed up toward the end of the seventies, Chester invested the brick in a condo in Hawaii—a move that further demonstrated his hands-on ability, according to Doug Price, since he not only bought the property but built the condo himself.

Meanwhile, true to form, the wizard died, leaving a cool million of his own stashed somewhere around his desert shack, never to be found, to the consternation of his in-laws, who thoroughly dismantled the shack. This, however, is irrelevant.

If Millar's personal view is that Afton was the most significant accomplishment in his life, few contemporary mining men would agree with him. His contribution to heap-leaching technology has been enormous, not only in his own operations but also in the consultative capacity in which he has served for other people and companies.

It was during the Voit encounter that Millar had his first chance to experiment with heap leaching. Ironically, it was because of his previous close relationship with the Placer Development people that he was able to do so. In the early seventies, anyone knowledgeable enough to engage in heap leaching kept it as closely guarded a secret as the V-2 rocket locations were during World War II.

"The Cortez Mine in north central Nevada," says Bill Thompson, public affairs manager at Placer in Vancouver, "was more or less the only heap-leach operation around. Commercially. A lot of work had been done on the process, in universities and in the field, but the technology was only one dimension. You also needed the right geological factors, not to mention the right gold-price level to make it all work."

Millar made a pilgrimage to see Placer, and to his surprise he was allowed to look, touch, and smell whatever he wanted. Undoubtedly, this lapse in security was a result of Ed Scholz's intervention. Scholz must have remembered with fondness the enterprising young mine-finder who had dealt off Afton, even as a minority shareholder.

As a result Millar came away from the Cortez mine ready to heap leach. He had conducted a test run on the Voit property, and then an even longer production test. Both had met with resounding success. It is regrettable that he and the Voits were not able to agree.

The name heap leaching, logically enough, derives from the fact that gold is leached out of the host ore, which has been piled up in heaps, real heaps, perhaps hundreds of thousands of tons of ore. The process is often referred to as "solution mining".

The most outstanding feature of heap leaching is that it extracts the most minute amounts of gold from the ore. Conventional gold extraction, for example, can feasibly produce gold of a grade as little as 0.1 ounces per ton (imagine one ounce of gold in ten tons of ore). Heap leaching enables the extraction of gold at least a quarter of such a grade; i.e., down to 0.025 ounces of gold per ton, or one ounce of gold in forty tons of ore.

In addition to the minuscule grade, heap leaching separates the gold out at a speed that Anthony Garson, gold analyst with Haywood Securities in Vancouver, describes as "providing a copious cash flow and return on capital assets which is almost an embarrassment to the traditional open-pit or underground gold mining operation."

The process is simple but large-scale. Huge heaps of ore are piled up on impervious bases, looking like giant inverted cake plates. Then a light cyanide solution is sprayed continuously on the ore, so that the gold is literally percolated out in solution, and then transported to a collecting pond. Then the gold is separated out either by zinc precipitation or absorption on activated carbon. More filtering, reduction and firing produce a dore bullion (perhaps 50% gold or more) which is then transported to a gold refinery for further refining into pure gold.

Heap leaching is not for everybody, or every ore body. Garson points out that apart from the necessity for finding the right kind of ore other problems present themselves along the way.

Laboratory and pilot tests are necessary to determine if extraction can be made economically. Even these are not conclusive.

If the ore has a heavy copper or zinc content these metals may have to be roasted before the leaching solution can be applied. (Copper, according to Garson, has been subjected to a leaching form of extraction since before 1750.) And excess clay in the ore may block the flow of the leaching solution through the ore, thereby inhibiting the action of the solution. Also, varying degrees of oxides in the ore may present a uniform-leaching problem. Since oxidized ores are usually more concentrated near the ore's surfaces, particularly in arid climates, the degree of recovery may be reduced toward the interior areas. Means of increasing the oxygen content in such cases may be successful.

Temperature variables are an important factor in leaching operations. The whole process unfolds best in dry temperate climates, and when the temperature dips below 50° Fahrenheit, gold solubility is reduced sharply. Moreover, when the temperature falls below freezing the solution may freeze before it percolates through the heap. For this reason production schedules must be sharply curtailed in the operations located in mountainous or wintry climates.

Similarly, rainfall's effects can be critical and such effects must be forestalled in the leach pad's design. Heavy rainfall can substantially dilute the solution, reducing its effectiveness, and can cause loss of gold in solution around the edges of the impervious underpad. And storage ponds can overflow in sudden downpours, not only floating away potentially valuable pregnant solutions but also driving environmentalists up the wall.

When Millar first heard about the process, he was immediately aware of heap leaching's potential. (Two visionaries named Potter and Salisbury in the U.S. Bureau of Mines had experimented extensively in the field, but Placer, as far as Millar knew, was operating the only commercial leaching operation in North America prior to 1974.)

Leaching meant that lower grades of ore could be exploited. Such deposits were often located in veins that had been ignored previously, lying on or close to the surface. The overhead, particularly at a time of rising gold prices, could be drastically reduced, with the effect that smaller players could operate profitably.

Millar, it should be noted, later placed the Picacho location in production at a cost of under $2 million. Picacho was a mine that was to become the hallmark against which all future heap-leaching operations would be measured. The Breakwater mine at Wenatchee, while it is not a comparable operation, required a capital investment of close to $90 million to reach full production.

Perhaps most important, mining, as a result of heap leaching, was no longer simply for fat cats and large corporations. Small companies that explored and found their own ore bodies would no longer face the constraint of selling their interests to the majors.

An example is Beaver Resources of Vancouver, a modest but well-managed gold producer. At a location in the Kramer Hills of California, Beaver is engaged in a 50,000 ton-per-month heap-leaching operation. It is likely that the company could not be a successful gold producer under conventional circumstances.

And of course large companies themselves are not averse to more economical operations. Placer Development pioneered heap leaching, and it was its strategic turn to precious metals early in the seventies that allowed the Vancouver giant to maintain profitability and lead the industry much later, when most of its contemporaries were floundering, locked in a base-metal tradition.

"Placer may have had the first commercial heap-leach operation," says Millar, "but we were the first in California, Arizona, and Honduras."

The "California" in that statement refers to Glamis, the name linked with that of Chester Millar the way the Yankees are linked with Joe DiMaggio.

Millar's acquisition of Glamis was accomplished without mirrors or wizards, but it was not without its problems. In the beginning, a corporate shell known as Renniks Resources had been acquired in Vancouver in 1972, and for five years that company underwent several changes in capitalization and name. In 1977, under Chester Millar's control, it assumed the corporate name of Glamis Gold Ltd.

You win some, you lose some. Near the town of Glamis in California, Millar became enamoured of a property unromantically named the Mesquite Diggings. He believed the relatively low grade there would make the property a logical contender for a heap-leach operation. (As a graduate of the Voit experience and a witness to Placer's operation, he was at this point one of the ranking heap-leaching experts of the western world.)

But when gold eased off to just over $100 an ounce, Millar and his group were forced to abandon the property. Moving from bad to good, he heard about the Picacho spread and determined to acquire it. That was finally accomplished, despite one or two occasions when, according to Millar, they were given a "hard time" by the owner of the property, a mysterious "New York lady." "In fact it was a continuous battle," says Millar.

The owner finally agreed to make a deal, but on a later occasion she called everything off because her visiting emissary had found "some mess lying around," left no doubt by the caretaker. She evidently failed to understand that a working mine site could not be as immaculate as her New York apartment. However, Millar and his management gamely persevered, and Picacho, in the fullness of time, became the heap-leaching model of the western world and the flagship of Glamis Gold Ltd.

If a mine can be said to have versatility, Picacho fits the description. From its humble beginning before the turn of the century it has been operated at one time or another as a placer, underground, or open-pit heap-leaching operation.

From the thirties until the seventies, numerous mining companies looked at the property, ran test-drilling programs and failed to be impressed. It was commonly understood that ore reserves ran into the millions of tons, but at grades of 0.04 or 0.05 ounces of gold per ton, conventional mining companies could hardly rhapsodize about Picacho's worth.

It was 1979 when Chester Millar acquired a 25% holding in Chemgold, the company that owned the Picacho property, later vending his holding into Glamis. Subsequently, Glamis acquired Chemgold as a wholly-owned subsidiary. By 1979, Millar was a five-year veteran of heap-leaching operations, and knew just what to do with the property. After drilling 500 test holes all over the Picacho property Millar had all the confirmation he needed that a substantial gold producer under the heap-leaching process was just waiting to be opened up.

Having commenced production in 1982, Picacho today operates year-round, pumping out gold at the rate of about 2,000 ounces per month and at one of the lowest cost levels of any gold mine in North America, on the sunny side of $125 an ounce. At the current rate of production it is estimated that the mine has sufficient reserves for ten years of continuous operation, unless further reserves are developed in the meantime.

More recently, an independent geological report has established proven reserves of close to 1.5 million tons of ore, and additional probable reserves of close to 8.5 million, grading an average of 0.045 ounces of gold per ton, far superior to those of many heap-leaching properties which have produced adequately under the process, working with grades as low as 0.02 ounces gold per ton.

One of the problems of the leaching operation at Picacho is that, while the ore is well suited for the leaching process, a relatively high clay content slows it down. Instead of taking days, weeks, or months for cyanide leaching to takes its course and percolate the last of the gold out (most recovery ratios run around 70% of all gold content) at Picacho it is expected that final leaching will continue perhaps years after the mining operation is depleted.

Picacho's gold extraction is almost a textbook case for the established practice of heap leaching, with two or three exceptions. Picacho ore is not crushed. It is highly oxidized and contains no base metal. It is also piled in higher heaps than usual, as much as fifty feet. And at the other end of the process the ore bullion produced is of a higher gold content than that of most producers, as much as 90%.

Since he has achieved substantial success with Picacho as a pioneer in a new medium, all eyes are naturally on Chester Millar now to see what he intends to do as an encore. That question is not difficult to answer. There are two or three properties that indicate the answer is—more of the same.

The Yellow Aster property about 125 miles north of Los Angeles has all the earmarks of a Chester Millar property: well over 6 million tons of proven and probable ore reserves grading an average of 0.026 ounces of gold per ton. Substantial metallurgic testing has established the leachability of the ore. Like that of Picacho, the location has a long history of having been mined, and in fact the extensive tailings that have been stockpiled in the past are quite likely suitable for further working under heap leaching.

Several major mining companies have examined the property in the past, passing it up for the usual reason—the grades simply did not justify conventional extraction. Millar's group, on the other hand, know whereof they leach, and have a long term option that includes a continuing production royalty which, as long as it continues to be paid, maintains the option in good standing.

In addition to several other properties it is closely considering, Glamis, spearheaded by Millar, has farmed in on properties operated by other companies. One such company is Amir Mines, also based in Vancouver and a relatively junior company blessed with excellent management, which operates twin properties in the Idaho gold belt.

Ian Johnson, Amir president, summed up what he considered to be an excellent arrangement for his company:

"You might say we had two deficiencies before we made the agreement with Chester. One was a lack of senior financing capability. The other was production experience. The partnership with Glamis takes care of both shortcomings."

In taking Glamis in as a joint-venture partner, Amir, to quote one financial writer, "has done a deal the equivalent of a man going into the stand-up comedy business, with Bob Hope on for fifty-one per cent and agreeing to put up all the capital costs while he's at it."

While some such farm-ins are obviously part of an overall strategy on Millar's part to develop a continuity of future producing properties, others provide direct access to current gold production. Beaver Resources, a Vancouver company, is involved in heap leaching on a small scale. Millar provided technical consulting for Beaver for some time.

Inevitably perhaps Millar and Glamis have been bracketed with the heap-leaching sub-industry, along with giants such as Pegasus and, more recently, Galactic Gold. One has the impression that Millar would rather be characterized as a prospector and developer than as a devotee of a single process.

Doug Price makes the point:

"Ches is a great guy, and the perfect partner. When I say he's hardworking, I don't just mean mental work. He likes machinery and he likes muck. I remember once going down to the Glamis property, and there he was, up to his waist in muck. I don't really know what he was doing—old barrels, old pipes. Whatever it was, he had the usual big grin on his face. And he built *two* houses in Bullhead City, Nevada. Not to mention his condominium in Hawaii. He didn't buy houses, he built them himself."

If it is true that Millar would rather be in the field than in the office, his latest major commitment should fill the bill. La Teko is a Vancouver-based company, as its president, Chester Millar, may be classified as Vancouver-based.

La Teko has developed the Ryan Lode property in Alaska and, at the opposite end of the continent, the San Juan Mine in California. Both locations are moving rapidly to production, completing final permitting, both slated for heap-leaching operation.

La Teko's Alaskan property seems to be on the gargantuan scale of most northern developments. Indicated ore reserves total 15 million tons, grading an average of 0.06 ounces of gold per ton, much of which is of much higher grade. A sizable metallurgic test involving 4,000 tons indicates that the ore is eminently suitable for the leaching process.

Which has come to be Millar's signature on each project. In fact, the process by which La Teko was put together has followed the by now familiar Millar pattern: a consummate mine-finder, Millar first finds a promising ore body (in recent years that has meant one that is amenable to heap leaching) then wraps a company around it, and finally he seeks out the appropriate financing, first to prove up, then to go into production.

From Glamis to La Teko, the companies that Millar has developed as heap-leaching operations have been paralleled, in fact led slightly, by another group which came to be known as Pegasus Gold. This group was initiated by the same Ed Scholz who formerly, as a vice-president with Placer Development, was one of the true heap-leaching pioneers. Three years before his death in 1980, Scholz sold his interest in the vast Landusky ore body in Montana. This was the nucleus of today's successful company, Pegasus Gold, which rivals Glamis as the most famous heap-leaching organization, both historically and in terms of current operations.

The financing imperative once caused anguish and concern, says Doug Price, recalling the travail he and Millar had over financing the old Afton project.

Millar agrees.

"Those bosses of mine," he recalls, "who insisted on diamond drilling destroyed our financing ability before we could come up with anything good. It literally lost the property for us. Of course, we got it back again in 1972 with the discovery hole. Then financing got easier."

Today Millar's batting average on outstanding properties assures him of a steady stream of financiers beating a path to his door. More often than not he is forced to turn them away, like most proven producers.

In an always mixed outlook for gold, Glamis, because of Millar's diligence in lining up a steady progression of present and future projects, all of them major, would seem to have a continued brilliant future. McLeod Young Weir, the largest integrated Canadian investment dealer organization, made the following comment on the company in mid-1987:

"We consider Glamis to be one of the few bargains left among North American gold stocks. Its growth prospects make it particularly attractive for longer-term investors."

Prominent among Glamis's longer-term investors, of course,

is Chester Millar, who never takes himself or his company one hundred per cent seriously.

"You know, Glamis," he says, "meaning the town, not the company, is not just the home of the Picacho Mine. It's also the dune-buggy capital of the world. I wouldn't recommend a visit on weekends."

When he is not looking at mining properties Millar tends to look ahead at mining technology. With his son (Millar's family includes a grown daughter and son) one of Millar's preoccupations recently has been with bio-leaching, an extraction method that involves bacterial action rather than cyanide solution.

Millar is convinced that bio-leaching will not only render conventional mining and extraction obsolete, it will also displace heap leaching, which eventually will be seen to be primitive in its recovery potential and in its effects. Reputed to be much more effective and cost-efficient, bio-leaching will also prove more popular with environmentalists.

The ultimate economics of metal production will make the conventional costs of mining seem unconscionable. Once the sulphides within ore are broken down, Millar maintains, the doors are open to far lower cost production.

"We have an ideal property for bio-leaching," says Millar. "When the technology is there, we'll be ready."

Millar is bullish on gold, but he is more enthusiastic about the future of mining in general. The rewards will be there, he is convinced, only for those willing to stay abreast of mining technology.

"The mines of the future," says Millar, "will be technological, not geological, discoveries."

———

CHAPTER 8

Lou Wolfin

Bridge River revisited. . . .

Any good miner will tell you that lightning doesn't strike twice, that history does not repeat itself and that a moving target is always best. Lou Wolfin, a man of thirty years' tenure in B.C.'s mining wars, prefers to think otherwise. Gold having increased in price tenfold in that period, since the early fifties, Wolfin asks the simple question: "Wouldn't *you* strike twice?"

Gold is like no other commodity. Apart from creating wealth, allaying nervousness, and leading to gouged eyeballs wherever it occurs, gold has a further effect. It consistently makes for the damnedest history.

For example:

(1) The magnificent gold overlays on Cleopatra's utensils, works of art, and jewellery brightened her otherwise prosaic life (and caused Mark Antony, Julius Caesar and other assorted dates to home in on the Queen of the Nile as if interested only in her Dun & Brad).

(2) The glory of discovery aside, we all know what Cortez was doing in Central America, and it was not checking out Mayan temples. Almost everything below the Rio Grande was colonized because of the strong rumours about the biggest gold play since the Inquisition.

(3) One cold winter night in Winnipeg in the early 1960s, a Transair cargo aircraft landed at Stevenson Field and taxied up to the company's air-freight building, where it was met by a panel truck and two men dressed in white overalls.

"We're here to pick up the gold," said one of the men in white, no doubt being answered with "Be our guest," or something equally trite from the aircrew.

The aircrew even helped the panel truckers to offload $400,000 in gold bars, chatting and making poor jokes about the weather as they did. One of the men in white then signed a receipt—a receipt, yet—and he and his companion trundled off in their panel truck into the Winnipeg night. Never to be seen again. Correction: to be seen briefly in the prisoners' dock a few months later.

Royalty, discoverers, and audacious thieves are all part of gold's rich history; the play on words is intended. And Lou Wolfin, who grew up in Winnipeg but left to seek his fortune ten years before the Transair heist, is a firm believer in gold cycles, not just in price but also in the recurring patterns in men's hunt for the big yellow. Being part of the gold history tradition, he is susceptible to it, accepting a sort of "life is short, but gold is long" philosophy.

The best possible example is Wolfin's thirty-year involvement with the Bridge River area in the B.C. Interior, where gold of bonanza proportions was mined at least a century before Wolfin arrived. 1858 was the year B.C. became a province, when membership in the confederation club leap-frogged Manitoba, Saskatchewan, and Alberta, and prospectors on the Bridge River were doing a little leap-frogging of their own.

The area at that time was the locus of a full-bore gold rush. When the scene had achieved the inevitable shake-out, two of the companies well staked out were Bralorne and Pioneer. In the following forty years of operation the two companies produced four million ounces of gold—close to $2 billion at today's prices. Pioneer was billed as the "World's Richest Mine," which sounds rather like B.C. chauvinism; but it was a pity that all that colour had to be dealt off at $30 an ounce, or whatever it went for in those days.

By 1930, when the area was probably the only game in North America (the only profitable one, anyway) it had also become a base-metal producer, turning up copper, lead, zinc, tungsten, and molybdenum. But who could get excited about anything else when gold was being churned out in such happy numbers? In foreign exchange good money drives out bad; in mining precious metals drive out base.

In 1958, when Wolfin hit the Bridge River area known as Skukakum (Land of Plenty), about one hundred miles northeast of Vancouver, he didn't exactly precipitate a great Bridge River Renaissance. The vehicle he was using, Ace Mining, turned up reasonably good values by today's standards, but Wolfin and Ace nursed an idea twenty years ahead of the technology their ore grades required—that gold mining could be profitable with low grades and high tonnage.

In the thirty years since, Wolfin has ranged widely in mining projects out of his Vancouver office, from Mexico to the Yukon, but Bridge River has never failed to be the focus of his attention. Currently five of his operating companies—Levon Resources, Avino Mines, Coral Energy, Berkley Resources, and Fairchild Resources—while they may have properties elsewhere as well have been deployed throughout Bridge River in a huge pattern collectively over 25,000 acres.

Anyone who had known Lou Wolfin in the sixties, and had then inexplicably fallen asleep for the interim period like Rip Van Winkle, might marvel on awakening today at this man who has graduated from the status of Howe Street promoter of positions to his current state with five companies, every one of which is flirting with a substantial ore body, and at least two of which are in production. Did he just sit around for thirty years until the markets were just right?

"Listen," says Ted Turton, long-term Vancouver broker, "When you grew up in the North End of Winnipeg, you appreciate *everything*, and it's part of your nature not only to work like hell but to hang in there. That's why there are so many terrific people who came from the North End."

(Like Cockneys, Winnipeg Northenders have their own geographical parameters. If you were born within the smell of Kelekis's potato chips, you are a Northender. You cannot become a Northender by adoption, and you never abdicate. In fact, never quitting is what it's all about. The following well-known public figures are among the distinguished group that has emerged from the North End over the years: Magistrate Isaac Rice, novelist Adele Wiseman, marathon MP Stanley Knowles, and Manitoba Attorney General Roland Penner.)

"In Lou's case," says Turton, "there's more than one good example. Of all the Canadian mining outfits that went down to Mexico to develop silver mines, Lou's is the only one that hung in and made it. And then there's Bridge River—the same kind of story. The North End spirit did it. That's it."

The Bridge River holdings of Levon Resources alone exceed 18,000 acres. And Levon, at least in this key area, is Wolfin's flagship. Eight of Levon's properties are joint-ventured with Veronex Resources. The richest potential seems to lie in the Congress property, site of the former Congress Mine. Just eight miles north of the ancient Bralorne and Pioneer Mines, the Congress property features eight important gold zones.

Originally staked in 1915, the Congress is fortunate in terms of its location in this generally mountainous terrain. Just five miles from the town of Gold Bridge on the highway between Bralorne and Lillooet, it has readily available hydro power, water, and timber, and buildings for the housing of exploratory crews.

Over the past three years extensive drilling has taken place on the Congress property and elsewhere in Levon's holdings. The most recent, in early 1987, took place in the course of working on the Howard tunnel underground on the Congress property. Assays from a 36-foot section averaged 0.74 ounces of gold per ton.

Dr. Franc Joubin, the discoverer of Blind River and one of the most highly respected mining men in Canada, made this comment about Bridge River in 1985, writing in Vancouver's *Northwest Prospector*:

"My association with this 1.6 billion dollar gold camp (present value of past production—over four million ounces) goes back almost 50 years.

"It was in the Depression year of 1936, when I was one of four UBC undergraduates who , in a rattle-trap Model T Ford , joined the original Bralorne-Pioneer 'gold-rush' to find work and earn a stake to finance the next year of university . . ."

And it was in the sixties that Joubin, following outstanding financial and mining success in eastern Canada, returned to organize a new management group for Bralorne-Pioneer, which included Cy Manning and Howard James. Joubin's second coming was heralded by the legendary Ma Murray in her newspaper as "the return of the Messiah."

Joubin went on to describe how he left the Bridge River area for the second time, after helping in the Bralorne-Pioneer reorganization, and then his recounting of his third contact with the famous valley in the eighties is perhaps the most fascinating of all—at least for Bralorne-Bridge River-Wolfin watchers. The year was 1983.

"The economics had improved considerably," says Joubin, "from $35 an ounce for gold to a tenfold increase and the earlier unmined sub-marginal material (below 0.25 oz. per ton) was now ore grade."

This had brought on a rash of "boomers" staking over older prospects, in addition to many pros, some of whom had been there before in the sixties or the fifties—and perhaps even the ghosts of some of the old originals from a hundred years before that.

Joubin noted: "The *Northern Miner* recently described some of the more impressive current discoveries, the parade-leader of the moment probably being the Levon Resources/Veronex Resources 'born-again' Congress property."

Just to clarify what was going on in the 1983 revival, Joubin spelled it out in language you are not likely to encounter in your basic Grade XII geology:

"This epithermal type mineralization commonly occurs in quartz-deficient shear zones, apparently cutting and not conformable to volcano-sedimentary rock assemblages. Perhaps significantly, several such shear occurrences (including the present most impressive model, the Lou Shear on ex-Congress property) are specially close to later, generally acidic dykes which, in one or two reported instances, themselves contain near-ore quantities of gold."

For the benefit of non-professionals, the implication would seem to be that Lou Wolfin was holding aces back to back.

Pointing out that these current formations are distinctly different from the characteristic deposits of Bralorne/Pioneer, Joubin adds that the comparison is not meant to downgrade the new types of epithermal discoveries now under development:

"If depth development of such structures as the 'Lou Shear' maintains its near-surface promise, then its total gold content per vertical foot will equal or greatly exceed that of the average Bralorne/Pioneer type vein."

If a geologist of Franc Joubin's stature sees fit to consider Bridge River "born-again" country, Lou Wolfin's years of work would seem to have been vindicated. In addition Wolfin, although he has been staking and working in the Valley consistently since the early sixties, has recognized the subtle shifts that have occurred in mining, the new ball-game made up of new technology and booming gold prices to offset rising costs. Against these factors, he has recognized that a get-rich-quick approach when you are playing with a real ore body is more likely than not to lead to financial disaster.

"My concern has always been for conservative, long-term corporate development," says Wolfin characteristically. "Success cannot be achieved overnight."

Whatever the time span, there is no denying the success attained on almost every level by Lou Wolfin. It is evident also in Levon's other major holding, Carbonate Hill in Colorado's Cripple Creek Mining District. That property consists of 300 acres adjoining some of the area's richest mines.

In the course of three years of development drilling, a large low-grade gold deposit has been identified ranging between 0.04 and 0.08 ounces of gold per ton, depending on the cut-off. According to Richard Dwelley, Levon's project geologist at the

Carbonate Hill site, after the most recent drill program, a series of six-column leach tests showed gold grades that averaged about 40% higher than those obtained by fire assay results.

The Company has estimated reserves at Carbonate Hill of approximately 10 million tons grading an average of 0.04 ounces of gold per ton.

While Standard & Poor's Corporation in New York indicates that Levon produces no revenue and is defined by the SEC in the United States as an "exploration stage" company, two things perhaps illustrate the financial versatility of the company at this stage of its development.

In 1986 Levon completed a private placement with the Union Bank of Switzerland and the Christiana Bank of Oslo for a total of 30,884 shares at $4.08 per share, together with warrants to purchase a like amount at $4.33. A year earlier a public offering of 600,000 units had been made in Canada, which netted the company approximately $2 million.

Levon has no long-term funded debt and has a strong working-capital position of approximately $3 million. It was the story so often experienced during the new gold rush of the eighties: in a world full of cash-heavy investors, particularly investors in gold, it is not necessary to be in production to draw the active buyers. As development companies have shown evidence of a sound ore body combined with intelligent management and the capability of coming to production, investors from Europe, Asia, and North America have lined up, often causing the entrepreneurs an embarrassment of riches.

But it was not his concentration on Bridge River alone that brought Wolfin to the edge of success by the 1980s. In the cycle of production and earnings, Avino Mines & Resources was one Wolfin company that was well on the road to success. With its principal operations near Durango, Mexico, Avino produces silver, gold, copper, and lead. It is also diversified with an important property in the Bridge River area.

The Durango mine is operated as a joint venture between Avino and Cia Minera Mexicana de Avino, the operating company. In recognition of the Mexican practice of involving domestic companies in the operations of offshore organizations, Avino owns 49% of Cia Minera Mexicana de Avino.

"The Avino mine," says Lou Wolfin, president, "raised silver production by 15% over 1985 and lowered costs to US$3.36 per ounce of silver equivalent. Avino now ranks among the lowest-cost silver producers in the world."

At any other time that might be taken as just some sort of hyperbole, but recent years have not been kind to the price of silver, so Avino's efforts have been doubly important.

Late in 1986 the *National OTC Stock Journal* of Denver published a profile on Avino by Zbigniew Lambo, executive vice-president of an investor relations firm in Portland, Oregon. In part, Lambo extended Wolfin's statement concerning Avino's cost-cutting efforts.

"If you subscribe at all to the contrarian investment theory," says Lambo, "you should find the following discussion intriguing and worth closer study.

"Avino's joint-venture silver mine has lowered production costs to US$3.36 per ounce, increased production by 15% and earned a modest profit of CDN$300,000. All of this took place while at least fifteen of the largest silver mines in the United States closed or curtailed operations due to depressed silver prices."

Lambo goes on to point out that—no flash in the pan—Avino has been plodding along for seventeen years (a Wolfin trademark), weathering upheavals in the silver market and emerging debt-free and unscathed.

What Lambo does not mention is the further action Wolfin took a year ago in an even more pronounced effort to minimize cost and maximize profitability. Wolfin says that the company's central philosophy is to remain debt-free while exercising maximal cost efficiency. One productive measure was to complete a 375 million-liter reservoir at the mine in 1985, which proved capable of meeting the mine's requirements during the following dry season, so production ran 13% ahead of the previous year

Total production for 1986 ran well over 500,000 ounces of

silver, as against 473,000 ounces the year before. Gold production, employed as a cost reducer, was up in the most recent year by 54%.

"But the year was not without problems," says Wolfin. "Our recovery rate for silver averaged 51%, which was below our previous average of 58%, and well below our goal of 85%."

Since even a slight increase in recoveries would mean much higher revenues, Avino turned to Lions Metals in London, world-renowned experts in precious metals mining, milling, and financing. Lions was asked to examine Avino's facilities with a view to making recommendations for the improvement of recoveries and profitability.

The Lions organization, which maintains an associated office in Mexico, submitted its report on Avino in March 1986, detailing several suggestions for raising recoveries.

"Also," adds Wolfin, "their detailed analysis of the milling system will greatly assist our mill expansion plans."

Since many of the Lions recommendations are being adopted immediately, one of that company's most senior executives has been invited to join Avino's board, not only to assist in implementing the improvements but to add management strength.

After ticking off all the good news—low production cost due to open-pit operations, production being the primary ore variety rather than as a by-product, and Mexico's low labour costs—Zbigniew Lambo turns to the bad news.

Silver tends to bore the equity markets, which are led by metals analysts who are more interested in gold and platinum. Also, Mexico is an unfortunate place to have a company of any kind these days, with economic tales of woe being exported wholesale. Will the country cave in, or simply default on the interest on its $98 billion in debt? Whatever the outcome it will probably not be as disastrous as expected.

Meanwhile, Wolfin has on Avino's active agenda early geographical diversification, most likely into the United States and South America. Already diversification of a sort exists in the company's Minto Mine in B.C.'s Bridge River field.

The Minto operation is a "mine," not a property, having produced gold and silver from 1934 to 1937, and later in 1940. The extent and grade of mineralization, according to Wolfin, are being determined by exploratory drilling, with a surprisingly large unexplored area north of the existing workings still to be developed.

Lou Wolfin has a favourite expression, "I'm an optimist." In the period ahead he sees the top priority for Avino to be an expansion phase, with the twin objectives of increasing rates of production and improving mineral recoveries.

With the problem of water supply as a production factor largely alleviated, the mine's three ball mills have been increased to four, adding 1,000 tons per day to throughput. Two additional mills with projected total capacity of an additional 2,000 tons per day will be part of a near future expansion.

The other priority will be the implementing of the recommendations of the Lions Metal report. It is expected that with very little expenditure recoveries can be raised to about a 65% level, while with further expenditure an 85% level of recovery can be achieved for both silver and gold.

Achieving all this calls for an ambitious program on the part of Wolfin and Avino. Diversification is as basic an instinct with Lou Wolfin as tenacity. If the Rip Van Winkle observer mentioned earlier were told of Levon's heavy position in B.C.'s Bridge River Valley, and Avino's operating mine in Durango, Mexico, he might then hypothesize that Wolfin would also have a major property halfway between the two—say, slightly north of Reno, Nevada. He would be dead right.

The property in question, Coral Energy Corporation, exemplifies several features of the Wolfin corporate philosophy. One, it is a respecter of technology. In the 1980s in the gold mining industry, and particularly in warm climates such as Nevada's, where low-grade ores are prevalent, new technology can be summed up by the term "heap leaching." Although the process has become almost commonplace, its popularity has reached the greatest expression in the western States, where even the higher altitudes, short of actual mountains, can escape heavy frost with which cyanide leaching is not compatible.

Another Wolfin characteristic is keeping good company. At Bridge River, Lou accumulated property close to a gold producer 130 years old. In Durango, he tied into a silver mine that was older than most settled areas in North America. And in Nevada, Coral Energy participated in a property that was a gleam in prospectors' eyes before the turn of the century, and it is also comfortably tucked in between the Carlin Belt and Battle Mountain in order to qualify as one of the most prestigious gold mining areas in North America.

Coral Energy is in fact almost completely surrounded by active producing gold mines: Battle Mountain's Fortitude to the northwest, Carlin Gold's various deposits to the east and northeast, Gold Acres to the southwest, and to the southeast is that classic in the annals of heap leaching, the Cortez Mine owned and still operated by giant Placer Development of Vancouver.

The site is large enough to encompass the former townsite of Tenabo, one of Nevada's historic gold-rush towns. In 1907 a gold and silver rush took place that resulted in the town's creation. Underground and placer mining were carried on for more than two decades. Two attractions have greeted more recent developers: tailings dumps from those early-in-the-century mining operations, and the possibility of deeper targets because the pioneer operators extracted ore only at shallow depths.

Mill Gulch is an excellent example. In 1938 this ore body was the largest placer mining location in the United States. Current exploration being carried on by the Coral group indicates the possibility of as much as 20 million tons of ore-grade deposit still.

Known as the Robertson Gold Project, Coral Energy's Nevada location already has drill-indicated reserves of over 3 million tons, grading 0.03 ounces of gold per ton. Continued drilling is expected to delineate additional reserves. Coral Energy holds a 70% interest (its joint-venture partner is Aaron Mining of Vancouver) and is the operating company on the site. A bulk-testing program is expected to lead directly into full-scale gold production.

The Robertson Project takes its name from Andrew Robert-

son, chairman of Aaron Mining. Among Robertson's credentials
is the development of the Endako moly mine in B.C., which he
successfully brought to production in 1965, and which is now
the largest producer of molybdenum in Canada. Placer Development still operates Endako today, at a capacity of over 35,000
tons per day.

Operations manager at the Project is Jack Archibald,
formerly smelter manager over a twenty-five-year period for a
major mining and smelting company in Laredo, Texas.

Lou Wolfin, as president and chief executive officer of Coral,
completes a strong operations and management group for the
Robertson Project.

Paul Wilkman, analyst with Pacific International Securities
in Vancouver, notes that, while it was little known a decade
ago, heap leaching in low-grade ores has become so commonplace that it is now responsible for half of all new gold being
produced in the United States (as distinct from North America). Many of the new major heap-leached discoveries in Canada are distinctly high grade.

Wilkman also points out that while Coral Energy's reserves
are carried at 3 million tons, geological reports tend to suggest
an ultimate figure of at least 12 million tons to be proven up as
exploratory drilling progresses. Bulk testing will involve a block
of ore of close to 100,000 tons.

Expanding the ore body potential will be Wolfin's next priority, following bulk testing and full production. Wilkman indicates that two or three ore zones surrounding the bulk-test site
indicate extremely high grades, as high as 4.0 ounces of gold per
ton and, due to the inadequacy of earlier drilling, much ore
probably remains to be discovered. For one reason, straight vertical drilling often does not fully sample the fractured systems,
and angle drilling will seek to intersect such systems more effectively.

Financing a project such as the Robertson Gold usually en-
tails either giving much of the project's interest away to a farm-
in partner, or else issuing so much equity in order to finance
the project alone that the management group's position is sadly

diluted. With a combination of factors, Wolfin may have evaded both eventualities. Much of the capital expenditure normally expected will have been saved by the circumstance that initial plant facilities and equipment are already on the site. These include a carbon stripping operation and a complete assay office. Water in sufficient supply is readily available from an adjoining property.

Development financing, totalling $2.9 million, was completed by Coral Energy over the previous two years by a series of private placements. Those funds will meet the company's requirements for the bulk-testing phase, exploring for additional ore reserves, and a full pre-production feasibility study.

One indicator of Coral's exceptional rate of growth, and of Wolfin's ability to move quickly in all departments from finance to production feasibility, is apparent in Coral's rapid balance-sheet development. In January 1985, total assets were just over $77,000. In January 1986, the year-end report indicated slightly under $1 million in assets. By January of 1987, a total of approximately $3 million had been raised by private placements of the company's stock with European institutional investors, and gold production was imminent.

One of the most interesting of Lou Wolfin's companies is Berkley Resources, for two reasons. Early in 1986 Berkley merged with two other companies, Kerry Mining and Fortune Island Mines. In addition, prior to the merger Berkley held 58 producing oil and gas wells, all but one of which are located in Alberta. This alone provides the company with a strong revenue base, enabling management to turn its attention to mining projects—which of course is exactly what the other two companies are all about. The amalgamation brought the combined companies' total assets to $2.7 million, and total revenue to more than $400,000 per annum.

As might be expected the new and stronger Berkley has extensive property in the Bridge River Valley of B.C. All three components were previously Wolfin Group companies.

In addition to tripled assets, stronger revenue, and more extensive mining property, Berkley, according to the *Broker's*

Guide of Portland, Oregon, will effect administrative efficiencies and lower costs. One of the reasons is the new company's unusual concentration in its two operating divisions. Virtually all its oil and gas wells are located in Alberta, while all of its mining properties are centred in the Bridge River area.

In addition, Berkley will be better positioned to generate funding for exploration and development. At the time of the merger the company showed a liquid position of close to $2 million, and no debt (another Wolfin trademark).

Even more recently, Wolfin's group took another company public, in July 1986. Fairchild Resources is a small but well-endowed company within 21 kilometres of the town of Gold Bridge and 17.5 kilometres east of the Bralorne and Pioneer mines.

The Fairchild property was originally staked in 1933, and was worked from time to time until 1940. While extensive drilling has not as yet been carried out by Fairchild, one exposed vein has assayed at between 0.2 and 0.36 ounces of gold per ton over strike length, with much more substantial grades pertaining to silver content.

At the time of the public issue, Fairchild raised $600,000 with a view to commencing a detailed exploration program. Canarim Investment Corporation acted as underwriting agent for the issue.

Recently, Wolfin has been joined by his daughter, Lee Anne, a law-school graduate and a member of several Wolfin Group boards.

Lou Wolfin's corporate concentration in precious metals, particularly gold, might raise the question of the future price of that metal. Is he concerned?

"I'm essentially an optimist," says Wolfin. "And there's also the fact that we *are* diversified. There's the silver operation in Mexico, and oil and gas in Alberta."

So much for outlook. And Wolfin's quiet, cumulative success suggests that sometimes, in mining as in other forms of magic, the real wizards are those who demonstrate tenacity and hard work over a long period of time. Thomas Edison came close to that theory with his statement that genius is ninety-nine per cent hard work. If that is so, there is no denying Lou Wolfin's genius.

And his chapter is one of considerable significance in the long history of gold.

———————

CHAPTER 9

Norm Keevil, Jr.

The beat goes on. . . .

To mention "Teck Mining" or "Teck Corporation" in British Columbia is to conjure up a tall, Bauhous-style office tower encapsulating a massive, corporate structure, much in the way one envisions MacMillan Bloedel. That Teck is involved in a different line of business and is nowhere near as large seems not to matter; Teck represents the solidity of corporate Canada.

In command of this edifice is Norman Bell Keevil, Jr., who in 1980 took over the presidency of Teck from his father, Norman B. Keevil, Sr., after nearly two decades of working at Teck. Father and son have vastly differing personal styles, but they both embody the Teck spirit, which is individualistic, less conservative, and more entrepreneurial than is usual in the annals of large corporations. The company has never submerged its original entrepreneurial instincts in its vast corporate structure, and the Keevils have been noted not only for their bold moves but for their impeccable timing and visionary tactics, solidly tempered with caution.

"Free-wheeling" is the term most often heard in connection with the Keevils. Wrote the normally low-key *Northern Miner* in 1986: "Recognizing a diamond in the rough has long been a trademark of Teck and its entrepreneurial staff. Style without substance doesn't go far in the mining business and Teck appears to have an abundance of both. Emphasis is placed on the individual, who is given a free hand in the decision-making process and is allowed to develop his or her area of expertise. Self-starters are encouraged and Teck's free-wheeling attitude has made it a favourite among junior-sector companies, which correctly perceive it to be a tough but fair dealer, laying all its cards on the table."

Norman Keevil, Jr., concedes Teck's philosophy is more uninhibited than is the norm. "We're basically opportunity-driven in our business," he says, thoughtfully drawing on his cigar. "What we look for is a good mineral deposit we can make money on. Latterly these have tended to be gold, because a lot of people are looking for gold, but when Murray Pezim found Hemlo we moved in, not because it was gold but because it was a good ore body. People ask, 'are you looking for gold, or zinc, or copper,' or whatever—I think a company in our business that says it is 'basically a gold company' or 'basically a zinc company' doesn't see nearly as many opportunities as one that says 'we're basically an *opportunist* company'."

Teck certainly has taken its opportunities wherever it has found them, and Keevil explains that Teck has no hard-and-fast plan, but does have a strategy. "Part of our strategy is based on the fact that mines always have a life," he says. "Our business is mine development. It's not just running out the life of a mine; we have to go out and get the opportunities, wherever they are, and in whichever metal, to replace other things that we might be mining." This future-oriented thinking is largely what has given Teck the reputation it has—while many times puzzling the experts who gave it that reputation.

At one time Teck had one hundred or so small companies in its coterie, prompting one business writer to exclaim that while Teck seemed adept at financial deals it seemed rather slow in bringing mines into production. "We were aiming at building up a portfolio over a period of . . . years," says Keevil now. A wise program, but one which did not endear Teck to financial analysts and stock-market experts. According to the *Vancouver*

Sun in 1980, Teck was "ignored by the stock market and treated like a penny exploration stock, bounced around mainly on drilling news with little consideration being given to earnings potential."

Those nay-sayers would have done well to examine Teck's history more closely. In the early seventies, while the vast majority of businesses moaned about the NDP government's attitude toward business, Teck took control of Afton Mines Ltd., buying about 1.3 million shares for $16 million. It proved a timely purchase; the gold and copper mine in Kamloops had an average reserve grade of 0.82% copper and 0.022 ounces gold per ton. The Afton mine deal sparked a string of expenditures for Teck in B.C., and in the Yukon, where, as Keevil explained later, they foresaw the opportunities of the future.

In the early eighties Teck, like many other companies, slid into the red. "We had never had a loss in our history since 1911," says Keevil, "until 1982." That was when the recession hit. "We were faced with costs which were going up due to inflation," he explains, "particularly in petroleum cost. Oil was going up forever, and the cost of gasoline and diesel fuel. . . . So our costs were going up even faster than inflation, which was bad enough, then world commodity prices plummeted and forced us and virtually every other mining company in the country into the red."

Teck decided to change tack in 1981, even before the recession hit full force. "We could see it coming," says Keevil. "The very high interest rates, they had to cause a recession. We started to sell off assets we didn't need, parts or all of them, and also to look at cutting costs where we could. The costs we were really trying to cut were interest costs, to get our debt down so that whether interest rates were 22% or 10% we would be solvent. We had too much debt anyway," he adds, "as did most companies, because the previous years had been so heady."

Because Teck reduced its debt before the recession, its turn-around was quicker than most. "We still had about a year and a half of losses, but we got turned around reasonably quickly," Keevil says. "In fact, we've made pretty good profits since then, considering metal prices haven't improved—other than gold."

[A bit of an understatement; Teck has a book value of $599 million.]

Teck moved to Vancouver just prior to the Afton mine move, for two reasons: first, the ore bodies in the East, though higher-grade, were in much smaller quantities than were those in the West; and second, the Ontario Securities and Exchange Commission had begun to over-regulate the mining industry. "They didn't understand the nature of Canada's mining industry, and strangled it with regulation," says Keevil. He was simply waiting for an excuse to come out west anyway, he admits. The Vancouver Stock Exchange was an added incentive, as that was where the junior mining companies were making their finds and he says that Teck saw its job as "tying in with them."

Keevil never liked the East much anyway. He laughingly says that he'd be just as glad if we gave away the "golden band of Toronto, Ottawa, and Montreal" to the United States. "We'd get a much more interesting country by trading them for Alaska," he says lightly. But isn't he *from* the East? "Well, not really," he says. "We didn't really consider ourselves 'the East' in northern Ontario—northern Ontario is hinterland as much as B.C. and Newfoundland are."

Teck Corporation's roots are in the East, though, and so is the Keevil dynasty's connection with it, beginning in the forties when Keevil Senior, then a University of Toronto professor of geophysics, decided to set up a side-line mining consulting firm. He maintained that double lifestyle for a few years, then, in the post-war boom, decided to give up academe altogether, a decision he says he has never had time to regret. He quickly established a reputation for technical expertise mixed with solid entrepreneurial instincts, and, in 1954, hit it big with the Temagami Mine in northern Ontario. Temagami was a copper ore mine, one the richest anywhere.

"It was 150 feet long and 50 feet wide, covered with a growth of forest and 25 feet of gravel," reminisced Keevil Senior to the *Financial Post* in early 1987. "When we uncovered it, the ore was just glistening there in the sunshine. A fantastic sight. It was almost a shame to cut into it." He did cut into it and became an instant millionaire—and the *wunderkind* of the moment. "Temagami showed that Keevil's knowledge of the then relatively-young technique of airborne geophysics could find mines," the same publication had proclaimed in 1958.

Much was made of Keevil Senior's academic qualifications (B.Sc. and M.Sc. from Saskatchewan, his home province; Ph.D. from Harvard, and post-doctoral work at MIT, scholarships all the way) and of the many scientific papers he had published. He was credited with developing the application of geophysical methods in the hunt for new mines, and particularly with pioneering the use of the magnetic airborne detector after it was declassified by the U.S. Navy in 1946.

"The Keevil Empire," as it was dubbed, with Keevil Senior at the forefront, had gained control of the Teck-Hughes gold mines at Kirkland Lake in northeastern Ontario, which in turn owned 81% of the Lamaque gold mine at Val d'Or in Quebec. (The current Teck Corporation is a result of the amalgamation of Lamaque and Canadian Devonian Petroleums.) Keevil Senior made a practice of buying just enough shares to gain controlling interest in a company, usually, if not always, with the owner's consent. This, and the fact that he was articulate, charming, educated, and wealthy made him every newspaperman's dream, the perfect embodiment of the archetypal postwar success story.

Keevil Junior was born in Boston in 1938 while his father was at Harvard, and attributes his entry into the same field as his father to the trekking the two did in the bush. "I got interested in geology by walking along the beach on Lake Ontario and seeing all the fossils in the rocks and reading books about volcanoes," he says now. "Things like fossils and volcanoes attract you when you're a kid." He pauses, then adds, "Actually, I hate fossils now." It appears that his present dislike of fossils is the result of his having had a very boring paleontology professor in college.

Keevil Junior followed in his academic father's footsteps by attending first the University of Toronto, then the University of California at Berkeley, getting his Ph.D. there in Mineral Technology, a fairly new discipline at the time and one which

encompassed geophysics, geochemistry, and geology. He joined
Teck in 1963 because his father "kind of twisted my arm." He
says his being the eldest of nine and the obvious heir-apparent
had nothing to do with it; "I was simply the first one to get the
twist of the arm," he says wryly.

At the time his entry was hailed by the media. "This hot
father-and-son team is flying," cried one headline admiringly.
Business publications were most impressed by the Keevil ploy,
begun in the fifties by the father and continued subsequently by
both, of snapping up control of early-stage mining companies.
According to some, that tactic earned them the tag "The Evil
Keevils" (Keevil Senior once boasted that at one point their various mergers and takeovers knocked twenty-one companies off
the Toronto Stock Exchange), but those in the know say the
Keevils, far from being perceived as evil, were actually considered fair and generous, with a reputation for honest dealings.

Following in the footsteps of his more flamboyant father has
not been so easy for Keevil Junior, although he never actually
says so. "We always thought pretty much the same way," he
says simply. Journalists did not seem to agree, and have tended
to confuse the son's reserve with colourlessness and have preferred the father's more extroverted ways. "Keevil Jr. . . . 49,
short, balding, and cigar-smoking, looks and often acts like a
mining president cliché," wrote the *Financial Post* unkindly.
(What, precisely, a mining company executive is supposed to
look and act like they never actually made clear.)

There is, if anything, an aura of academic coolness about
Norman Keevil, Jr., which may explain why he has not been
loved by the media. Although his dark-blue suit is impeccable,
it somehow gives the vague impression of being professorially
rumpled. The *Financial Post* notwithstanding, he is tall (two in-
ches taller than his father) and well-proportioned, with a quiet
and thoughtful manner. His descriptions and explanations tend
to be cerebral; he sometimes pauses to reflect, then speaks
quickly. It is easy to see why the press would denigrate him, as
he is neither chummy nor confiding.

Nevertheless, his measured words and his detailed descriptions of ore bodies, of mining them, and of how he sees Teck's

rolc are concise and explicit. He leans forward to demonstrate with a brochure and an ashtray just how a mineral formation looks, and it suddenly seems that Keevil's natural habitat is not the boardroom but the classroom. That was exactly where he intended to go when he finished his doctorate. "I had a chance to set up a new geophysics department at the University of Utah," he says almost wistfully. "It was close to the ski hills. . . . I had my eyes on an academic career, and then I got talked into coming to Teck instead."

The "ski hills" comment demonstrates another aspect of Keevil's personality, his love of the outdoors. This does not seem surprising in a man who remembers childhood hikes with his father so fondly. "I used to go out on field parties with him," he recalls. "Just wandering along. It's nice being out in the bush." Keevil still loves the outdoors. His hobbies are skiing, golfing, fishing and gardening. He has a cottage on Whistler Mountain next to the lake and he has said it reminds him of Temagami, where he spent much of his childhood.

Keevil says he is not really a workaholic, he is more "results-oriented" than that. He adds, "As a matter of fact, Bob Hallbauer (now president of Cominco) and I used to take one afternoon a week to play golf—and we probably got more accomplished than in more recent years when we've been busier and had less chance to do that."

Keevil makes time for his main hobby, growing orchids. It seems characteristic that this rather reserved executive would enjoy a pastime that is "quite a challenge," as he says, and is, at the same time, a solitary and fairly complex task. The hobby evolved from his love for gardening, which he took up after he stopped managing exploration for Teck. "I didn't really plan to grow orchids," he says almost apologetically. "But I like being outside and I love gardening. Then, it started to rain, so I built a greenhouse. Someone gave me one or two orchids. . . . It was a natural progression from there." He laughs at his own circuitous logic. "What I'm saying," he concludes, "is that there's a natural progression from being in the bush to growing orchids."

Keevil has a dry sense of humour and laughs easily. He does

not guffaw, as does Murray Pezim, but now and then succumbs
to a hearty laugh—never, however, at his own lines, which he
delivers with the serious mien of a Woody Allen. A writer recently quoted him—with a touch of malice—as having said
"with the slimmest of smiles" that he had "3.1 grandchildren,
which includes two 1.0s, a 0.6 and a 0.5." Now, with another
"slim smile" he elaborates: "I had two grandchildren and two in
the oven. Since then one has come out and one is nearly due, so
I have 3.9 grandchildren." He still enjoys in retrospect the previous reporter's discomfiture at the statistical recital. [To complete his statistics—he has 1 wife (his second) and 4 children
from his first marriage.]

Teck has come a long way since its inception as the Teck-
Hughes gold property originally discovered in 1911 and taken
over by Keevil Senior in 1963. By the time Teck moved to B.C.
it had "mines all over the country" and since then Teck's
market capitalization (its total stock issued multiplied by its
market value) has grown from $26 million to more than $750
million. Along with the assets came the reputation of a company
with a propensity for making good. "Teck has a habit of turning
successful beginnings into successful outcomes and the reason
starts at the top," wrote the *Northern Miner* in 1986.

Keevil Junior, whose track record at Teck certainly provides
proof of his creativity, seems weary of epithets like "conservative" that have been applied to him. His father's style is perceived as "visionary" according to David Thompson, Teck's
vice-president of finance, who says, "Senior is more of a broad-
brush person, while Norman is more a hands-on sort of person
with an eye for all the little details and how to put everything in
place."

"When you're just starting a company," says Keevil Junior
patiently, "or when your company has one operation, you're still
scrambling for more operations. Your company simply has to
run differently when it's larger." He could add that after a dip
in its corporate fortune in 1982, Teck made an amazing turn-
around, and that all his attention to those "little details" has
made a massive difference. Of his father's and his differing

styles he says, "If the positions had been reversed we would have done it in the same way. It is more the nature of the beast we're driving."

That "beast," which has the reputation of being one of the fastest, most successful dealmakers in all of Canada, is said to have a dizzying acquisition rate. "Well, I don't know how 'dizzying' it is," says Keevil. "We've done a lot over the years—in the early seventies, maybe two or three a year—but our rate is probably every two years." He looks amused. "We'd have a new mine every second week if we could, but historically that's just about the rate. I don't know whether that's dizzying or not, but it seems to appear that way to some people," he finishes dryly.

One takeover that seemed to make onlookers positively vertiginous was the Cominco deal in October 1986. "Bold Keevils" and "The Tecking of Cominco" were two of the colourful headlines used by amazed—and often aghast—business publications. "Cominco surprised a lot of people for many reasons," says Keevil. "First, because Canadian Pacific (the sellers) had been in for eighty years and hadn't let on to the public at all that it was for sale, so it seemed like a real bombshell. It even surprised me," he admits. "And yet, it was first brought to us in April 1986. The news was out in the senior mining companies. C.P.'s agents, Dominion Securities, talked to twenty-two mining companies around the world—Falconbridge, Placer, Noranda, ASARCO in the U.S.— because only the very senior ones could afford it."

Teck's deal was shocking, primarily because Cominco just did not seem like a very good prospect. Although it had a book value of $1.96 billion, its debt was $1.13 billion. Keevil has gone on record as saying that their objective with Cominco is to reduce that debt substantially, "in much the same way as Teck did a few years ago, through divestitures and/or the taking in of partners". The general negative reaction was summed-up by *B.C. Business*: "It's good for Cominco and Canadian Pacific, but it's a rat's nest for Teck."

Nevertheless, although Cominco has been plagued by an obsolete plant, unprofitable mines, and the aforesaid debt in recent years, Teck, by contrast, has been characterized by steady growth and increased profits; so who better to turn Cominco around than Teck?

"Our first reaction was to refuse," confesses Keevil, "because Cominco had a lot of debt problems. We decided to look into it anyway. We could see that there were a lot of things happening within Cominco already that hadn't been taken into account." Those "things" comprised a continuing program of cost reduction and cash conservation in the metals division, according to Cominco's then-chairman, Norman Anderson, and "production cutbacks and layoffs continued at most operations, with major cost reductions being achieved at the Trail smelter and the Sullivan mine."

"It took us maybe two weeks to decide that we probably wanted to do it," says Keevil, "and after about two months we were red-hot. We wanted to do it with partners, and it took us two months to convince the Germans (Metalgesellschaft) and the Australians (M.I.M.), in that order, to commit. It was around mid-August, and by then we couldn't find C.P. or Dominion Securities because they were all on holiday! The good part was that no one else was dealing with them either."

Teck decided all it needed for effective control was 31%. (Taking the minimum necessary for control is, after all, a Teck landmark strategy.) "If we had bought the whole 54% it would have cost us a substantial amount, $500 million," Keevil points out. "That was too much." [It would be; that is practically what Teck is worth.] "31% was $280 million," he adds, "and was still too much, so we decided to bring the partners in. It was partly for financial reasons and partly for their expertise. We cut that down again to $140 million, and then we had C.P. take back a note for $35 million of that, which left our cost at $105 million. So, we went from what initially looked like a half-billion-dollar deal (and easy to turn down) to the point where it was something we could handle. Part of our job was to sell that extra 1400 shares to the public."

Many of those shares were sold in Europe. Keevil went on a "show-and-tell" trip, as he calls it, to Frankfurt, Paris, Zurich, Geneva, and London. "A lot of people hadn't heard of us at that point," he says, "but we convinced them it was good underwriting." [He is being modest: the well-circulated London *Economist* said many Europeans were viewing the Keevils as the emerging OPEC of the world zinc market.] The rest of the shares went to Japan, Australia and Canada. "It was done a lot faster and a lot more successfully than anybody had hoped for," says Keevil, "and it *has* been successful, since they've all made a lot of money."

The reason the Cominco operation is the type best done internationally, Keevil explains, "is that Cominco markets internationally." He goes on to say, "Cominco has operations in Australia; they're in the same business as M.I.M., so both of these partners bring expertise to add to ours." He could add that Germany's Metalgesellschaft is a strong marketer of zinc, which is used extensively in galvanizing metal and in die-castings and coatings for cars. The use of zinc is on the decline in North America, which is leaning toward car bodies with more aluminium, but it is still strong in Europe. "Metalgesellschaft is basically a smelting and refining company," says Keevil. "Engineering, construction, chemical plants, things like that. The nice feature of the package just happened to be that the shareholders we picked also fitted very neatly with the Cominco package."

That does not seem purely accidental, somehow, as Teck's connection with both Germany and Australia began many years ago. Germany's Metalgesellschaft has a 16% voting stake in Teck; it sold 3.4% of its holdings to M.I.M. (formerly Mount Isa Mines) of Brisbane, Australia in 1984. "The attraction of the international connection is that it gives us a window on what's going on in other parts of the world, which we wouldn't otherwise have, based in Vancouver—or even based in Toronto," says Keevil. "If you don't have that window it's too easy to think only of North America, or of Canada, and really not have a full understanding of the European markets, or opportunities that might come up in Australia."

Keevil originally met Karl G. Ratjen, Metalgesellschaft's chairman, by accident in 1977 at the Temagami mine in Ontario. The German company acquired an interest in Teck in 1978 and lightened Teck's debt load with the Highmont Mine by buying 20% of it, then by interesting the Kuwait Investment Office in buying another 29%, so Keevil is not exaggerating when he says their international connections give them more opportunities. "We get exposure to their trading knowledge and to their knowledge of international affairs," he says happily.

Teck also has a relationship with Japan; Teck's Bullmoose project in northwestern B.C. has been selling coal to the Japanese since 1983, about two million tons a year. Keevil looks a little secretive as he starts to say which Pacific Rim country Teck will be dealing with next, then becomes expansive. "The possible linkage of this sort that might come would be with China," he admits. "Our interest in China is twofold: doing business with the Chinese *in* China, and doing business with them *outside* as well, providing the materials they need."

Keevil thinks the Pacific Rim region is, in many ways, the wave of the future for the west coast. "Simply from a transportation point of view," he points out, "and also from the point of view of investment coming from there to here. This 'International Banking Centre' concept right now is keyed to getting more connections between countries. Still, Europe is still a good market, and the U.S. is still our biggest market," he finishes.

Keevil feels that Canada, generally, is better off when it is opportunistic and diverse—like Teck. "I think the same applies internationally." he says. "We should be looking for opportunities, whether it's to market products (and I'm not just talking about mining) or to develop new producers. If we confine ourselves to our own country we're like the mining company that says it's only looking for gold. You miss opportunities in other areas."

Opportunities. Keevil's favourite word. And there are very few, internationally or locally, that Teck has missed. One major deal was Pezim's Hemlo gold mine in Ontario, what many observers called "a golden opportunity" for Teck. The Teck-Corona partnership (Teck 55%, Corona 45%) demonstrates Teck's commitment to junior-sector mining companies and to B.C. Pezim says his deal with Teck was made over a handshake, adding that Teck not only gave Corona the best deal (most companies wanted 80/20 deals), but it also provided needed expertise for development. Keevil says the gold reserves at Hemlo stand at 9.5 million tons, averaging 0.35 ounces of gold per ton—which translates into a lot in layman's terms.

Keevil isn't quite as obviously gleeful as Pezim at the fact that a western concern "scooped" a gold mine right from under the noses of the eastern establishment ("It was right in their own back yard!" crows Pezim), but he does exhibit a restrained satisfaction at Teck's perspicacity. "It's interesting that the results were coming out and it was a long time before the *Northern Miner* did more than print a little tiny story on it," he says. "It prides itself on being the country's only mining newspaper, but at the time it didn't have a very good Vancouver connection and this was a Vancouver story. . . . They finally realized it was a major ore body." The paper has since rectified the error with a major story on Teck and all its interests, and with a long bit on Hemlo.

Another major ore body, gold again, in which Teck has an interest is Bruce McDonald's Golden Knight. Keevil says they originally heard of that deal through his brother, Harold Keevil, a stockbroker with Canarim. "He was quite excited about it," recalls Keevil, "so I looked at it and talked to one of our geologists who knew something about the area and we dashed off an offer in handwriting, on one piece of paper. We came over and visited Bruce— I'd never met him before—and we had a cup of coffee; within ten minutes we had signed the deal. The association grew after that into other projects. Now, we're a shareholder in his newest vehicle, Noramco." (Teck owns about 9% of Noramco.)

Keevil likes doing deals over a handshake and coffee, or golf, and says he's generally had good luck with these. "We've done handshake deals where the other guy's reneged," he says, "but never in Vancouver. A guy like Murray Pezim or Bruce McDonald, in my experience, when you shake hands with them it's a deal." He adds that one deal made with Bruce McDonald was to be drawn up at a Teck board meeting three weeks later, and during that period "they hit a couple of enormous drill holes, and the stock went 'way up. A lot of people might have tried to renegotiate, if nothing else, but Bruce held to the deal." He adds that the only people he's ever had welch on deals were in Toronto. (McDonald is equally complimentary in his talk of Keevil.)

Keevil doesn't profess to have a "nose" for which mines to invest in, as Pezim claims to, but Keevil does admit that his background in geology enables him to see what someone whose sole specialty is finance cannot. "I see things that any good geologist or mining engineer would see," he says. He does keep up with the technology and says the basic technology has not changed much in his time, although there were quite significant advances in the late fifties. Keevil Senior was one of the people actually involved in mining who used the changing technology to discover ore bodies. "People used to say you could find gold with a magnetometer [an instrument that measures magnetic intensities, of which minerals emit more than do non-minerals]," he says, "but there was no way, unless one had a geological background." "The technology is always changing," says his son, "but since the early sixties things have been evolving more slowly, always getting more refined. The more recent changes are in the drilling techniques."

In spite of his obvious familiarity and ease with the technical aspects, Keevil Junior is a little cautious about trying to outwit everyone by getting into metals that might be on the "cutting edge" of the future, as it were. "Going into exotic materials that might not be much in demand now, that's a bit of a mug's game," he says. "You always try to think about what might be important in 1990 or 1995, but when I think back to the early sixties, when berylium or lithium were both supposed to be 'metals of the future', well, neither one has performed very well." The same applies to neodymium, he adds, which sounded exciting because it could apply to superconductivity. "We made a solid profit on neodymium," says Keevil, "but we were selling it to prosaic steel mills. The superconductivity applications have never grown very much, and now you don't see a lot written on it because they've found some new materials which are much better. So you can't really predict," he finishes.

Very little is predictable in this world, but it seems reasonable to predict that Teck's future is assured—particularly as long as there's a Keevil at the top. If they can't find a mine to invest in, well—no problem; they'll just go out and discover one.

CHAPTER 10

Richard Hughes and Frank Lang

Exploring the anatomy of risk

In March 1987, when Richard Hughes and Frank Lang were declared co-recipients of the Developer Of The Year Award by the Prospectors and Developers Association of Canada, it came as no surprise to mining-watchers along Howe Street and in the Vancouver Stock Exchange. Few if any are the mining entrepreneurs who have contributed more than Hughes and Lang to the definition of "developer" as a sub-species in the hierarchy of Canadian mining.

Their entry into the industry during the sixties, in fact, coincided with a critical mass being achieved by that group of developers who were in the game for more than a penny stock play, but had not reached major status.

"The fortunate thing about entrepreneurs in this market," says Jim Bartlett, mining analyst with Odlum Brown Ltd. in Vancouver, "is that in the current mining scene the majors would not be maintaining nearly the pace of activity that we're seeing, if left to their own devices. It's the developers, with their flexibility and expertise, who are really making things happen."

Dick Hughes and Frank Lang are two of them.

The Hemlo gold development in Ontario is an outstanding

example in recent years of the importance of the independent mining entrepreneur. Discovered in 1944, the mineralization that was to become one of the most significant gold plays in Canadian history was bandied about so much that it became a prospector's joke, a sort of local "fool's gold" gag. It remained so until a geologist named David Bell in 1980 did some drilling east of the main centre of interest under the auspices of Murray Pezim's Corona. Hughes-Lang's two companies, Goliath Gold and Golden Sceptre, were in place a short time later bracketing the Corona holding, and the rush was on.

Yawned at by the majors, passed up by Bay Street, Hemlo's two junior companies were financed in Vancouver by independent developers, including Dick Hughes and Frank Lang. The Norandas and the Tecks came later, earning their positions by bringing the Hughes-Lang and Corona properties to production. Billions of dollars in gold, thousands of jobs, and the sweet smell of success were to reward the ingenuity and farsightedness of the developers who had quickly graduated from the status of promoters.

In many cases the explorers and developers who occasionally become the mine-finders do follow the practice of dealing properties off to the majors. In fact there was a time when a prospector's fondest dream was to develop an interesting property, with the sole objective of selling it to one of the integrated companies before heading into the bush to find another one.

Today, if that strategy is considered shortsighted it is probably because the influence of people like Hughes and Lang has made the middle range of mining innovators more independent, more prone to form their own companies. Somehow the qualities of patience and painstaking work have enabled those that follow this model to tame the odds of mine-finding, even though they are still astronomical.

Control of a company, of course, is often surrendered or bartered away along the long rocky road from discovery to property, and from property to producing mine. Recently, Frank Lang casually made the comment that if and when Noranda exercised all the options on Goliath and Sceptre stock surrendered in the course of their joint venture agreement on the Hemlo property, it would own an effective 33% of both Hughes-Lang companies—obviously, effective control.

That is often what it costs to get to the situation where 330,000 ounces of gold is being poured each year. And Hughes and Lang long ago learned the equations that apply in hardball mining.

But in addition to their seasoned professionalism Hughes and Lang are different from most other mining venturers by any measurement. Even when they first met, when they were both employees of B.C. Hydro in the mid-sixties, they were the most improbable mining duo you would be likely to find, before, then, or since. Each quiet and reserved, it is rumored that their first mutual interest was in stocks they were trading. Then they progressed to their mutual interest in prospecting, geology and mining. Both have families and live in Vancouver, but in their early acquaintance the weekends were largely given over to prospecting.

"They're both completely unlike anyone else in the game," says Martin Gibbeson, westcoast mining financier. "And it's probably because they're *both* that way that they teamed up in the first place. A couple of quiet guys. They go about their job without any fanfare—and that's it."

An engineering physicist at Hydro in his "straight" life, Frank Lang had for some time made it a habit on weekends to put a pack on his back and tramp around in the bush and over the mountains—environmental background that is readily available in B.C. He had begun the practice much earlier in life, hiking around and staking claims back in the Ottawa Valley where he grew up. Dick Hughes gladly joined the club.

From the very beginning of their association, one that was to develop into a business partnership spending tens of millions of dollars annually for exploration alone, Dick Hughes and Frank Lang shared a common philosophy leading to their ultimate objective, which was to pursue those mineral projects which demonstrated the potential for long-term production. It was a realistic goal, but it was a long time before they realized their first producer of *any* kind.

In one of those ironies of the industry, Cream Silver Mines

Ltd., their first joint project, which might well have proven to be a significant producer, was frustrated and stalled for many years. But recent developments have indicated that it may yet become as successful as originally expected.

In his role as a weekend prospector, Lang had for some time been examining a property in the wilds of Vancouver Island that had been named after the adjacent Cream Lake. The lake, surrounded by rock formations that had been ground into powder by glacial action, had literally been transformed into a geological milkshake. Early on, the two prospectors established that the property had a high gold-lead-zinc content. This they determined through innumerable four-day jaunts into the property.

One colleague suggests that both Hughes and Lang would rather tramp four days in the woods than around the corner to the bank. But the very length of that hike to the Cream Silver property might well have contributed to the end of their status as weekend prospectors—the weekends simply were not long enough. But for years Cream Silver lay idle, its true potential yet to be plumbed. There was nothing wrong with the property except for its location. A law that went on the B.C. statute books in 1973 (coinciding with a certain provincial government not exactly held dear by B.C.'s mining industry) prohibited the carrying out of any mining activity on land designated as park land. And Cream Silver is located just inside Strathcona Provincial Park on Vancouver Island, adjacent to the location of a Westmin Resources producing gold mine that has been operating profitably for several years.

It is only recently (mid 1987) that, aided by a Supreme Court of Canada ruling on a similar case in favour of the mining company, there is a likelihood that the provincial law will be amended. If this should occur the first Hughes and Lang prospect may come alive beside a lake which, if it looks like a milkshake, is the most expensive milkshake on earth.

Cream Silver since the beginning has been generally accepted as one of the finest base-metal properties in Canada; gold as an additive would contribute to lowering the effective production cost.

For many years both Hughes and Lang found it expedient to remain employed at B.C. Hydro while they pursued the career they loved as part-time prospectors. Hughes was in the gas division, while Lang sold electric power and gas to commercial users.

"Even long after that," says one prominent Vancouver broker, "I can remember Dick manning a modest little office on Hastings Street, while Frank was still punching the clock at Hydro."

It was not until 1975 that Hughes and Lang achieved what they themselves considered to be their first major breakthrough—the discovery in the Val d'Or area of Quebec of the ore body that was to become the Belmoral Ferderber gold mine. One of the interesting things about that property is that since the mine became operative it has been continually and significantly expanded, both laterally and at depth, in terms of the delineation of greater reserves.

It all began when Peter Ferderber, a prospector-geophysicist based in Val d'Or, suggested a course of action scoffed at by a whole corporal's guard of geologists—drilling in the middle of the Bourlamaque Batholith, a formation around the rim of which a group of gold mines were already known to be clustered.

Since nobody involved in these mines was a geologist, according to Fenton Scott, a Toronto consulting engineer, and they could not afford to hire one, they took the plunge, to the merriment of every mining company in the area. The 20-cent stock they managed to flog subsequently saw a high of $40 and Peter Ferderber was a regular team player from that time on.

Lang says they were almost out of money when they hit on their eighth drill hole and knew they had the real McCoy—right where all the experts had been sure they would never find gold.

This foray into eastern Canada was also a watershed in the Hughes-Lang organization, with much of their total effort from that time on being concentrated in Northern Ontario and Quebec. Today, Hughes-Lang major projects in eastern Canada outnumber those in B.C. and Yukon by approximately two-to-one. Hughes-Lang represent a rare phenomenon, that of absentee landlords calling the shots over a large spread of eastern Canadian mining operations from a fifteenth-floor office on Vancouver's Hastings Street.

To run such a show at three thousand miles' distance, says Scott, the partners have three infallible operational rules:

1) If it works, leave it alone;
2) Local knowledge beats experts from out of town;
3) When you hire the best people, rely on their judgment.

Its eastern orientation is just one more indication of the sharpness of the Hughes-Lang judgment. Vancouver might be the world centre for mobilizing venture-mining capital, but Quebec for several reasons is the most receptive area in Canada for mining investment. And that was the pattern Hughes and Lang adhered to in the nine years following the Belmoral mining development, during which period they raised $40 million for various Val d'Or properties through sixteen corporate entities in the Vancouver market.

What prompted these two apparently normal unilingual Vancouver citizens, with no particular financial background other than the taking of an occasional flutter on the VSE, to pull off such a wholesale haul? According to Fenton Scott, there was a concatenation of events that looked something like this: gold prices were rising in that almost-decade, so that most of us believed there was no tomorrow; the securities industries in Quebec and Ontario, still smarting from their own scams of the sixties, had not yet awakened to the reality of venture capital in the resource field; meanwhile an excellent batting average in large base-metal deals in B.C. and decades of hard work had engendered a mature taste for risk and a healthy understanding of its anatomy by the highly professional Vancouver financial infrastructure; the practice of carrying out exploration in Quebec for twelve months of the year, compared with a much shorter season in the West, was enticing to developers constantly faced with financial and other deadlines; and finally, all of these factors allowed Hughes and Lang to be the first Vancouver players to take advantage of the charms of flow-through financing.

But as Belmoral-Ferderber hit the charts, the bringing of their first solid producer to production did not diminish the Hughes-Lang enthusiasm for searching out and developing other properties. And oddly, with Hughes and Lang the incentive of striking it rich never had a prominent place in their priorities. Their attitude almost seems to convey the notion that the profit motive, if it is there at all, weighs in the balance about the same as other considerations such as office rent and joint-venture agreements.

As the seventies gave way to the eighties, the string of Hughes-Lang discoveries began to make the business of finding profitable properties seem routine. In two decades they made the following gold discoveries: Perron Gold Mines, Standard Gold, Gabriel Resources, Arbor Resources, Gallant Gold Mines, Easter Mines and Silver Sceptre Resources, Kangeld Resources, Goliath Gold, Golden Sceptre and Val d'Or Mines. (While only two of all these became producing mines with any speed, almost all the others have demonstrated excellent mine potential from the beginning.) Hughes and Lang have compiled an outstanding, if not unique, record in the sheer numbers of likely properties they have developed over two decades.

Golden Sceptre and Goliath are two of the most unusual, not only in their position in the Hemlo camp but because they were the first in production in that mind-boggling scenario. A jump in the price of gold in 1982 coincided with the financing of Goliath in order to conduct further work on the Hemlo property. Drilling went ahead quickly, but the joint-venture agreement with Noranda came along soon thereafter, obviating the necessity for further work. But before that happened, the drill operating adjacent to Lac's Hemlo property hit a 90-foot swath of 0.5 ounces of gold per ton, lighting up every switchboard on Howe Street.

According to Vancouver financial columnist Frank Keane, at that point Lang had an opportunity either to dance attendance on the unveiling of one of the largest gold mines in Canadian history or to join the Canadian Mount Everest expedition for a jaunt up to the base camp. What would any red-blooded Canadian entrepreneur choose? No contest.

"We hiked around the mountains (Himalayas, that is) for twenty-three days with porters and sherpas," says Lang, "and we finally got into base camp at 18,500 feet. It was a great trip . . ."

Meanwhile, back on Hastings Street, Dick Hughes was fending off financing deals from all quarters. But for a mine as huge as Goliath-Sceptre's Golden Giant, a major financing or a deal was unavoidable. When Lang got back to town, they ruled out financing on the basis that they needed a minimum of $40 million, and with the stock selling at about $3 they would have been diluted out of their shoes.

They accepted Noranda as joint-venture partner, partly because Noranda is Noranda and partly because the latter had a nearby mill capable of 1,000 tons per day, which was compatible with what Hughes-Lang saw as a hurry-up schedule. At that time, several world-class gold analysts, such as the Aden Sisters of Puerto Rico, were predicting $3,000 gold within two years, and they didn't want to miss all the fun.

To earn its 50% position, Noranda agreed to spend $292 million to place the mine in production. Prior to the agreement, John Harvey of Noranda argued with Lang that the ore body was a mere 2.5 million tons; Lang's bet was 10 million tons minimum. Stakes were set modestly at a case of whiskey. Lang says he still has a little of it around. (By the time the agreement was signed, the Golden Giant reserves had been established at about 22 million tons and counting, and grading an average of 0.3 ounces of gold per ton.)

Initial target capacity was 240,000 ounces of gold per annum, rising to 330,000 ounces, well in excess of one tenth of the national total of gold production. Even more surprising was the relatively low production cost, US$100 per ounce.

The detail of the Noranda agreement is such that all initial profits from mining operations flow to Noranda until the production cost is recovered. According to estimates by Tony Garson, research director with Haywood Securities in Vancouver, repayment of the Noranda investment proceeds at about one-third of the total per annum. Thereafter Goliath-Sceptre receives 50% of all revenues.

Sceptre and Goliath in fact had been true pioneers in the fabulous Hemlo Gold Belt. While they were not the first in the Hemlo play, their Golden Giant mine very rapidly established itself as the most successful producer in the area.

In the aftermath of the Noranda deal, Goliath-Sceptre attracted considerable attention both here and abroad as an investment medium. Among other notable shareholders were the three branches of the Rothschild family. "We gave them a private placement at around $4.50," says Lang, "and before the ink was dry on the agreement the stock was $21."

But it is neither accurate nor true to depict Hughes and Lang as a hugely successful partnership in terms of financial success, at least following the establishment of its first two gold producers.

"They're not normal miners," says Howe Street financial publisher George Cross. "And that applies to everything they do. They've shown wonderful management, had reams of luck and good advice, and have stuck to their job for many years, all of which has resulted in their finding a percentage of promising properties that is quite unusual. And they've got an organization now such that, if they can keep things developing for the next four or five years, I think they'll be in great shape and will start to realize some of the rewards they've earned."

Meanwhile, both partners live quite modestly, completely in keeping with their personalities—unostentatious, conservative in their habits, and more prone to giving than receiving.

"I know for a fact," says Cross, "that as individuals they have been plagued by those trappings of wealth, or let's say by the people who assume they have wealth, when in fact they haven't yet truly made it. And on many occasions, they've had to sell stock in one of their companies in order to buy stock in a new company, in order to keep it alive. And they're generous like you wouldn't believe—far beyond their means."

To develop a continuous sequence of promising ore bodies is like a game of dominoes in reverse—the game creates its own necessity of propping up one company in order to prop up the next—until such time as a significant number of them stand by themselves as revenue sources. Again, there's nothing unusual about that process, but in Hughes-Lang's case it is the numbers involved that are unusual.

Even though the Val d'Or (Belmoral Ferderber) mine should have meant that their ship had come in, it did not spell real financial success. It was not until 1984 that success of that kind began to look possible. Now, with the solid production of Hemlo and Val d'Or behind them and innumerable properties to be brought along in sequence, Hughes and Lang, if they were preoccupied about such things, could logically expect a large payoff at last. Instead, they are more concerned with their common objective—to build a continuing group of producing mining properties and a strong organization to house them.

One of the top priorities, to which they have so far not given much time, is the internal development of a senior and middle management team to handle an organization of their potential size. This has been a preoccupation of Dick Hughes particularly, as president and administrative head of most of their operating companies.

Even in their decade of rapid expansion following the Belmoral discovery, the project management Hughes and Lang have been able to exercise on all their eastern holdings has been impressive. Typical was the development of the Val d'Or Mines Beacon property, which is positioned in such a rich mineral environment that an ore body might seem almost a matter of course.

Since 1909, when gold was first discovered in the horseshoe-shaped area of Quebec and Ontario known as the Abitibi Belt, this area has been the foremost gold-producing region in the Western Hemisphere, more prolific, for example, than the total of gold-producing mines in the State of California. In addition to the major mining companies and the established producers that have followed the rush since the early eighties, eighteen mid-sized companies joined the group involved in exploration and development. Seven of those were Hughes-Lang companies.

On the Beacon property, an exploration shaft was sunk to a depth of 1600 feet, with numerous crosscuts made to explore veins delineated by previous diamond drilling, not only to confirm the earlier drilling but to seek new structures.

The results of that pre-production program, according to Anthony Garson, were a consistent increase in reserves and a continuing improvement in ore grade.

On completion of the vertical shaft an extensive secondary program was begun, with a major exploration drive at the 770 foot level, to evaluate the area of three diamond drill intersects where grades of up to 0.54 ounces of gold per ton were encountered over a 3-metre depth.

Even while this exploratory work was under way, at a cost of several millions of dollars, a mill facility was being put in place (completion set for late 1987), and the development ore from the advanced exploration program was stockpiled to provide the first mill feed. And it was planned that when the mill came on stream, production would coordinate the Beacon property's output with ore produced by other Hughes-Lang properties in the area.

The Beacon property is a good example of Hughes and Lang in action; their usual reticence does not apply when the commitment of funds to a potential producer is involved. Nor is there evidence of ultra-conservative management as the large investment flows into production and the mill is allowed to operate at optimal capacity.

Perhaps Hughes and Lang have consistently made the mine-finding exercise look easier than it was over the years, simply because they believed that the game for them had to do with the commitment to finding ore rather than seeking personal wealth. Their efforts have had the appearance of a moonlighting distraction rather than the go-for-broke desperation that characterizes many westcoast players.

Long after they had attained at least nominal success (anyone who finds a commercial ore body even once has, in our scheme of things, surmounted odds that George Cross sets at 10,000—1) Lang maintained his job with B.C. Hydro, as if the mining thing, however promising financially, was still not part of the real world. But at last, in 1980, Lang reached normal retirement, and after accepting it he was then free to work even harder than before.

Although Hughes and Lang have been atypical of most others in this capital-oriented industry, they have always been more than prepared to throw any amount of funding necessary at a promising property. "They seem to be really consistent in that respect," says a colleague. "Every time they make $1 on one property, they tend to plough back $1.25 somewhere else."

The history of Perron Gold Mines Limited illustrates that point. Having successfully contracted a farm-out to Noranda on the Hemlo property, Hughes and Lang asked Noranda management if they would like to return the favour. Noranda responded with a property farther north in Quebec where 500,000 tons of ore grading 0.15 ounces of gold per ton had been delineated.

"Obviously on the back burner," says Lang, "because it was too small for them."

Hughes-Lang's Perron Gold farmed in for a 50% interest by spending $2 million on the property. The end result was that Perron Gold proved up as a pleasant surprise, with well over one million tons of ore grading 0.25 ounces, of which both grade and tonnage are likely to increase with further testing.

The initial shaft, sunk to 800 feet (the commitment to Noranda had been to expend all the money underground), was followed by crosscuts on four levels 150 feet apart. This development demonstrated several ore structures not indicated previously by surface drilling. A feasibility study and further exploration pointed toward production by 1988.

There was a humorous postscript. When the farm-in was done, both Noranda and Hughes-Lang retained an option to fall back to a 25% position. Noranda beat them to it, just prior to the completion of work that indicated much larger reserves than had been estimated. As a result of being too slow off the mark, Hughes-Lang ended up with a 75% interest instead of 50%.

It was another case of Hughes-Lang's seeming inability to miss in Quebec and Ontario. The consistency of their success is sometimes explained by the lack of primary junior financing in eastern Canada, and the circumstance that, to a degree, Hughes and Lang, as strong players in the junior market with the resources of the VSE behind them, have the junior resource field in Ontario and Quebec all to themselves.

"It's no mystery at all" says Bruce McDonald, Vancouver mining merchant banker. "Mining developers in Vancouver understand the structure of risk in a way that just isn't known in the East."

Still, in perhaps the most promotion-minded industry in the world, Hughes and Lang have an attitude that is sometimes incongruous. They seem to run from rather than toward publicity, and their stocks tend to languish unless enterprising brokers come along and make a secondary market for them.

Hughes-Lang's abiding objective is to find ore bodies and then develop them for the long pull. That may not be exactly novel but their *modus operandi* on the promotional side is more than unusual.

If Mark Twain described a mine as a hole in the ground surmounted by a liar it is quite apparent that he never met the likes of Dick Hughes and Frank Lang. Where the B.C. woods are chock-full of moose pasture specialists, Hughes and Lang stand out like a high-grade vein in a tailings dump. Their reluctance to hype any of their own stocks is legendary.

"Hell," says one of their employees, " we're probably the world's worst promoters. That may not be entirely a bad thing. But on the other hand, there's the shareholder to consider. We'll probably spend $35 million this year, largely on one or two properties. I can think of one of our stocks sitting at about $3—if anyone else was running this show, with the kind of potential earnings we're looking at, it would be $15 to $20."

These particular gold-dust twins, however, seem to intend to progress in the manner to which they have become accustomed. They continue to hold the theory that if they produce the metal, the stock will eventually reflect its value by itself without any unnecessary urging, and so will ultimately take care of itself—and the shareholders.

From this one might deduce a theorem good for the mining industry: when you find a stock that's good but distinctly undervalued, you will probably find a conservative management group that's non-promotion minded.

But with Dick Hughes and Frank Lang it goes far beyond that; they simply believe that some activities are more important than others. "Off-duty hours?" says George Cross. "Their idea of entertainment is hiking, climbing a mountain, or skiing—both cross-country and downhill. Both are excellent skiers. I'd say they were conservative rather than aggressive skiers, mind you."

Which is entirely in character. But whatever they're doing Hughes and Lang never stand pat, no matter how many current projects they have under development.

Gold analyst Tony Garson has a standard model for the life cycle of a junior mining company over its first five years of development. Typically, the stock surges upward in three distinct waves—in the first year or so on the speculative strength of a discovered property, then over the following year it rises to a second interim peak with the production decision, and finally in the following two or three years the stock moves to a level that reflects the production phase.

The market commonplace that anticipation produces a rise while a sell-off always follows the news is illustrated in the Garson gold-mine model. Those three advances are interspersed with two substantial sell-offs, says Garson, the first following the news of the discovery, usually by way of diamond drill results, and the second as a reaction following the production decision, coupled with the anticipation of more and bigger problems in the pre-production phase.

Either Goliath's or Goliath-Sceptre's chart could be superimposed over Garson's model if the chart were dated from the beginning.

Whatever the revenue being produced by the Hughes-Lang companies, the total exploration budget generated year in, year out is enormous—in the tens of millions. And if Hughes-Lang stocks are not overvalued, at least the investor is getting a bargain in the organization's lack of overhead. Someone counted heads not long ago and determined that the administrative bodies on the Hughes-Lang payroll worked out to half a person per company.

And Hughes and Lang have this persistent habit—they keep moving along. Lang has said they are now excited about a new play in the Yukon, which they believe not only has great potential but also could lead them to the source of the Gold Rush of '98.

But why should that impress a partnership that's been conducting its own private gold rush for over twenty years?

CHAPTER 11

Doug McRae

Actions speak louder than words

There is a story Doug McRae likes to tell about one of his first selling trips into the European investment market. Today he has the largest share of European support of any Vancouver financier, but then, in 1979, the name "Doug McRae" had yet to set any continental hearts racing.

McRae was in Europe with another broker and they were "knocking on doors, making ten appointments a day and getting nowhere."

Finally he got a break. He was told he could make his pitch to an influential investor over breakfast the following morning. "I went through the whole presentation," he recounts. "This is the property. This is what it has done and this is what it is capable of doing."

Before McRae could get to his summation, however, the businessman stopped him, and in broken English said, "I have not understood a word you have said, but I like you. You seem to know what you're doing. I'd like to buy half."

It was one of the highlights of his career, the kind of happy circumstance every salesman dreams of. But that first sale taught him that a different approach would be necessary in Europe. It was a lesson that would help him make subsequent contacts and ultimately achieve his present success.

An instantaneous decision to buy that is based on positive first impressions (like that first European sale) is much more likely to happen in Europe than in North America, according to McRae. The difference in the European business environment, in his experience, lies in an emphasis on personal integrity and management ability over tangible assets. It's an emphasis that has worked well for McRae, who has integrity and ability to spare.

McRae is a salesman's salesman. But banish the image of the Purina-checkerboard jacket and the back-slapping greeting. We're talking classic tailoring in the navy pinstripe suit, white shirt and burgundy tie. A courteous demeanour and soft voice that project genuine warmth. Kind, smiling eyes and an easy-going humour that make talking in millions as natural as talking about the weather. He is gracious, elegant, funny and generous. In a business arena where personal referral is often the only access, McRae has gained entrance and won trust and respect everywhere—for himself and for Vancouver.

But very few people know any more about Douglas McRae after ten years than they did after the first ten minutes. He is an intensely private person who would rather be known as a family man. In an industry of lone wolves, McRae is one of the most solitary and most travelled. He flies a quarter of a million miles a year, and spends enough time in transit to keep up with all the bestseller lists.

"McRae is a guy who has been around the street long enough to have made all his mistakes and learned from them," says stock-market watchdog Frank Keane. Doug McRae was the youngest junior broker ever registered in B.C.; now, at thirty-seven he is almost a twenty-year veteran.

Doug's father was a CP Air pilot who retired to farm life in Langley, an ideal place to raise five sons. Doug was in his first year of economics at Langara College when his father died. There was not enough money to continue college so Doug went to work for the Hudson's Bay department store. Because the Bay offered an in-house management course, Doug saw this as a way to continue his education while he worked. His marks at Langara were "not that great," and he did not fare much better in the management course.

Doug's older brother was an investor at the time and helped him land a job as a junior broker at Hemsworth Turton. There Doug worked under Peter Brown. Later, Brown was to take control of the company and turn it into Canarim Investment Corporation.

"Peter's training program was a phone and a phone book — and you often had to share those," McRae remembers dryly. McRae learned early what he considers to be one of the most important sales skills, how to present one's self well on the telephone. "Most people are afraid of the phone," he maintains.

"I'll tell you how naive I was when I was just starting out," he smiles with a trace of mischief, "One of the stocks trading at the time was called Early Bird. Being a junior broker, I had to be at work early in the morning. As the other brokers came in, they would occasionally ask, 'How's Early Bird doing?' I thought, 'isn't that great? There's a whole market that runs early in the morning.'"

McRae was an eager student in the real-life learning environment of Hemsworth Turton. "The market was different then — a lot of action," he recalls. Caught up in the spirit of the job, McRae invested his small savings in some stocks and promptly lost everything. "I decided that the label 'broker' was just that. You got broker and broker."

Disillusioned, McRae went on to other sales jobs, selling everything from ladies' clothing to cars. While in the car business he worked his way up from the showroom floor to owning his own dealership, and got a taste of the excitement of dealing in large numbers. A little more financially secure, McRae purchased some VSE-trading shares again and discovered a different investment climate.

A new focus on resources in the seventies put the VSE in a unique position in the world market. As borderline properties that had been uneconomical when oil was $3 a barrel and gold $35 an ounce suddenly became profitable, a wildly speculative attitude developed. When the OPEC nations drove the price of gas and oil up, the search was on for other petroleum sources and the financing for these exploration projects.

The number of listings and the size of the underwriting on the VSE have increased considerably since McRae's phone-room days in the sixties. In the old days, a $50,000 underwriting was commonplace; today, anything under $500,000 is considered a very small-scale equity financing. During McRae's junior-broker days, a company coming on the Exchange offering shares at 15 cents would probably yield a maximum of $60,000 in commissions. As a point of comparison, he points to his own company, Granges: "This year, we'll pay between four and five million in commissions to brokers alone."

On the basis of the new opportunities for making money in stock promotion, in 1977 McRae put his sales and business skills into arranging financing packages for gas and oil ventures and found himself on Europe's doorstep.

After his first fortuitous sale, McRae worked his contacts in Europe and built an impressive portfolio.

"We had orders for $90 million." He pauses and then, as if some explanation is necessary, adds, "They have large amounts of money; they need places to put it."

Although he was representing such sure bets as Exxon, the oil-market activity was short-lived; McRae managed to lose $23 million for his European associates.

Today, the subject of loyalty comes up often when McRae talks about his European clients—with good reason. In 1982, when McRae came back to his European partners after losing $23 million, and told them of an opportunity that he'd just heard about in a bar in Munich—shares in a gold mine in Wenatchee, Washington—they were interested. The foundation of trust McRae had established with his Swiss partner enabled him to get the financing to engineer one of the VSE's more spectacular takeovers.

In 1982, as mentioned above, McRae ran into a man named Carl Whigby in a hotel bar in Munich.

"He told me they had this wonderful project in Wenatchee and he needed $290 million to pay Asamera, the operators. I told him I didn't know anything about mining, but I did know oil was no good. I flew back to Switzerland and showed my partner the deal.

The Cannon Mine in Wenatchee is one of the richest gold mines in the United States. Through the finance-packaging efforts of Doug McRae, Breakwater Resources, owned by McRae's group, purchased 49% of the Wenatchee operation from Goldbelt Mines. Several big players had shown interest in the property over the years, but the mine had drawbacks that took decades to overcome.

Bern Brynelsen remembers trying to interest Noranda in it, almost fifty years ago, but it was, as he put it, "too complicated." "They wouldn't touch it with a ten-foot pole. The mine is practically on the edge of town. There are apple orchards and everything around."

He even took his nephew Dal Brynelsen, who is a realtor, to see the property on the assumption that if it didn't make a mine, it was an excellent opportunity for a subdivision.

Bern Brynelsen and his partners worked the property for a while and extracted silica from it. Drill samples indicated much greater things were possible. But the proximity of the mine to the town of Wenatchee limited the extraction methods that could be used.

Eventually, Brynelsen took a colleague named Don Carmichael to see the property. Carmichael, who was a partner with Don Cannon in Goldbelt, saw the same potential and took an option on it, and Cannon, a director of Asamera also, was able to interest that company in investing. Over the years, Asamera invested a substantial amount of money in the Cannon Mine without its reaching full production.

"It had the ingredients, if you like. It was operating; it had proven tonnage and it looked as if it could have some production. So we arranged the money to pay off Asamera. Breakwater was a shell that we had and we rolled the assets of Carl Whigby's company into it and acquired control of what is now Cannon Mine."

McRae continues. "Breakwater has invested some $40 million in it since Asamera, which is way over budget from what

Asamera expected." With his usual understatement he adds, "It started out as a very nice stock, shares were going well. Then they drilled the discovery holes and we all drank champagne."

Others have sung the company's praises more enthusiastically.

"It will be, without doubt, the largest gold mine ever found in North America," Breakwater president Robert Hunter announced exuberantly at the annual board meeting in 1986. "I suspect we'll get more than one million ounces of gold from this program.

"We have 600 feet of proven resources. So go home tonight and walk 600 feet. Remember that every step of the way you're earning $1.5 million."

In his regular column in B.C. Business magazine Frank Keane wrote, "McRae has raised over $18 million on the VSE and in Europe for Breakwater Resources. In the past couple of years, Breakwater has been one of the spectacular performers on the VSE, going from 12.5 cents to $25 before being split two-for-one."

The Cannon Mine, which constitutes only a fraction of the Asamera-Breakwater Joint Venture, has reserves of its own sufficient for eleven years of operation. The mine went into full production debt-free, leaving earnings available for dividends to shareholders—due largely to the financial efforts of Doug McRae.

Surpassing Breakwater as a success story for Doug McRae is Granges Exploration Ltd. In 1983, Granges AB in Sweden decided to sell off its nonferrous mining interests in Canada. The company's founder, Dr. Marcus Wallenberg, had died the previous year and the family decided to dispose of all mining interests to concentrate on their many major holdings in Europe.

The buy-out of Granges's Canadian holdings through Pecos Resources, one of McRae's holdings, resulted in the creation of a formidable team, Vancouver's leading international financier, McRae, with one of the world's foremost mining explorers, Mike Muzylowski.

In 1976, before the takeover, Muzylowski had led the Canadian Granges team in a number of mineral discoveries, including the most important Granges discovery to date, at Trout Lake near Flin Flon, Manitoba. He had come to know this area of the country well in his earlier fifteen years with Hudson Bay Mining & Smelting.

With Muzylowski and McRae at the helm, the performance of Granges has been meteoric, to say the least. The ink was barely dry on the takeover papers when Muzylowski was on the acquisition trail. They even made a bid to purchase Muzylowski's old employer, Hudson Bay Mining & Smelting, but were turned down. Currently they are operating more than fifty active explorations projects specializing in gold and high-grade base metals like silver and zinc. Muzylowski has found thirteen proven, productive operations for the company. Several, like Trout Lake, report steady cash flows in spite of lower metal prices and have decades of productive life ahead of them. To illustrate their commitment to exploration, McRae points to the fact that of a total staff of twenty, fourteen are directly involved in exploration and development.

It is not surprising, then, that Loewen, Ondaatje, McCutcheon & Company calls Granges "the most exciting mining exploration company in Canada, if not North America." If further testimony were needed, it would be amply supplied by the investment of 30 million Eurodollars into Granges in 1986 by European investors. This translates to approximately CDN $42 million with which McRae and Mike Muzylowski can go after even more acquisitions.

McRae shrugs at the question of what plans they have for these funds, making a vague reference to Australia and the Pacific Rim countries.

While McRae settles back on the sofa in his panelled corner office, a staff member has helped himself to McRae's desk and is shouting to assist the transmission of his voice across the miles: "I CAN'T SELL FROM AN EMPTY BASKET. SEND ME SOMETHING TO SELL WITH."

McRae seems unaware of the distraction and carries on. "We're looking at various acquisitions. We've probably looked at fifteen to twenty deals so far that don't meet our criteria. The right opportunity will inevitably present itself.

"We've become known for our diligence in taking over at a stage that shows it's a good deal, something that's going to work."

The criteria they have adopted to assess investment proposals reflect the lessons McRae has learned in the European investment market. It gets back to what McRae believes is a fundamental difference: "Generally, in Europe, they buy management before they buy property." North Americans tend to look at the asset sheet to see what can be liquidated in a worst-case scenario. This can result in undermining the human factor.

Even the best idea, or product, or property will not develop or market itself. Above and beyond the assets, McRae was instrumental in the largest financing ever done on the Vancouver Stock Exchange when Nelson Holdings bought Embassy Home Entertainment from Coca-Cola for $85 million.

"The biggest deal in Vancouver Stock Exchange history," the *Vancouver Sun* proclaimed on 5 August 1986, "has Los Angeles-based Nelson Entertainment Inc. buying a home video company from the Coca-Cola Company. Nelson is a subsidiary of a VSE-listed company (Nelson Holdings)." Peter Brown, who owns 700,000 Nelson shares, was quoted as saying that the Nelson acquisition was a "huge, world-class deal" and an international "public relations coup."

Originally little more than an idea on the part of some industry veterans for starting another film studio, Nelson Holdings had the management expertise that McRae felt could make it a reality. Indeed, the board of directors reads like a cinematic Who's Who: Richard Northcott, the wealthy British financier and retailing executive; Barry Spikings, former chairman of the London studio where *Star Wars* was filmed and Oscar-winning producer of *The Deer Hunter*; Lord Antony Rufus Isaacs, whose last major movie productions were the successful 9½ *Weeks* and *Hot*.

Raising the necessary $85 million on the VSE to buy Embassy Home Entertainment Division from Coca-Cola turned Nelson into a major film studio overnight. The $85 million bought them a library of 900 video titles, of which only half have been released. Additionally, Coca-Cola agreed to a $200 million production deal that gave Nelson total authority over any films they produced. Coca-Cola will release these "A" films in a minimum of 650 theatres throughout the U.S. and spend a minimum of one million dollars per film on promotion. "So there's no question in my mind that Nelson *has* to be a success," McRae concludes.

McRae maintains that it's not in Nelson's mandate to produce any of these films in B.C. but concedes that a Vancouver-based directorship and VSE financing could contribute to a significant part of the work coming to the province.

This leads to another deal that McRae has recognised as having a strong management base. A former president of U&A Records has plans for starting Cable Radio. Soon, nine channels of compact-disc-quality radio will be available for the home market, just like cable television. "It doesn't sound like a very big deal, yet five percent of the market is three million people. That's US$24 million for a $5 or $6 million investment."

Opportunities like this are as much a hobby as a business to Doug McRae. It is what he was referring to when he told a reporter from the *Financial Post Moneywise Magazine*: "My success gave me recognition in the community, like a degree for another level of work. It's not the money itself that matters. What counts is what the money lets you do next."

What McRae's money has allowed him to do is indulge in "two-foot-itis" to the point that he now owns a 36-foot sport fishing yacht called Granges. "I do a lot of boating. Our Pacific is one of the most beautiful places to go out—no doubt about it. I'm playing with the idea right now of going in with some people on a destination resort."

McRae enjoys hosting his European associates when they visit Canada, combining a tour of the mines in Manitoba with some lake fishing, or taking some guests to where the best steelhead can be found on the coast.

He wanders over to a corner cabinet in his office where the memorabilia and gifts of his career are displayed.

"That's a bottle of Aqvavit given to me from the people from Granges AB, Sweden, because we signed the deal over a full bottle of that . . . there's a bottle of malt whiskey from one of my

British investor friends... there's some of the discovery drill core from the Cannon Mine in Wenatchee..."

There's also the ticker tape that announced Granges's listing on the AMEX, the New York-based Stock Exchange. A Boda crystal bull, symbolizing the stock market, was presented to him in Stockholm. "There's a bottle of Auditor and Port, which they give to their best clients. That is copper from Trout Lake Mine."

A photo of a thoroughbred racehorse crossing the finish line brings to mind another hobby. John McPherson, an associate from the old Hemsworth Turton days, and McRae jointly own several horses. The latest addition has McRae as proud as a new father as he searches on his desk for a photo. Akureyri is a seven-year-old stud out of a Northern Dancer daughter, a dark bay as near perfect as it's possible to get. His sire was descended from the great Buckpasser.

"The only reason we were able to get him is that E.P. Taylor wants to concentrate on the Northern Dancer line," McRae continues. The new owners plan to stand him in Canada for about a third of what he was commanding as a stud fee at Taylor's farm in Kentucky. "We think he'll still pay for himself."

This is where the fun comes in for Doug McRae. "But I don't have any desire to be a horse mogul," he says. "We have six horses and they pay for themselves. We don't lose anything and it gives us something to do."

McRae insists that his life is as simplistic today as at any other time in his life. He owns practically nothing outright; all his investments are on a partnership basis. He doesn't believe in the customary corporate jets or other material trappings of those who have arrived financially.

Before investing, he researches thoroughly and looks for experience and loyalty in management, and stability and staying power in assets. "Every time I invest in something I don't know quite a bit about, I lose money," he jokes with characteristic modesty.

"My net worth in 1977 was maybe $10,000. Now, it's several million. My personal assets in 1982 when we listed Breakwater publicly rose by several million dollars. But I am still the person I was when I had $10,000. I drank Chivas then and I drink it now."

He was a salesman then and he's a salesman now. It is just infinitely more comfortable to be a *rich* salesman.

"I think it's the most stimulating, most enjoyable job there is," he concludes with quiet conviction.

———

CHAPTER 12

Peter Brown

The getting of wisdom

Mention the VSE to anybody and invariably the name of Peter Brown will crop up. He has been called "The Immaculate Conception of Howe Street," and "Mr. VSE." For many, Peter Brown epitomizes the Vancouver Stock Exchange; without him it might never have changed from one vast bucket shop to the world-acclaimed venture-capital market it is today. He is, simply, a Howe Street legend. Yet he got into his field by accident, and never planned on staying in it. Twenty-five years later, he cannot imagine leaving.

Peter Brown sits at his desk in his office looking like what he is, a very busy and successful man. Canarim occupies four floors of the VSE building, one of the three black towers that so obviously symbolize money and power. The outer offices are understatedly elegant, all coral and taupe and marble, reflected in mirrored glass. Brown's office is not quite so elegant; it looks rumpled and lived in—which, given his long hours, it almost is. Brown himself is anything but ostentatious; he works in his shirt sleeves, his only ornament a gold family signet ring. The face is still boyish, although he looks tired; the hints of silver in his dark hair, his glasses, combined with a tendency to heaviness around the middle show that the young hotshot has entered gracefully into middle age. But his energy and his enthusiasm for the business are still as vital and alive as when he started, perhaps even more so.

After completing two and a half years of university (which took him five years), Brown joined the brokerage firm of Greenshields Inc., largely because he did not have any other particular career in mind. When a friend of the family offered to send him back east to learn the ropes at the Greenshields Toronto and Montreal offices, he accepted promptly, "not because I liked the investment business," he says, "but because I thought it was a lark . . . I took the job because it was a free trip to the East." He thought it might be an "interesting experience" but confesses he never imagined it would be a business he would stay in.

Instead of dabbling, he surprised everybody, including himself, by becoming dedicated to his new career. Brown gives credit to Brad Firstbrook, his boss at Greenshields, for changing him "from a wastrel to a workaholic." Firstbrook took a brilliant but undisciplined young man and, Brown says, "really got me interested;" and with that interest the hard work he could not settle to at university became easy. The man who was unable to concentrate long enough to graduate became fascinated with the process of underwriting and financing companies. "It changed my whole life," says Brown. That interest became an overwhelming passion which has stayed with him all his life, and has probably changed the course of the Vancouver Stock Exchange.

Brown, who believes he has spent his life "reacting to events," came back to Vancouver in 1967 and reacted to a new challenge, a job in the company of which he would eventually become president. At that time it was a brokerage firm called H. H. Hemsworth, after its founder. Brown started as vice-president of sales. Murray Pezim was Hemsworth's partner at the time, and in one of his spectacular dives (in which he indulges from time to time and from which he always recovers) he lost his shirt when a company called Bata Resources collapsed. Ted Turton, who later became Brown's quiet and less flamboyant partner, stepped in and bought Pezim's nearly worthless shares. (Brown already had 5%, which came with his job.) Said one article, "The place was a zoo." It only reflected the Vancouver Stock Exchange, which was pretty wild and woolly—as was Peter Brown himself. The same article added, of Brown, "He was twenty-six years old, brash, arrogant, loud-mouthed—and incredibly smart."

It was the late sixties and the VSE was still rather small-time. Its members were charged with fraud too often for most investors' liking. Most of the people who came into the market then, Brown feels, did not have much judgment, common sense, or management experience. He denies that his company was involved in anything dishonest, but admits they all made a lot of mistakes in those early years. Brown, who was only in his twenties when he was appointed president of what was by then called Hemsworth Turton, says he personally made numerous mistakes, a lot of errors in judgment.

The chance for change came when Harold Hemsworth died —on the golf course, as he had hoped he would. Brown and Turton had already bought 51% of the company in 1969 for $23,000. The company was at this time a "bankrupt bucket shop," according to Brown, but one he wanted. So he and Turton purchased the other 49% from the Hemsworth Estate for about $140,000. "That's really all the money we ever put into the business," says Brown. "We poured our profits back into the company, built the capital, and built the firm up."

Brown wanted to change the image of the company from flim-flam to quality, and acquiring good people became the first priority. "The quality of our salesmen wasn't what it should have been," he said. "My idea of quality control was to throw a phone book at a prospective salesman; if he could catch it he was hired." No more. He fired two-thirds of his sales staff and started over. He persuaded Chan Buckland, then a highly-respected mining engineer, and former bank manager Brian Harwood to join him. "Then," says Brown, "the flood-gates opened," and in came M.B.A.'s, engineers, special consultants; people from Wood Gundy, Midland Doherty, and Merrill Lynch; and out went the mooches and boiler-room types. With the change in personnel and attitude came a change in name.

"Canarim" was a combination of "Canada" and "Pacific Rim", symbolic of Brown's desire to make his company the best venture-capital firm in the world, not just in Vancouver.

Brown was, and is, an aggressive workaholic, and in those days he played just as hard as he worked. He started his day at six in the morning and worked intensively until seven-thirty at night, then it was time to party. His bacchanalian revels were legendary. The man turned carousing into a fine art, and he was always the last to leave any good party or nightclub. He managed this regime, which would have killed a lesser man, by sleeping only four or five hours a night.

The combination worked for him. From 1972 to 1975, during the NDP reign, when everyone else was cutting back Canarim was expanding. When the NDP took office it temporarily destroyed the market, yet Brown still pursued underwriting aggressively during the lean years, certain in his own mind that the NDP would be gone sooner rather than later. Writes author Frank Keane, in his book *The Vancouver Stock Exchange: from Bucket Shop to World Venture Money Capital*: "When it was impossible to obtain financing, Peter Brown's Canarim could be counted on to give the good promoter a helping hand, if the deal was up to snuff. A firm believer in the Vancouver market, Brown was always willing to put his money where his mouth is . . ."

Many believe Canarim's current dominance in speculative underwriting is a result of Brown's bold actions during those years, plus, of course, a few of his better gambles on behalf of other companies. Because he was there when they needed it, some companies who could now obtain capital from larger houses still give their business to Peter Brown.

It doesn't sound very risky when Brown talks about it today, but few other houses had the courage to follow his lead. "I could clearly see that the NDP were going to be defeated," he says. "They were vengeful, inexperienced, not ready to govern. They made a lot of serious mistakes in mining and resources . . . they were a cinch to get defeated for a lot of reasons. So," Brown adds, "in the three months following the election we went out and underwrote everybody in B.C. that needed money to start." He smiles in reminiscence, "Everybody said we were crazy."

Crazy like a fox, perhaps. After the NDP defeat he had predicted with such confidence, his stocks did very well. "Made a fortune," says Brown. "That's the kind of risk I like to take. A good risk." For Peter Brown, a bad risk is, naturally, one that does not work.

Expanding while others retrenched worked for him again in the 1982 bear market. Once more he had faith that it could not possibly last, so he bulled forward, expanded his Vancouver headquarters, and opened an office in Calgary. "This is not the Titanic," he said at the time. "The ship is not sinking. We've just stopped to pick up some ice." Brown firmly believed that during poor market conditions, with drastically lowered profits, the best thing to do is prepare for the next upswing. "The first guy ready for a good market does 60% of the business," he says, "and the other firms split the rest." That attitude has helped to make Canarim the Vancouver Stock Exchange's leading underwriter.

He never forgot his clients in all this; his risks tended to be calculated ones. "In a bad market, we have to find the special situations. Clients must make money. Pricing of new equity has to err in favour of the retail guys," he states practically.

Practicality and caution are not, however, what made Peter Brown's name a household word among stock market aficionados. In the late sixties and early seventies he was the visionary of the Vancouver stock establishment. He had a dream of what the Exchange could be, and how to achieve it. For Peter Brown, the VSE simply was not big enough; he wanted it to cut the apron strings that tied it to the East and do what he felt it was meant to do, raise venture capital for Vancouver people, Vancouver resources.

"The Exchange at that time was controlled by people like Mike Ryan of Pembertons and Ernie Drake of C.M. Oliver. They weren't venture-capital people," says Brown, "and they never understood the kind of exchange and the kind of regulations that were required to attract and bring venture-capital companies and venture-capital investors here." He adds, "I don't blame them for that. There are very few people in Canada that *do* understand it." Peter Brown does, and did. He knew just what he wanted, and what he wanted to get rid of, and his main concern was the attitude towards junior companies. "In the late sixties," says Brown, "I came into an investment industry that frowned on the raising of venture capital. The Ontario Securities Commission and the Montreal Stock Exchange and Securities Commission closed down junior financing in Canada, not because they had any mandate to do it but because they were a bunch of bureaucrats who didn't understand how to operate or control it." Brown also attributed the closure to fear, the fear that junior financing might cut into the $800 million or $900 million that was the investment capital at that time.

Brown disagreed completely with that attitude. He decided that venture-capital financing was "the most needed area of financing in the country . . . *and* the most exciting area to deal in." He wanted to make it a business, partly because no one else was doing it. But he had to deal with the status quo, and that meant the people who controlled the stock exchange, and the Investment Dealers Association (IDA). They all had what he calls "the Toronto Stock Exchange mentality," the conviction that junior financing was an activity that was unsuited to public investment.

This attitude infuriated him. "You could buy a lottery ticket," Brown says, "but you couldn't buy a share in a junior company. What a load of crap." He was not the only person to feel that way, and gradually a group of like-minded individuals was formed: Murray Pezim, Bruce McDonald, the Granges Group and several others. By the mid-seventies they were ready to act. Traditionally, a nomination committee controlled by the established order comes up with a list of nominations for the VSE board of governors, which is accepted by acclamation. Not this time. In a break with tradition, Brown and his group forced nominations from the floor, a move that shocked and appalled the old guard. It was shocking but effective. Brown was elected, along with three others in the group: Ian Falconer of Midland Doherty, Warren Clark of McDermid Miller, and Bob Atkinson of Loewen Ondaatje. VSE president Cyril White resigned. It was 1974 and the young upstarts had control of the Exchange.

"Critics," laughs Brown now, "said that they'd turned the keys of the bank over to the burglars." But Brown and his group had even more surprises in store. They brought in Bob Scott, formerly president of the Securities Commission in Alberta, to replace Cyril White as president of the VSE, and together they tightened up the rules considerably, while giving penny-stock players more leeway than ever before. Brown feels that too few people know how good the Exchange really is. "We have a security liaison committee that meets regularly to review policy and make recommendations," he said. "There's no other financial jurisdiction in the world that has that." By tightening the rules they also inspired more investor confidence than had ever existed before.

For Peter Brown, shocking people was not a new development. He had done it often throughout his life, but this time it was for a sound and constructive reason. A far cry from his school days at the exclusive Shawnigan Lake Boys' School, where the bright if unruly Brown was known as a prankster. As punishment for one of his misdeeds he was ordered by the German gardener to "pull veeds" in the flower beds that bordered the school's half-mile-long driveway. He pulled out the daffodils instead, hundreds of them. Pretence of ignorance did not help him; he was given a detention for the rest of that year. "But it was worth it," he claims, smiling happily at the memory.

Brown's roots are more established than the antics of his younger days would suggest. His father and grandfather were provincial managers of Crown Life Insurance Co., an uncle was one of the city's best-known Q.C.s. One of his brothers (he has three) is now headmaster of St. George's School for Boys, from which Peter was graduated at the age of fifteen. Thirteen generations of his family have been born in British Columbia, all of them generally quiet, distinguished, low-profile individuals. Then along came young Peter.

Brown was only fifteen when he was enrolled at the University of British Columbia, and had gone to sedate, private (boys only) schools. His youth and immaturity, and comfortable background perhaps explain why, when he hit UBC, he ran amok. Soon his escapades entered into legend. "There were women," he says, "and stuff I'd never seen before..." A lot of hard drinking and wild parties went on in his rented coach house on Southwest Marine Drive and, needless to say, his grades suffered. "I was taking arts, but I was aiming at having a good time too," he says.

He certainly did. One of his more spectacular experiences earned him a lot of press coverage later on. "Brown's parties were legendary," said one report, "but the bash the night before had been like a scene from *Animal House*." During the party, in the early hours of the morning, two of his guests decided to engage in a tree-felling contest. The winner is long-since forgotten, but no one can forget that one tree thundered down across department-store magnate Chunky Woodward's driveway, while the other destroyed the treasured flower beds of the founder of West Coast Transmission, Frank McMahon.

The next day a horrified Brown found a terse McMahon on the doorstep, with just one thing to say: "I'm here to tell you I want you off the property by tomorrow." This was no idle threat, for he added, "I've just bought the place."

His reputation followed him for many years and he did his best to live up to it. The partying continued, but now he worked just as hard as he played. As he became "obscenely wealthy," as one writer phrased it, he found ever new ways of spending that wealth. (His income has been conjectured to be anywhere from $5 million to $10 million—"only his accountant knows for sure.") The stories tell of sixty pairs of identical Gucci shoes and a special cupboard to house them; of three houses, four boats, a storied Rolls Royce convertible, and of the time when, shopping for company cars, he went into a Mercedes shop and dumbfounded the salesman by buying three.

Another article told of Brown and a friend lounging by the hotel pool in Las Vegas. When the friend mentioned that he liked bullshots, a drink made with vodka and bouillon, Brown ordered him thirty of them, at $6 a shot. In a later story, he claimed that the first reporter got it wrong, "Actually I ordered

150 bullshots." (Whether they were finished is anybody's guess.)

Comments like that caused him to be labelled obnoxious, and egotistical. Brown denies the former but admits to the latter, quoting Earl Louis Mountbatten of Burma, "I am the most conceited man I have ever known." Detractors aside, even his worst enemies have had to admit he is brilliant, and that without him the VSE would not be the respected place it is today.

When talking about the change in the VSE, Brown gives an impression of modesty, not arrogance. "It was a group of people," he says, "not any one person . . . that made it all happen. It wasn't Peter Brown or Bruce McDonald or any one player by himself. It was a lot of experienced guys who, at the time, in the early seventies, already had ten years' experience under their belts, who knew what could be done, and who worked damn hard to make it happen. They travelled, sacrificed their social life, family life, to make the Vancouver Stock Exchange grow." His pride shows. Adds Brown, "It was probably two dozen people who made it happen. Had you taken those same two dozen people and plunked them down in Calgary, then the Alberta Stock Exchange would now be the big venture-capital market." He is probably right.

The VSE has changed dramatically, and Canarim reflects that process. Canarim is first in financing and volume of trading, and accounts for nearly 20% of VSE trading. It raises some $300 million in venture capital a year. Canarim has over two hundred salesmen, who earn about "twice the industry average," according to Brown. He laughs at a reported figure of $250,000 a year for his top salesmen. "We have people that make over a million dollars a year," he says. They trade for around 200,000 clients, filling up to 5,000 orders a day in which 2 million to 3 million shares trade hands. One study showed that in ten months alone, Canarim raised money for 132 companies, and netted a massive $5 million in commissions, more than twice that of its nearest competitor, Continental Carlisle Douglas.

Peter Brown still does sixty-five per cent of the underwritings personally, and fields hundreds of phone calls a day. Still a workaholic, his average day has not changed much since the beginning. What has changed is his partying habits. Brown doesn't like to talk of his early notorious exploits, considering them past history. "At forty-five you don't do the same things you did when you were twenty-five," says Brown. "It just doesn't interest me to go roaring around the bars anymore." Now it is only on rare occasions that he gets into what he calls "fiesta drinking;" the saturnalian has settled down.

He may have given up his former festive habits, but his love of pranks and practical jokes has never died. "You've got to laugh," he says. "In this business you lose your sense of humour and you're dead." Friend and colleague Murray Pezim agrees: "If you don't laugh a lot during the day, God help you. This is one tough business on the nerves."

Brown, known to his friends as Peter "the Rabbit" Brown, used to receive rabbit hats, rabbit shirts, rabbit paintings, sculptures and so on. He even has a $25,000 gold-plated replica of an oil rig entitled "Petro Rabbit," that was presented to him by a Texan client. In keeping with this theme, one morning the VSE staff sent a beguiling live white rabbit adorned with red ribbons to Brown's office. Later that day, a whole, roasted rabbit with the same red ribbons was delivered to the Stock Exchange for lunch. The staff were horrified; they thought Brown had cooked their present. Instead he had found one, "the exact size" he chuckles, and had restaurateur Umberto Menghi cook it. The original bunny was safe, and became a family pet.

"Most stockbrokers have a good sense of humour," says Brown seriously. "It's a stress business—if you don't have a sense of humour, you die. All the good brokers I know are very funny people." Murray Pezim is certainly one of them. Pezim has known Brown since his early days at Greenshields, when he called Brown a "snot-nosed bond salesman." In spite of this they have been friends and colleagues for years, but the banter never lets up. "Peter's got a great sense of humour," says Pezim, "but he tells terrible jokes."

Pezim, who once called Brown arrogant, feels he has mellowed a great deal. "He's not as arrogant as he used to be." Serious for once, he adds, "Peter's really a very good person, very philanthropic. A lot of people don't know that about him, but I do. He gives his heart and soul to it."

Brown himself has commented that he and his wife have been very active in the community, "but nobody ever writes about that." He has a right to complain. Every year Canarim gives a million dollars and raises a million for charity. "We support just about any cause," he says, "from giving a quarter-million to keep the Emily Carr Gallery in the Vancouver Art Gallery to putting up a mural in the Children's Hospital." (They had a painting competition, which was won by an eight year old, and then the winning painting was incorporated into the tile mural.) They have funded cabins for the Y.M.C.A., built a Fine Arts Centre at St. George's School, Brown's old Alma Mater, and contributed to many more causes and projects.

He believes in giving more than just money to his community; he also gives of his time. The list of boards and committees he has served on seems endless. He was recently named Chairman of the new B.C. Enterprise Corp., the result of the merger between B.C. Place and the B.C. Development Corp., and last year he was on the boards of Expo 86 and the Vancouver Art Gallery, as well as on twenty other boards and committees. Jimmy Pattison, who served on the same board as Brown for a year, has nothing but praise for the man, calling him a "very smart, attractive guy" with an "excellent sense of humour." He also lauds Brown for being community-minded and, all in all, a "great guy."

The man who flunked his freshman year three times was appointed to the University's Board of Governors, no small honour. "Do you need a degree to know how to be a good director?" he asks rhetorically. Perhaps what provided final proof of his transformation from wild young hotshot to pillar of the community was his appointment to the national executive committee of the Investment Dealers Association of Canada, "the same IDA," says Brown gleefully, "that tried to put me out of business ten years ago."

Any prejudice concerning Peter Brown's market tactics has long since disappeared. "But," he says, "there is always a prejudice towards the West." He sounds resigned, and recalls that back in the early 1980s, 50% of the share volume on the stock exchanges of New York, Vancouver, and Toronto was in oil. That collapsed, oil went from shortage to surplus, and the senior stocks plummeted by about 65%. So did the juniors. In Toronto and Montreal, the reason given was obvious: oil prices had gone down because of the surpluses. "Yet in Vancouver, according to the easterners," says Brown, "the reason was that the game was crooked. There will always be that suspicion if you run a venture-capital marketplace. You just have to get used to it." On a more positive note he adds that he is "glad that they think that way, because if they knew what a neat business it is they'd want to come into it!"

In 1971, when Brown was first getting into the game, the VSE had $19 million worth of financing. In 1985 it had $348 million. In 1986 financing took another leap to over $705 million. In most recent years Canarim has earned a 100% return on its pre-tax investment capital. Says Brown, "Between our parent company, Intercan, and Canarim today we have about $38 million in capital."

His clients profit too, particularly if they invest in some of the big winners like Highland Pro, which Canarim underwrote at 90 cents and which had reached $10 when last heard of; or Emerald Lake—they did the first primary at 30 cents and it later hit $11. "They just go one after another," says Brown. "There's a very big market and there are very big gains." Not every stock has been a gold mine, so to speak, which doesn't surprise Brown. "If you're in a high-risk business some deals just won't work out," he ways. "You expect that." But by and large he feels he does very well for his clients. "There'll be some investments that don't work," he admits, "But if you can be right even two or three times out of ten, you can double the client's money."

So how does he know which deal is going to be right? "It's an automatic computer sort of thing," he says. "Part of it is having been there before, and knowing when something won't work.

Some call it instinct, but for me it's more like twenty-four years of experience. A deal's got to have the right people, the right price, the right assets. I got to know that by doing hundreds and hundreds of deals." [More like thousands and thousands; Canarim reputedly does a deal almost every day.]

Peter Brown has not always had the ability to choose wisely, however; he has gone broke twice, experiences he profited by both metaphorically and literally. "I've made a lot of mistakes," he says. "You learn by it. You show me a young man who's gone straight up and never had a setback and I'll show you a potential disaster. It's the setbacks that train you and teach you how to think." He muses, "When you start out in business you're just there to do everything you can. You don't have the defence mechanisms. And if you get successful early you think you're a genius. You've got to learn that stock markets are bigger than any individual; market cycles, depressions, are bigger than any individual."

Brown would not trade the tough days for anything. "Everybody does well in good times," he says, "but you have to have been through bad times before you're any good." He survived five or six years of bad times, of bear markets and recessions. Canarim had to close its prairie offices and recall Ted Turton, who had been heading up the Winnipeg office. For Brown, it was all part of the learning process. "It's getting kicked around a few times that teaches you that balance between optimism and cynicism that allows you to operate effectively." Wisdom, for Peter Brown, "comes from having made a lot of mistakes and having learned from them." Tough times may have forced them to close the prairie offices, but expansion is not over yet; they recently opened an office in Toronto and acquired a seat on the Toronto Stock Exchange for about $215,000.

Brown does not dwell on his past successes or failures, preferring to live in the present: "What you made or lost yesterday is irrelevant." With the changes in the market due to deregulation there has been no shortage of new challenges to occupy his time. The latest one is the fund-management business. Their mutual fund, called the Multiple Opportunities Fund, came as a surprise to many, as it is the first fund of its kind to specialize in speculative issues listed on the Vancouver Stock Exchange; that is,"the juniors," or low-priced mining stock. It upsets the traditional concept of mutual fund as "conservative-investment vehicle." Somehow it comes as no surprise that this shocking new concept is doing very well. "Canarim scores with fund," said one headline. "Investors flooding Canarim," said another, as enquiries (and cash) poured in. "It's the top performing fund in the country," says Brown proudly. "It's up 75% in its first fifteen months."

It is only one of the funds in which Canarim is and will continue to be involved. The company is also doing a flow-through fund with CMP, the biggest tax fund people in the country, 35 points ahead of its nearest competitor. Brown's next project will be a merchant-banking fund. "We just have to do the final paperwork," he says. He'll be funding it, about $20 to $25 million to start with, through several institutions, including Loewen Ondaatje of Toronto and Beutel Goodman, a New York-based dealer. This fund may help improve the calibre of company listed on the VSE, for it will finance companies ready to go public. Says Brown, "You end up with a better class of company going public on the final day, as more money's been spent prior to going public."

Brown puts the same energy and enthusiasm into collecting art as he does into underwriting companies of managing funds. The VSE may be a monument to money-making, but in Canarim art has not been forgotten. Seven exquisite Toni Onleys line the walls of the spacious waiting room and boardroom. "About half the art," says Brown, "is mine; the other half belongs to the company." A large painting tries to dominate his office, but has to fight for supremacy with the magnificent view of the harbour and the sails of the Pan Pacific Hotel. "I've got personally one of the largest collections in North America," he says, "all of it Canadian."

But for him, at the moment, the biggest thrill in his collection of Canadiana is his antique duck decoys. "It's the fastest-growing art form in North America," he says enthusiastically—and he has the largest collection in the country. For Brown, the investor, it is also important that they are one of the best investments around; in recent years they have increased one hundred per cent in value. Two years ago the highest-priced American decoy sold for US$97,000. This may sound like a lot for a wooden duck, but, he says, "the record is now US$390,000 for a single decoy. I own about 3000 birds."

Brown collects for love as well as for investment purposes. "Art is both," he insists. Whereas in the past people sent him rabbit memorabilia, now, he laughs, "they send me ducks." He dismisses scoffers. "It's a real art form; they've been recognized as *the* three-dimensional art form in Canadiana and Americana. I have the largest collection in Canada," he reiterates.

His competitive spirit spills over into other aspects of his life. He and his wife live in what he grandiosely calls "the finest home in the city of Vancouver." They have, in addition, a home at Whistler (where he is on the board of the Whistler Mountain Ski Association), and a 4,000-square-foot summer home on Bowen Island.

When queried about all this luxury, and his accession to wealth as a very young man, Brown responded, "I've worked like hell for twenty-five years. In the early days I worked nights and weekends, and if you didn't want to talk business, you didn't talk to me. It didn't come quickly," he maintains, "it came very hard."

Yet after twenty-five years in this grinding business, Peter Brown has no intention of slowing down. "I love it," he says. "If I didn't I wouldn't be here." Although his partner, Ted Turton, recently sold all but 5% of his shares in the company in order to slow down a bit and let new and younger shareholders get more involved, Brown shows no signs of slackening his pace. Not, at least, while there are still new challenges to confront and conquer.

"With deregulation," he says, "the whole marketplace is changing very fast, and you've got to change with it." The man who helped to change the stock market from nickel-and-dime action to the premier venture-capital marketplace in the world, and who has always said "I believe in the future," should have no trouble keeping up. Especially now that, as Brown says, "the speculative pool of money that's available is a thousand times as

big as it was ten years ago." He adds, "You've got investors looking for a higher risk and a higher return." And Canarim and
Peter Brown will be right there to help them.

Although he insists that it was a group that changed the face
of the VSE, many feel that Brown's contribution was the
greatest. Rupert Bullock, former superintendent of brokers,
said, "He's probably had more to do with the way the VSE is
now than anyone else." One article claimed that "Peter Brown
is to the VSE what Wayne Gretzky is to the Edmonton Oilers."
So closely are they identified that it is hard sometimes to separate Peter Brown from the Stock Exchange to which he has
dedicated his life. Both were brash and wild in the early days,
and both have since matured, come of age. The former rebel is
now respectable; the wild one is no longer wild; the toppler-of-
the-establishment has *become* the establishment. Vancouver
and the Vancouver Stock Exchange are the richer for it.

———————

CHAPTER 13

Robert Hunter

Raising the standard of gold

The success of Bob Hunter's first big gold producer, Break-water Mines at Wenatchee, Washington hung by a thread in 1982—on the price of gold. And the price of gold has been just as crucial in all of Hunter's activity since, including his most recent achievement, the bringing to production of his North American Metal Corporation mine at Dease Lake, B.C.

But while the price of gold was usually the catalyst the projects that spanned the five years between Breakwater and North American Metal Corporation were fast-moving, complex enough to be bewildering, and often as exciting as a Hollywood screen play. Involving offshore financing, machinations and counter-machinations, the progression in mine creation and management also marked the evolution of Bob Hunter as an entrepreneur. While the mine development showed steady improvement, the accomplishment in human terms was even more impressive.

"It's people like Bob," says one Howe Street broker, "who have raised the standards of this industry, and its image."

A comparison with the late sixties, when Hunter first entered the mining-promotion game, is almost amusing. Then the norm was for promoters to sell "position plays," a sort of endless game of Monopoly where promoters, brokers, and investors circled a variety of properties but where few, if any, ever passed Go. Talented geologists and mine-finders tended to gravitate into honest jobs with the majors, leaving the promotion of scarcely visible traces of mineralization and "potential reserves" to the scam artists.

Today a substantial sub-culture has grown up in B.C., as in central Canada, a young and innovative group of entrepreneurs, geologists, and financial specialists who are consistently exploring and developing honest-to-God mines and then finding the financial resources to fund their production. These modern mine-makers have steadily reduced the still-astronomical odds against separating the producing mines from the barren ground.

Over the past decade Bob Hunter has been at the forefront of this new mining generation.

But the learning process that constantly takes place in handling the problems that beset mine creation and management is very evident in the many ways in which the North American Metal mine has profited from the Breakwater experience that unfolded five years earlier: But even with the benefit of that background, bringing Dease Lake in as the largest gold producer in B.C. did not come easily.

The real story began with Hunter's upbringing and the legacy of his family's four generations in the Lower Mainland.

Contrary to other Canadian cities, Vancouver seems to have been built by people who have come from just about everywhere else. But Bob Hunter is not one of these. His grandparents on both sides arrived in New Westminster, he declares with pride, not too long after the Canadian Pacific Railway had bypassed that riverside city in favour of the foot of Granville for its western terminus, a quasi-political move on the part of Van Horne that caused several New Westminster realtors to commit *hara-kiri*.

Hunter's antecedents were not the type to care much; with or without the C.P.R., New Westminster was their turf and much later Hunter echoed that feeling. Even today he lives in Coquitlam, not far from the place where he was born.

He grew up in New Westminster, attended South Burnaby

High, and did all the things you would expect of a future super-achiever. Active in athletics, he did his stint with a Province paper route (a mandatory entry in all successful resumés, as you may have noticed) in the days when it was an evening paper. And as his first up-town job he was a busboy at the old Palomar.

As a native of the Lower Mainland it would have been quite natural for Hunter to gravitate to mining, the way a retired Saskatchewan farmer homes in on Vancouver; but he went about it indirectly, his first adult occupation being with a Big 8 accountancy firm. Here the first twinges of attraction to the mining industry stirred in his bloodstream.

"I was auditing small mining companies," says Hunter, "and it occurred to me that not only was this a fun way to make a living, but also that it was tremendously exciting—far more so than accounting."

What he failed to realize at that point, of course, was that successful mining depends very much on the prosaic world of accounting which, when it involves funding, can be anything but dull. His early introduction to Doug McRae corrected his thinking on that point.

But Hunter did not move directly to mining. Instead he launched himself into an insurance career with Occidental Life of California. "Launched" understates what was more like a blast-off. With his usual intensity he reached the level of *world* leader in sales for the Occidental organization.

"You can see the traces of that experience later," says John Woods, president of the Howe Street newsletter *Stockwatch*, "As a mining executive he utilized all the important attributes of an outstanding salesman, such as constantly widening his contacts and consistently treating people well."

There was something else, a certain compulsion in addition to his attraction to the excitement and challenge of the mining industry, a compulsion best expressed by George Cross, Vancouver financial publisher: "Bob *had* to get into mining," says Cross. "By that time he had seven kids."

But the transition was gradual. Having completed his CLU with Occidental, for a while Hunter (in partnership with Vern Mayer, then a recent graduate from the compliance department at the VSE and anxious to utilize his experience), developed junior mining situations in his spare time, including that of Lincoln Resources in 1969. Call it his apprenticeship.

In actual fact, Hunter's first lesson in the mining curriculum revolved around the importance of being earnest, or at least the importance of having an earnest geologist.

Don't forget, this was the sixties, when "bizarre" was the watchword. The engineer had rendered glowing reports about the property. Then two things happened simultaneously: the stock went to $20, and Hunter's management group, which consisted of himself and Vern Mayer, went to the High Sierras, where the property was located. There they found their ore body under twenty feet of snow, hardly consistent with the detailed appraisal the engineer had just turned in.

"Since we fired that engineer," says Hunter, "I've never been a paper player. Any group I've been associated with has always been oriented to the property's potential and production, rather than to the stock's action or the financial side of the operation."

This in a way is a classic understatement. Hunter, because of his upbringing, education, and training is as uncompromising, upright, and straightforward in business as he is in everything else.

"There are a lot of characters in the mining industry," says one colleague, "who are given to hyperbole. So it sometimes comes as a pleasant surprise to work around Bob. You know what I mean? Occasionally it can be a refreshing change to have someone around who invariably tells the truth."

In fact, taking a poll of his business associates is like writing the minutes for a Bob Hunter fan club. Except that with Hunter such testimony is convincing because it comes across just as naturally as the way in which he does the most commonplace things.

"Dress is not a thing people are too concerned about in the mining industry," says Doug McRae, senior vice-president of Granges Canada, and an associate of Hunter's in the formation of Breakwater. "But Bob is always flawlessly turned out, whatever the occasion. We kid him about whether or not he wears three-piece pyjamas."

John Woods's point about the carryover of Hunter's training as a salesman has a good deal of relevance. The presence Hunter brought to an industry not usually noted for the charisma of its senior executives, at least in the junior companies, explains another enigma. Hunter and his group in recent years, Doug MacRae, John McPherson and two or three other regulars, have built a reputation for the ease with which they can arrange financing.

On either side of the Atlantic their excellent financial connections and, naturally, their track record have made this condition possible. They make the raising of capital appear to be easy when, in this day and age of mine financing, major funding is one of the central problems for any organization.

At the same time, the systematic exploration and development of a series of outstanding properties has also seemed to come naturally, at least since Hunter's group broke through with the success of Breakwater.

"People are always approaching us with the most innovative deals," says Hunter, "often organized around financing packages that show real ingenuity. And even though we often have to turn this kind of offer down, it shouldn't be concluded that mine financing is an easy thing to accomplish."

The fact is of course that the number of financiers beating a path to Hunter's door is more a commentary on his management group than an indicator of the availability of funding. And financing—as well as mine-finding, which in a way is the other half of the equation—is fraught with anxiety and perennial problems that must be overcome. But like a ballet dancer, the real pros consistently make accomplishment look easy.

In the early eighties Bob Hunter and his group acquired a tired VSE performer named Goldbelt Mines. Goldbelt did have one redeeming feature—it held a forty-five per cent position in a gold property near Wenatchee, Washington, of which Asamera Minerals owned the other fifty-five per cent.

The Wenatchee site had history on its side. The area, according to Frank Keane, a Vancouver financial columnist, had been explored for gold as long ago as 1890, and commercial production for the two decades after 1949 had produced a million tons of ore grading 0.4 ounces of gold per ton. Now, with apparent current reserves outlined at 1.6 million tons grading 0.15 ounces gold per ton and with improved technology and higher gold prices, there was little doubt that Breakwater could be actively employed for some years, while with its partner Asamera it could pursue the logical strategy of attempting to prove up additional mineralization.

But getting Breakwater there was more than half the fun. The footwork became a little involved. Watch closely.

The players, according to George Cross, included the following: Karl Rollke of Vancouver, who controlled Kimberley Gold Mines (which in turn controlled Goldbelt); Carlo Civelli, a financier in Zurich; Lindsay Semple and Dieter Peter, both prominent Vancouver mining entrepreneurs, as well as McRae, John MacPherson and Hunter.

To resuscitate Goldbelt, at that time figuratively about to go down for the third time, Hunter's group needed a financial infusion of close to $300,000, fast. They managed to round it up from a dozen shareholders. As mentioned earlier the price of gold was crucial in the equation, and it bottomed under $300 just as the deal was being transacted with much trepidation on the part of Hunter and his group in July 1982. Within two months fortune smiled on New Westminster's favourite son, and gold was close to $600. The new management had made the right move.

Yes and no. As a vehicle to handle the Goldbelt interest, Hunter's group adopted a VSE shell company known as Breakwater, MacPherson having lined it up through certain business connections. The imagery was appropriate; the company was to become a seawall against the battering odds of creating a successful gold mine.

But problems began almost immediately. Since Asamera kept to its tempo of spending $180,000 a month on the Wenatchee prospect, Hunter and his group were under almost intolerable pressure. They had stretched themselves to the limit to make the acquisition and were now constantly scrambling to raise capital with one hand while staving off Goldbelt's old creditors with the other.

But the inherent value of the Wenatchee property gradually asserted itself and the Breakwater stock began slowly but steadily to move ahead. Constantly-expanding reserves and modifications of their production plans necessitated more and more financing. The original plan had called for $20 million to bring the mine to production; the final figure was $90 million.

One of the reasons for the quantum leap in costs was the elaborate tailings pond, a project that came to be faintly reminiscent of the Grand Coulee Dam. This structure, greater than the average concession thrown to the environmentalist lobby, cost $19 million and is the largest of its kind in North America, capable of holding 10 million tons of tailings with absolute security. The process of obtaining complete permits on this site was understandably somewhat like preparing for a small Normandy invasion, requiring twenty-six separate permits and the monitoring of wind, dust, light, and sound factors.

Meanwhile the juggling with the Goldbelt ownership went on. First the Breakwater management restructured and then eliminated the Goldbelt debt. Then acquisition of a total of 63% of Goldbelt by Breakwater succeeded in making Goldbelt cash-rich when the Breakwater stock went to $25 and was split two-for-one. Breakwater successfully came through that maneuver, but had more difficulty in the financing of its obligations at the Wenatchee property—until a public financing in Vancouver succeeded in strengthening Breakwater's status, as befitted its position as a 49% partner in a major new gold mine.

In the years since operations began at Wenatchee, Breakwater's success has not been unalloyed. Phase-in and technical problems reduced the company's targeted goal of 65,000 ounces of gold in the first complete production year of 1986. In that year Breakwater experienced break-even, with the likelihood of a marginal net profit in 1987.

Haywood Securities' Anthony Garson in Vancouver estimates that earnings over the 1988-89 period will approximate 15 cents per share per annum, suggesting that the stock, at close to $9 in

March 1987, may have been slightly overvalued.

But Breakwater represented something of a new departure for gold mining in North America in several respects, just as it represented a turning point for Robert Hunter and his management group. With start-up in mid-1985, its first official production and expense statements were made in March 1986. It has moved toward profitability in an extremely short period of time.

Partly because it has faced an unusually high-cost construction imperative, notably in the huge tailings pond that is a monument to environmental concern, its cost structure is such that, according to Garson, under a $400 price for gold, profit potential could be only marginal. But with higher gold prices operations will be highly profitable. And the outlook for expanded production is even more favourable because of the likelihood of increased reserves.

During Breakwater's formative stages a sound financial network was being built among dealers and brokers in Vancouver, Toronto, and Western Europe. While Douglas McRae is usually credited with arranging the offshore financing for any organization with which he has been involved, the importance of Robert Hunter's role has also been evident in spreading the word internationally concerning Breakwater and its potential. As a result the company has developed a strong worldwide shareholder group extending wherever Hunter has conducted his missionary activities— Zurich, London, Paris, and twenty-two American cities.

Once a world leader, it seems, always a world leader.

Parenthetically, it is worth noting that Hunter's seven children, who range in age from eighteen to thirty, have each in one way or another emulated their father's qualities in athletics, business and academic achievement, and community service. One of his sons, for example, has a post-graduate degree in physics. And on Bob's entry into full-time mining entrepreneurship another of his sons assumed his insurance clientele. To learn that they have political aspirations or that they play touch football at the gatherings of the Hunter clan would not be surprising.

"It's well known of course that Bob's a workaholic," says

Vern Mayer. "But it's not so well known that he's a charter member of the Lions organization. God knows where he finds the time, but he's done a lot of work establishing homes for elderly people, that sort of thing."

After Breakwater, Hunter's group tended to follow different interests, but they continued to come together again from time to time, practising their now-familiar gambit: injecting enough capital into a selection of sow's ears in order to come away with silk purses.

McRae, for example, became active in the development of Granges Canada, while Hunter, still chairman of Breakwater, devotes much of his energy to North American Metal Corporation.

"But we're always looking at new deals," says Hunter, "and in fact, Doug and I worked closely together on North American Metal."

Pecos, an 8-cent VSE shell company, was developed in 1983 into a formidable force able to provide the muscle to acquire Granges Canada, the domestic residue of a Swedish company of the same name. After Pecos became functional, thanks to some financing by offshore investors, Hunter's group learned that the Granges company would become available as its Swedish parent divested itself of the operation.

The Granges acquisition was significant in that, while Hunter and his Breakwater group had essentially decided the main purpose of the Breakwater organization would be the developing of the Wenatchee gold property, they were also sensible enough to realize that few realities in the mining game are permanent, and consequently mining success depends on a constant flow of projects.

In addition it is important to note that some of the group were to be more active in Granges than others. Hunter, as chairman of Breakwater, could not devote a great deal of time to the Granges deal, but he remains a director. Similarly, McRae became an active principal in Granges and later was actively involved with Hunter in the formation of North American Metal.

Granges, regardless of the management mix, is an interesting model for any aggressive mining holding company, with a superlative mine-finder in the person of Mike Muzylowski as a complement to a man of McRae's legendary money-finding ability. That Robert Hunter did not join them to round out the management team is more a commentary on the discretionary time Hunter had available then than whether there might have been room for him in this powerful emerging mining company beyond the directorship he assumed.

In any case, a long series of deals, takeovers and reverse takeovers left Pecos owning Granges, but being absorbed by it in the process. But before the Granges combination was achieved Pecos had entered into a joint-venture arrangement with the Fisher-Watt organization in Nevada, earning a position in two excellent heap-leaching properties, Hayden Hill in California and the Dexter Mine in Nevada.

That was a good start, but when the news arrived that Granges was ready to sell its Canadian arm, with the flagship Trout Lake ore body in Manitoba alone earning $3 million a year, the former Breakwater financing team swung into action. Using Pecos as the vehicle, they bought Granges for $12.5 million.

After the phenomenal success of Breakwater, Hunter and his group were the fair-haired boys as far as European investors were concerned. The details of any given offshore funding—such as the one that fuelled the Granges acquisition—were usually worked out by McRae. In the latter case, rumor has it that he sketched the financing plan on the back of an envelope, airborne while returning from Finland and the U.K.

It was almost routine procedure to line up European investors for a Swedish entity that was well-known, that was engaged in a Canadian industry they had come to understand, and that was producing a commodity most of the world's peoples revere more than they do their grandparents. (And the fact that the group borrowed the funds on the credit of Granges itself demonstrates that at that time, in 1983, they were not averse to reinventing Sam Belzberg's leveraged buyout technique.)

In addition, the Granges Canadian spread, in retrospect, just may have been the greatest bargain since the Dutch rip-off of Manhattan.

"It's amazing," says Hunter, "the values that get snapped up at clearance prices sometimes when a major mining company decides for its own corporate reasons to abdicate a certain part of its holdings. Sometimes it's a case of vacating a whole industry. Anaconda in recent years has been a good example—the properties that became Galactic and Quartz Mountain were both literally bargain basement deals. And in a different way, the Granges parent company, because of estate taxes and the disposition of a new major shareholder, also decided to relinquish its Canadian mining assets."

But the Granges development was more than a good bargain. The synergism developed by that hard working team that in the space of a few short years had produced Breakwater, Pecos, Granges, and North American Metal Corporation became such a powerful force in Canadian Westcoast mining that it can only be likened to a famous show-business equivalent, the Vegas "Rat Pack" (Dean Martin, Joey Bishop, Frank Sinatra and Sammy Davis). Even then, the comparison doesn't do justice to Hunter's group, which after all had more than entertainment value.

There was a huge bonus that did not appear on the financial statements the European investors in Granges perused. With Granges, the deep thinkers on both sides of the Atlantic picked up Mike Muzylowski, arguably the best mine-finder west of Kapuskasing. Muzylowski, when he was named president of the new Granges Canada organization, teamed with Doug McRae to produce the most powerful one-two punch in mining: a superlative mine-finder and a legendary money-finder. And while interlocking directors lingered on, Breakwater and Granges-Pecos tended each to its own knitting, with Breakwater's Hunter minding the Wenatchee operation and Granges devoted to a series of projects that Muzylowski had brought with him. The greatest asset Granges had to work with was obviously Muzylowski himself.

The diversity of Granges was well known. Frank Keane has pointed out that at the time of the acquisition the Swedish subsidiary had over one million acres of mineral holdings in Canada, including several proven ore bodies, not counting the approximate twenty per cent position in Hudson Bay Mines'

Trout Lake producing mine. And soon after, with the reverse takeover of Pecos, the promising heap-leach operations in California and Nevada also came into the fold.

Less than three years later, the Brotherhood, now with Muzylowski grafted on as president, had accomplished through Granges an amazing progression, juggling fifteen major projects that spanned the western provinces and the Yukon as well as Ontario, Nevada, and California. Granges had by this time set itself the corporate goal of bringing a minimum of one major property to production each year.

In a mining market that has witnessed the continual erosion of metal prices during most of a decade, this performance suggests the degree to which volatility in metals tends to separate the run-of-the-mill operators from the true innovators. Most of that innovation is summed up by the mine-finding expertise that has created thirteen proven mines in Muzylowski's career, combined with the established network of international investment bankers who routinely manage billion dollar portfolios and actively seek promising mining projects. The combination, as Hunter and his group had discovered earlier, is not only rewarding, it is indispensable.

More prosaic perhaps than finding new ore bodies or outside funding, but almost more germane to any emerging company—mining operations included—is the third indispensable principle that Bob Hunter practises: cost control. This, in fact, is doubly important in an industry as price-sensitive as mining.

In an operation such as Breakwater, where a moderate decline in gold price could bring the plant's revenue potential close to borderline, cost control is the ultimate discipline. (Elsewhere it is the sort of exercise that enables a Teck to produce copper in B.C., where copper mines are enshrined almost like dinosaurs.)

When Hunter's associates had digested the Granges organization through Pecos, or vice versa, the stage was set for Hunter's venture with North American Metal Corporation. An agreement was negotiated with Chevron Minerals whereby a fifty per cent interest in the latter's Golden Bear property near

Dease Lake B.C. was to be earned out by North American Metal Corporation as operating partner.

According to Tony Garson of Haywood Securities, original reserves of the Golden Bear property looked like 1.9 million tons of ore grading an average of 0.27 ounces of gold per ton, sufficient to ensure a reasonably long-lived mine, not counting the excellent prospect of expanding the known reserves. But the important point, says Garson, is not only that the reserves are subject to expansion as step-out drilling takes place, but that a factor of at least twice the current total seems to be realistic.

That factor, says Hunter, the potential for greatly increased reserves, is the extraordinary dimension that has management excited about the Golden Bear property.

Robert Dickinson, North American's managing director, goes even further:

"A modular mill will be utilized so that increases can be made up to 1,000 tons per day. By the time the project is in production, we will have developed sufficient reserves to keep us occupied for at least fifty years."

North American, by taking over as operating company on the site, will expend $9 million in order to earn its fifty per cent position in the joint venture. Chevron Minerals had already spent $12 million on the property. Wright Engineers of Vancouver performed a feasibility report, with production likely to commence in 1988. Of the current indicated reserves, 750,000 tons will be amenable to open-pit operations, with the balance being mined by conventional underground operations.

Hunter as president of North American Metal Corporation has taken an active part in the company's development, but like all good chief executive officers, he tempers a hands-on role with trust in the professional staff operating the project.

"Bob wants to be thoroughly briefed every day," says Dickinson."And he makes it clear what his end is and what he expects of the people—usually highly capable professionals—who are working in a technical capacity. There are probably two outstanding things about him as a senior executive. One is his tremendous enthusiasm—we constantly have people calling us who want to know all about Golden Bear, and usually when that happens it's because they've been talking to Bob and he's somehow infected them with his own sense of excitement. You can't buy that kind of quality. And when you combine it with his extreme consideration for other people you understand why he is such an unusual person to be associated with. I'm sure it's those two qualities—enthusiasm and thoughtfulness—that explain why he gets so many invitations to sit on boards of directors. More invitations than he can accept."

It is not only the North American Metal insiders that are enthusiastic. Recently Tony Garson of Haywood Securities in Vancouver released some figures on step-out drilling at the Dease Lake site. They were widely varied, but many of the holes intersected substantial widths (ranging from 23 to 50 feet) of ore which graded between .66 and an amazing 2.41 ounces of gold per ton.

"What this means," says Garson, "is not simply that the North American Metal reserves are subject to considerable potential increase, as we had thought. If these drill results are typical, a considerable improvement in grade can also be anticipated."

Hunter's own enthusiasm is characteristically understated.

"The project's current probable and inferred reserves," he says, "certainly warrant an aggressive work schedule with the goal of early production."

Golden Bear, which is Chevron's largest Canadian gold asset, is likely to become the largest gold mine in B.C. In the foreseeable future it is the major preoccupation of Bob Hunter, chairman of Breakwater and president of North American Metal Corporation.

Bob Hunter has made a life principle of raising the standard of every project he has ever headed: in mining, that can sometimes be a formidable challenge. "We're still looking for new deals," he says. "And we're always being offered new money. Just recently, somebody offered us a plan for a double conversion feature—a loan convertible by the holder either into equity or gold bullion."

A bullion-based instrument may not be unusual in a world

dominated by current gold prices, mostly bullish. And from the vantage point of one who has made a significant contribution to the standard of gold mining, Hunter is convinced that gold will continue to be strong.

"As long as inflation represents a threat," says Hunter, "we're in the right business."

———————

CHAPTER 14

Mike Muzylowski

Winning western ways

If they ever make a movie about the life of Mike Muzylowski, and they should, it might begin with this kid jumping off a rural school bus near Oakburn, Manitoba, and sprinting up to the barn, where he confronts his father with astounding news:

"There was a guy who visited our school today, and he says you can go to more school after Grade XII. They call it University."

To which the elder Muzylowski responds: "Well, do you want to do that?"

"Might as well," says young Mike. "Give it a try, anyway."

The scene dissolves to a counter in the Registrar's office at the University of Manitoba in Fort Garry. The Registrar, a little guy known to generations of Manitoba scholars as Rigor Mortis, is checking out Muzylowski's course selection.

"You need a science," says Rigor. "Like biology, botany, geology . . ."

"What's geology?" says Muzylowski, and decides on the spot to take it, if only to find out what it is.

He is to spend the rest of his life finding out. Today Mike Muzylowski is perhaps the most outstanding mine-finder in

Canada. The industry shakes its head over the enormity of Spud Huestis's find at Bethlehem Copper, and Morris Menzies's record of discovering three or four major mines in his B.C. career. But in the thirty-five years since Mike Muzylowski left those hallowed if flood-ravaged halls on the Red River, he has discovered *fifteen* commercial ore bodies, each capable of being placed in production.

It is difficult to isolate anyone's reasons for success, but in Muzylowski's case the major ingredients have been perhaps four: a driving personal philosophy about the business of exploration, a finely-honed methodology, the tenacity that is common to all great mine-finders and, perhaps most important, an innate love of geology (once he found out what it was).

"I've got to learn this," was his instant reaction in his first lecture on the mysteries of rock formation, and his first field trip as an undergraduate was an absolute revelation.

"I suppose I'd been looking at rocks all my life," says Muzylowski. "But they were something you picked out of a field. I'd never particularly paid any attention to them before."

When he saw his first rock outcropping, it was like Keats's description of "stout Cortez" staring at the Pacific.

Hooked for all time, Muzylowski burned through his science degree, impatient to get into action, and was graduated in 1952. His haste was unnecessary. Not only was the Hudson Bay Mining Company waiting for him but there was a lot of northern terrain just waiting to be drilled.

"I went straight into the boonies," says Muzylowski. "You name it, I did it, geology-wise. My first discovery was that the thing about Northern Manitoba black flies that distinguishes them from those of the rest of the world is that here they use diamond drills."

And in retrospect, even though he may not have acknowledged it at the time, there is no question that an important advantage to be gained in working for a large company when you are young is the breadth of experience available. Especially if for six years you are more in the woods than out.

"I had a taste of just about everything," says Muzylowski,

"electromagnetometry, logging cores, diamond drilling. We covered Northern everything—Northern B.C., Northern Alberta, Northern Saskatchewan, Northwest Territories, and of course Northern Manitoba."

The one exception was Southern Yukon. They covered that, too.

One of the immense benefits of this long and intense journeyman odyssey was his service under a brilliant chief geologist named Albert Kaufman.

"A colourful guy," says Muzylowski. "We fought a lot, which made me nervous until I discovered that the reason we fought was that he loved battles."

Kaufman also taught Muzylowski an invaluable principle that is part of an overall geological philosophy.

"The principle," says Muzylowski, "is that, in our approach to geological formations, none of us are really that clever. In other words, from what we see in one place we can't generalize in another. Every ore formation is unique."

Kaufman's philosophy at first glance seems to contradict that principle, but in actual fact it does not. It is a working philosophy that Muzylowski has made part of his permanent furniture ever since, and is probably central to his outstanding success.

"It goes like this," says Muzylowski, "If a geological environment is capable of hosting mineral formations, if the rock is in the right stratigraphy for such an occurrence, then it's to be assumed that the mineralization is probably there. Which may not sound too profound, but the follow-up is what's important. When you find such a formation, you go into a 'scorched earth' program, doing absolutely everything necessary to prove it up, without screening out other possibilities."

According to Duane Poliquin, now president of Almaden Resources in Vancouver and formerly a soldier along with Muzylowski in Kaufman's unusual task force for Hudson Bay Mining, one anecdote is sufficient to illustrate both Kaufman's principles and his philosophy.

"We were working in the Coronation area near Flin Flon," says Poliquin, "and we had identified twenty-five anomalies using airborne equipment, and then confirmed them on the ground. By the time we had drilled all but three, managing to come up with twenty-two negative results, head office had instructed us to forget the last three anomalies and move to a new area. Kaufman refused to accept that. He decided he could find another budget source for the three remaining holes. He drilled them anyway, and on *the last one* we hit. That anomaly developed into what later became the rich Coronation Mine."

That episode amply illustrates the Kaufman principles that Muzylowski absorbed as if by osmosis: (1) every formation is unique, so you don't generalize from formations you think are similar; and (2) when the host rock and the stratigraphy look right, assume they are and do everything you can to prove up the existence of ore.

By contrast, says Muzylowski, a far more conventional method is to look for a signature rather than the evidence of the host. Practitioners of this approach, like the head office response in Poliquin's example, may not even test an anomaly.

Along with his other capabilities Muzylowski's enthusiasm moved him along rapidly, after successes on the Stikine River and in the Northwest Territories, and the discovery near Flin Flon. He was made drill superintendent in 1960 and assistant chief geologist in 1963. In the bush and in head office he learned every facet of his profession, including geophysics and airborne procedure.

In 1970 the development that was to change Muzylowski's life happened along unexpectedly. He had always believed that, while a large mining company was usually an excellent environment for learning, it often presented certain drawbacks in that its lock-step bureaucratic movement tended to impede the upward freedom and progress of a rapidly developing individual.

Now, out of the blue, came Granges AB of Sweden, a large mining organization anxious to expand its operations in Canada. The company had obviously had its eye on Muzylowski and now approached him with the offer that he assume direction of Granges's Canadian operations. It was flattering for a geologist still not far removed from a Manitoba farm. It was also a little unnerving for a professional geologist who was as self-effacing as he was capable.

Muzylowski made a quick trip to Sweden to talk about it. If he was going to make a favourable move with Granges, he was intent on getting the right conditions in place. Granges proposed a complete package, including a set budget and an office in Vancouver (where the Swedish company already owned a 26% interest in Bethlehem Copper). Muzylowski was to have complete autonomy in running Granges's existing holdings in Canada and in exploring for and developing others.

By this time another trait had surfaced in the Muzylowski character. He had somewhere acquired, as one colleague referred to it, "a business nose" that was not always orthodox. He had a strong business sense despite his reticence. In any case, when the Granges high command offered to buy him a house and a car Muzylowski declined.

"In the first place," he responded, "I can buy my own house and car. And with that kind of money, I can probably drill enough holes to find an ore body worth many times more than that for both of us."

That gambit probably gave him increased bargaining power over the larger budget issues.

"No one knew better than I did," says Muzylowski, "how difficult it could be to commit myself just to finding new ore bodies. So my opening request—trying for elbow room and time —was for a $5 million budget stretched over a five-year time period, with complete freedom to apply both expenditures and operations in my own way."

To his surprise the company agreed with him, giving him everything he asked for, together with complete *carte blanche*.

In the next half decade, Muzylowski came close to meeting the objective he had asked for. A little under budget at $4.8 million, he took a little longer than planned. But in the five years and four months following his verbal agreement in Sweden, he brought in the first success, the highly profitable copper-zinc-gold Trout Lake Mine near Flin Flon. Given Muzylowski and his team, it was inevitable that he should find a major mine near the northern Manitoba town, practically his own back yard, where he had worked for much of the previous twenty years.

"After the dust settled," says Muzylowski, "they admitted to me that they had actually planned to allow me up to *seven* years if I had needed it."

That was 1976. Three years later Muzylowski arranged a farm-out on the Trout Lake property to his former employers, Hudson Bay Mining. Under the terms of the deal, HBM agreed to provide $30 million and the mill (actually in existence eight miles away) that was necessary to place the property in production, for forty-four per cent of the equity. This eventually escalated to a majority position.

Meanwhile, reserves kept being extended. At the outset, 2.6 million tons were indicated. Since then (production began in 1982) 2.3 million tons have been mined out, but known reserves have increased to a total of over 5 million tons. Subsequently, Granges obtained a healthy annual revenue of over $3 million from the Trout Lake base and precious metals mine, even though its participation was reduced to approximately twenty per cent, as Hudson Bay Mining eventually contributed a total of $33 million in equity investment to place the mine in production.

Shortly after Trout Lake went into production, Muzylowski's world was jolted once again, this time with an initially adverse development which again ended up favourably in the long run. The parent Granges company in Sweden fell upon evil days, and although it was in bankruptcy its considerable tax-loss position rendered it a favourable target for other companies. It was eventually acquired by the Electrolux organization.

It often happens, when a major company makes a corporate decision to divest itself of large divisions, or even of whole subsidiaries it does not wish to continue operating, someone standing in the right spot falls into a bargain.

It had happened to Robert Friedland with Galactic, and to Dr. William Bird with Quartz Mountain, both occasioned when Anaconda's parent ASARCO decided to withdraw from the mining business altogether. And it happened to Mike Muzylowski when Electrolux unexpectedly decided to stick to its own part of the globe; Granges Canada was suddenly up for grabs. But whereas Friedland and Bird had been able to acquire outstanding properties, Muzylowski won a company.

One Toronto group had actually submitted a bid for the Canadian subsidiary when Muzylowski made a flying trip to Sweden to let it be known that there could be other interested parties, and that the control group might be ill-advised to act hastily. In fact, Doug McRae and some of the Breakwater management group had been aroused to take action, realizing the value of Granges's one million acres of mineral holdings in Canada, its mining team that had been together for thirteen years and—the icing on that particular cake—Mike Muzylowski.

Operating through a recently-acquired shell company known as Pecos, which just before this time had been trading on the VSE for the princely sum of 8 cents, McRae and his group quickly assembled financial support in the U.K. and moral support in Finland (whose Outokumpu Oy had operated a joint account with Granges, Jr., in Canada), and bought the farm for $12.5 million.

That move suited Muzylowski, who was destined to carry on as president. He had not been known to McRae and the Breakwater group previously but he was a friend of Carl Toporowski, a mutual acquaintance. Realizing that Muzylowski represented the wild card in the hand being dealt in Sweden, the storied McRae crowd had swung into action.

Appointing Muzylowski president was actually a wise stroke on the part of McRae and Company, in preference to parachuting in a senior mining executive or a financial type as chief executive officer. First, because Muzylowski before and since has demonstrated that he is supremely capable in the executive suite, and second, because the keynote of the organization he had built in thirteen years was its orientation toward its mineral resources. With Muzylowski combining a "business nose" and his superlative field generalship with McRae's financial wizardry, a strong team was forged.

A year later, in November 1984, Granges became a public Canadian company with an issue of 2 million shares being offered on the Toronto Stock Exchange at $2.50 by Richardson

Securities of Canada. The European lenders who had backed McRae's group for $12.5 million had been vindicated; Kilborn Engineering subsequently valued Granges's assets at well over $18 million. And the public offering was effected by allowing the former Pecos holders to receive an option to buy Granges stock. Still later, in the spring of 1985, through a reverse take-over Granges acquired Pecos Resources and, in the process, certain assets such as heap-leaching gold properties in the U.S.

Muzylowski points out that Granges Canada in its short public life has compiled an impressive record financially as well as on the geology charts. The stock recently traded on the Toronto Stock Exchange in the neighborhood of $19, and has since been listed on the American Stock Exchange and also in London.

One of Muzylowski's first scores following the formal reorganization of Granges Canada was the Tartan Lake property near Flin Flon in Manitoba, less than five miles from the Trout Lake mine. It seemed that Muzylowski was intent on mining the whole of his home province.

The Tartan Lake property had been in the Granges portfolio previously, but Muzylowski and his team had only turned their attention to it when Granges Canada had become their own company, pouring on their characteristic concentration of airborne surveys and follow-up drilling on the ground.

The initial ore body weighed in at about 600,000 tons averaging 0.37 ounces of gold per ton, but subsequent exploration will no doubt expand the tonnage. Granges's mine plan at Tartan Lake involved the use of a decline rather than a conventional shaft in the initial stages of the operation. This allows for more rapid and cheaper extraction of ore, as well as continued exploration and development of further reserves.

Granges is joint-venture partner with Abermin Resources on a fifty-fifty basis at Tartan Lake, having declared it a commercial mine in 1984 and gone into production in 1986. In fact it was the exception to Muzylowski's announced plan to bring one mine per year into production. In 1986, both Tartan Lake and Hycroft saw light at the top of the shaft.

Hycroft, in Nevada, is an excellent example of Mike Muzylowski's other attributes, in addition to those of an outstanding geologist. As a profitable working mine, Hycroft is a tribute to both his negotiating strength and his innovative approach to business.

Muzylowski did not "find" Hycroft, that is not until it had attained full mining production capability. But he worked out a joint-venture partnership with Hycroft Resources and created the design for a total financial plan, by which Doug McRae's financial genius could fund Hycroft's development so that production on the Nevada property would come about without Hycroft incurring a load of debt, as is usually the pattern.

In addition, Muzylowski strengthened Hycroft's chances of succeeding by acquiring a neighbouring mine that was fully operational at the time, thus producing a source of early revenue that aided the funding of Hycroft in its pre-production phase.

But Hycroft was indeed a different ball game for Muzylowski. Approached from the air in the northwest corner of Nevada, the huge barren escarpment that hosts both the Crofoot and Lewis Mines looks like everybody's idea of badlands, or perhaps even terrain on the rougher side of the moon. Pockmarked, pitted, and gouged by the tracks of ancient long-dried rivers and streambeds, this wasteland is also traced by dozens of trails and roads that seem to reach into every corner of the totally dry stretch of terrain.

There is a good reason for these finger-like explorations. And it is also the answer to why Muzylowski could not be said to have "discovered" the Hycroft location, no matter how long he had worked on it. Because the Indians had done so before 1875, telling the first white men to appear in that corner of Nevada that there were valuable yellow showings in the form of outcroppings. Those showings turned out to be native sulphur, but that did not worry the pioneers, who proceeded to mine the stuff anyway—at the rate of six tons a day.

It turned out that there was more than sulphur there, and a gold-silver operation was carried on right up until 1940, when the ore seemed to peter out. And, ironically, in 1974 Homestake Mining came back in with a view to reopening sulphur extraction—only to find gold. It was of a low-grade quality to be sure, but meanwhile technology had caught up with the property, not to mention gold prices that could make a low-grade play feasible.

However, by a very narrow margin Homestake gave up on the property before heap leaching as a process became commercially proven. The price-technology combination came along in time, though, for another operator, Standard Slag Company, to dig in on the north side of the property.

In 1985, Hycroft acquired a bargain-basement option of the Crofoot property for $10,000, and within sixty days had drilled twelve holes, enough to confirm Homestake's painstaking work and to convince themselves that the ore could be heap leached. Then president Jim Yates sought out Muzylowski. They needed a joint-venture partner with access to money and capable of developing the Crofoot. Granges was their answer.

"I spend a lot of my time," says Musylowski, "wheeling and dealing—and also just listening to people. Once word sort of got around that we were interested in deals as well as developing mines of our own, everybody and his brother seemed to come around looking for money, deals, sometimes just advice. That's okay. I like to think that sort of time is well spent. My door, as the saying goes, is always open. You never know when a real winner is going to walk through it."

Jim Yates was obviously one of those. By early 1987 a production decision had been made at Crofoot, based on a likely ore body of 20 million tons grading an average of 0.035. To the Indians sulphur would have seemed a better deal, but then they had never heard of the leaching process.

Don Duncan, one of the foremost heap-leaching consultants on the continent, was brought in as a director and consultant on all aspects of the mine and plant design and the feasibility study. For an operation of its size, capital costs were amazingly low at $8 million.

The financial plan leaned heavily on Granges's famous capability. At the beginning Granges owned 14.6% of Hycroft, with options on over a million shares at $1 and $1.50. Granges took down an additional million Hycroft shares in settlement of outstanding advances for Hycroft's development work. When these options and payments were completed, the effect was that

Granges held a majority position in Hycroft. Hycroft did not seem to mind.

In addition Granges undertook a private placement of Hycroft stock and guaranteed whatever measures were necessary to fund Crofoot's production without incurring substantial debt.

An even more innovative development on Muzylowski's part came with the purchase of the Lewis Mine to the north of Crofoot from Standard Slag. At the time this mine was estimated to contain a residual 4 million tons of ore grading approximately the same values as Hycroft's Crofoot—perhaps 0.035 ounces of gold per ton. With a slight capital additive, the Lewis operation was dressed to support Crofoot in the latter's development stages. The Lewis property was vended into the Crofoot operation in return for additional Hycroft stock.

It is a measure of Muzylowski's mine judgment that, in a comparative study of six heap-leaching and eight lode-gold mines performed early in 1987, Hycroft, calculating in the Lewis Mine, had the highest production rate, 1.58 ounces of gold per $1,000 invested. This was not the case when the Crofoot property was calculated singly.

It was just following the appearance of that comparative study that Hycroft stock reached a level triple that of the fall months.

"It's quite evident," says Bruce Thompson of Hycroft Resources in Vancouver, "that Mike is not only a top technical guy, but also a very astute businessman. It's that combination that has really made him a success. In my opinion, Granges will emerge as a major player in the long term because of its really great team—Doug McRae, the financial architect of the company, and Mike, the mine-finder, who just happens also to have a keen sense of business."

Another dimension is suggested by Hank Ewanchuk, president of Mascot Gold Mines Limited in Vancouver.

"Mike and I have joint ventured together many times," says Ewanchuk. "A factor in his success has been that he worked so long in a given area (across the northern area of all the western provinces) that he came to know not only the area but everything in it. You can't beat that in the training of any mining man. Quite apart from knowing the geology, you could set Mike down in any town in the northern half of any of the western provinces and he'd know just where to find a cat or a drill or the right local guys for a given job. Mike has a positively encyclopedic ability to file this kind of stuff away in his mind. Over a vast territory that he covered for a twenty-year period, it's like today he's never out of his element."

Attempting to pinpoint the Muzylowski talent is largely a losing game. There are, however, observations that make the exercise a little more possible.

"In a way," says Duane Poliquin, "you can trace Mike's attributes to his training under Albert Kaufman, chief geologist with Hudson Bay Mining. I'm sure Mike would agree. Kaufman was a mine-finding son of a gun. But he had two distinct rules: he was extremely methodical in his approach to everything he did, and when in doubt, he drilled, drilled, drilled."

The latter, Poliquin emphasizes, is no empty rhetoric. More drilling, less rationalizing, is a subject over which geologists tend to disagree.

"Mike, like Kaufman before him," says Poliquin, "maintains at least 55% of total budget on drilling. Many I know don't spend more than 30% to 40%. You can spend an awful lot of time and money simply 'geologizing'. Mike doesn't."

It is apparent, according to Poliquin, why many geologists do. The need to "be sure" before committing the drill to the ground is a natural instinct, and geologists are not alone in such a sentiment. In most walks of life, the majority of people in a decision-making position usually tend to cover themselves before taking a risk. Muzylowski, on the other hand, invariably demonstrates the courage to risk being wrong more often, and, like most winners, he is rewarded by being right more often.

Perhaps the simplest explanation is the most obvious.

"Mike works hard and long," says Lou Parris, a prospector based in Flin Flon, who worked with him for many years. "And he knows when to stay with a situation. He's also very astute, and he received an education from Hudson Bay Mining that you can't buy. But I think the most important reason for his success is simply his willingness to work longer and harder than most guys in this game."

Jim McInnes, a Vancouver lawyer, who is more a personal friend than a business associate of Muzylowski's, sums it up in a different way.

"Mike is in a tradition with people like Ed Scholz (former Placer vice-president) and of course Kaufman," says McInnes. "It's not only a tradition of extraordinary talent, but it's really more in the realm of art than science, which is usually the way we think of geology."

The ability to divine mineralization by intuition as much as scientific principles is difficult to outline because it cannot be proven.

"You can't define an art such as Mike's," says McInnes. "If you could, everybody would have it. But in total, it's a matter of putting so many qualities together, not any one quality. Just the way a hockey superstar is what he is while any number of other guys are bigger, faster, and better stickhandlers."

For example, McInnes points out, Muzylowski is an excellent negotiator who can ferret out the essentials of a contract as well as a lawyer. He has an all-round talent for business, gets along well with people, in fact has created his own environment of key people over a long period of time, and he has steeped himself in knowledge of the terrain of half of Canada. And finally, he is extremely loyal and commands loyalty in others.

All these qualities add up to success. And they all leave out the factor of Mike Muzylowski's personal enthusiasm.

"I have a lot of other things to do these days," says Muzylowski. "But I still get out into the field as often as I can. I like it better than an office in the city. In fact the most exciting thing in the world for me is still pulling a great drill hole. I live for it."

It is a well-known fact around the Granges office that when a core is about to be pulled on one of the properties, no matter how far away, Muzylowski can be expected to drop everything and run.

Just as there is no defining Muzylowski's talent, there is no quantifying his relationship with Doug McRae.

"Doug's supposed to be the financial man," says Muzylowski, "and I'm the technical one. But there's no fixed rule as to what person initiates what things. We take it as it comes. It's a great relationship."

[When John Hirsch and Tom Hendry formed the Manitoba Theatre Centre, the prediction was that Hendry's accountancy degree and Hirsch's artistic talent would ensure success. Later it was revealed that Hendry's sharp critical sense and Hirsch's natural business instinct were the real winning combination. It may be just so with McRae and Muzylowski.]

Meanwhile Muzylowski somehow manages to do some joint venturing with his close-knit family, with an intensity not commensurate with the time he has available for them.

"I have four kids," says Mike. "Great kids. Two of them are already off the payroll." He laughs at that one, and then goes on to tell of his son going into science at the University of British Columbia, not necessarily geology.

"But if he did choose geology, I'd make sure he knew what it meant," says the former farm boy.

Mike Muzylowski is a respecter of very few government figures, and does not consider himself political. "Most governments never face the music. Everybody wants to be popular, and how can you be popular if you face real issues. That's why, if for no other reason, I admire Maggie Thatcher. She was courageous enough to make some unpopular moves, and now the pound is strong and unemployment is 'way down."

Muzylowski's stock-in-trade is something he feels more strongly about.

"I'm a short-term bull on gold prices," says Muzylowski. "Long-term may be something else. But right now we have enough uncertainty in the world to offset the growing gold supply. Plus a weakened U.S. dollar. There may be an oversupply of gold three years down the road, but even then, long-term developments are not all bad. There's a French fund that recently toured North American gold mines rather than South African —that's the first time in history, and I think it says a lot about our outlook."

Muzylowski is not really worried, even about gold's long-term outlook. Given three years' lead, it's an even bet that Mike Muzylowski can capitalize on two or three more gold mines and still have enough elbow room in which to diversify into something else.

Golf and fishing, perhaps?

————

CHAPTER 15

Lal Gondi

The broker who came in from the cold

Few can say if Lal Gondi is a geologist first and a stock broker second, or the other way around. But the fact that he works diligently at being both explains his meteoric advance in just over ten years from field geologist with a mining company to chairman and senior partner of Haywood Securities, a Vancouver stock brokerage house. In the latter position, Gondi runs a taut ship, a new-wave organization, VSE-oriented but strong in research and underwriting, specializing in mining finance and often relying on Gondi's essential background in the exploration, evaluating and development of ore bodies.

"I'll say this," says Gondi, "I actually practise far more geology *now* than I did when I was a geologist."

"There's not a doubt," says Robert Hunter, president of North American Metal Corporation of Vancouver, "Lal's a better broker for being a geologist. He called Breakwater at $3.80, took a position and introduced it to his clients. Then it went to $25 and split. You don't need too many of those to make the clients love you."

Almost everybody seems to admire Gondi anyway.

"A prince of a guy," says Hunter. "The kind who's always smiling—even when things are tough."

"Tough" is not an unusual condition in either the Vancouver market or the mining industry in B.C. At least, that was the way things were when Gondi landed here in 1967 from India, a freshly-minted Master's degree in geology under his arm. Gondi (his father named him Jawaharlal after Nehru, the famous statesman) went to work as a geologist almost immediately with the Cypress Anvil Mining Company.

"One of the first things I noticed," says Gondi, "and worried about a lot, was the relationship between a given mining company's active projects and the stock's trading pattern. Not only did the market almost always anticipate an important mining development, such as new drilling results, for example, but it anticipated *incorrectly* just as often as correctly. So as a leading indicator the market was a useful device only when it was properly interpreted by a broker who knew the score, geologically speaking. And there wasn't a plentiful supply of those."

Ten years before the event, Gondi was seized by the notion that would eventually make him throw down his hammer and follow the ticker. If a company was drilling on a project and the market in Vancouver was anticipating the outcome, he reasoned, where was the relevance of the geologist? Perhaps less on the site than on Howe Street? He thought about it for years.

But for the time being Gondi was too embroiled with his profession to concern himself about the stock market. Bob Dickinson, now managing director of North American Metal Corporation, recalls that in 1970, when both he and Gondi were with Cypress, they were dispatched to handle two projects in Manitoba. But within a short time Dickinson was recalled and Gondi, as always taking things in his stride, ran both projects. That was the way he did his job.

"There are quite a few good brokers," says Dickinson, "but what sets Lal apart is his disciplined background. It's the basis of his success."

In simple terms, the discipline of geology has trained Gondi to moderate his view of situations in a way that is anathema to most brokers. "Conservative" is not the right word to describe him but he does exercise a healthy restraint that is lacking in most mining brokers.

That is not to suggest a limitation on his enthusiasm. Page Chilcott, president of C.M. Oliver & Company in Vancouver, points out that Gondi is never lukewarm. "He tends to be hot or cold on any given situation," says Chilcott, "although he rarely likes to deliver a negative verdict about a deal."

Working in the field, it was not long before he became fascinated by the market that he considered to be a commentary on what he was doing. It was inevitable. His first investment, in 1969, was in a mining stock called Adanac, which was sitting at $2.20. With his total savings of $4,000 he plunged—and came up smelling of roses when the stock went to $8.10.

"The worst possible thing that could have happened to me," laughs Gondi. "I thought 'How long has this been going on?' and spent most of my time after that in looking at junior mining situations."

By the mid-seventies, with his children beginning to grow up, he decided he'd had enough of the travelling that was part of the geologist's routine. Hot market situations had come along, such as Dynasty, which he had correctly identified and just as correctly invested in himself, and he had become increasingly confident of his ability to profit by his forecasting of the market's movements. For these reasons, the stock market offered more appeal to him than the life of a straight geologist.

There is an extremely rare market sense possessed not too often by the market's practitioners. Brokers who have it tend to hit home runs seldom, rather than ground balls with regularity. The best of pension and mutual fund managers partake somewhat of this talent, but they can guess wrongly and still take refuge in the huge size and diversity of their bets.

It is not inaccurate to say that Gondi has that sort of market sense in the realm of junior resource issues. As a result it was only a matter of time before he gravitated to the function that would enable him to use that ability to the fullest.

"In 1977," says Gondi, "I took the plunge, moved into Vancouver and joined C.M.Oliver & Company."

This undoubtedly was a huge transition, in almost every respect. It was one thing to take an academic view of the market, or even to pick an occasional stock for his own benefit. But to develop a clientele dependent on his judgment, and especially to do so in sufficient volume to achieve almost immediately the status of a "producer" in the eyes of the Street, was something else.

For most people the basic requisites for being a salesman, which he had not been before, are of necessity the subject of study and practice for many years. Gondi seems to have acquired that sub-culture almost immediately.

In fact, by all indications, Gondi made the change without hesitation or strain of any kind.

"He was successful," says Chilcott. "right from the beginning. He seemed to know just how and when to make the right contacts. And many of the clients he brought in had been unrelated to mining previously. There was no doubt he was a better broker for his geological experience and training. His method was to develop his own situations and then use them for the benefit of his clients. He never attempted to impose those ideas on other people in the organization, but if you wanted him to look at a situation he was always willing to give you an opinion.

"He worked long hours and brought in underwritings from time to time. What more could you expect of a good broker?"

Quite a lot, to hear Gondi tell it. No sooner were his feet on the ground at C. M. Oliver than he delved into all manner of things, tracking and constructing his own charts on silver and gold prices, on inflation, and on commodities generally. He was obsessed, as he had been for some time, with the idea that the stock market's lead-indicator characteristic had real importance in more ways than one. Everything he did related to that factor, even though he was usually spotting his own "situations" in the junior mining field, coming to his own conclusions and then getting his own clients on board. With some regularity they were winners because he was right.

"Although he brought in underwritings," says Chilcott, "at this stage his primary objective was to be recommending one or two stocks at a time to his own people."

There was a certain mystery to Gondi's method in the first years of his activity as a broker. While he had a reluctance to be negative over a stock that was shown to him, and while he was the most affable of people in his relations with clients and colleagues, he remained essentially a loner.

"Both, in a way, could be seen as his strong points," says Ross Nursey, former sales manager at C.M. Oliver, now manager of Jones Gable & Company in Vancouver. "As a broker he was always positive, and yet around the office he wasn't given to small talk."

Even this early he had shown more qualities than simply those of a good broker. "His geologist's instincts are interesting," says North American Metal's Bob Dickinson. "He seems to have an instant grasp of the potential of a property."

That is a characteristic that has been attributed to some of the great mine-finders. It has been said of Morris Menzies, for example, that he could walk around on a property and "feel" the potential ore body. Given the huge ore bodies that stand to his credit, such as the giant Brenda copper mine, it would be hard to argue the point. Gondi has never claimed that sort of talent, but there is no doubt his early evaluative ability in junior mining situations placed him head and shoulders ahead of the average broker on Howe Street.

"The other outstanding thing about him," says Dickinson, "is his capacity to be helpful with his friends, not just his clients. I've known him to help mining companies out by tipping them off about properties."

Into each life—particularly that of a broker with geological overtones—a little rain must fall.

"In 1981 there was a substantial drop in the market," says Gondi, "mostly because of galloping interest rates, and a sort of collective loss of common sense. With bonds yielding 20% to 21%, people had a hard time convincing themselves that stocks were worth betting on. It was the collapse of the equities business—at least for the time being."

In 1982 Gondi moved over to Yorkton Securities, a Toronto-based house that does a substantial VSE business. The following five years was a period which saw Gondi setting new records in several departments. As one example, he completed three of the four largest VSE underwritings in history.

"As a broker," says Don Risling, Yorkton manager in Vancouver, "Lal has a surprising combination of talents. On the one hand, he has a high-powered personality. I didn't say 'high-pressured'. The strength of his personality comes through, but he's always pleasant. You can't imagine how effective that combination can be in the all-important realm of client relations. Invariably, he gives the impression that he knows exactly what he's talking about—and of course he does."

The other factor, of course, which after so many years has become finely tuned, is his technical strength.

"He's one of the few geologist-brokers I've seen," says Risling. "And the benefit to his clients is self-evident. Add the fact that the guy is virtually a workaholic—he works unbelievable hours, both in the office and on the road—and you have a combination that's pretty hard to top. He has a meticulous approach to everything he does."

In 1982, shortly after he moved over to Yorkton, Gondi did his own independent study on Breakwater Resources, as usual for his own and his clients' benefit rather than for any widespread distribution. He came to the conclusion that at its then current price of $3.80 the stock was a steal.

His next move was to take his clients into Breakwater wholesale. Within a year the stock had moved to a top of $25 and then split two for one. This was typical of several such calls Gondi made in the following five years, with the resultant growth of an enormous clientele—which in turn catapulted his personal remuneration into the six-figure category.

His other unusual endeavour during the Yorkton years was the bringing in of several immensely successful underwritings. The first and in many respects the most unusual was Galactic Resources.

About the time he was moving over to Yorkton a striking figure arrived on Howe Street, like the white-hatted stranger who rides into town in the first reel of your basic Western. The stranger was Robert Friedland. (On Howe Street they don't blast strangers with guns, but by brandishing short positions. But that was to come later.)

Gondi could not have been too interested in the stranger at

the outset, because there was nothing to whet a geologist's appetite. Friedland hit town and launched his embryonic Galactic Resources as a 50-cent new issue on the Vancouver Stock Exchange at a time when he had neither property, management, nor capital. Nor was he well endowed with contacts; he had nothing but good intentions. Nevertheless, within two years he had virtually a mountain laced with gold at Summitville, Colorado; within three years he had the best management team in the heap-leaching business and had raised well over $100 million in B.C., the U.K. and California, while Galactic stock had topped out close to $20; and within four years his mine was solidly in production ahead of schedule and under budget. All that is another story that will be told in another chapter.

Gondi and Friedland became close associates at some point. Friedland was a neophyte in gold mining and heap leaching; Gondi had spent most of his adult life exploring for and developing mines. Friedland still harboured a certain market naivety (early in the game he made a personal call on one of the more visible Vancouver players and asked him to please stop shorting his stock) while Gondi was a seasoned veteran of the Vancouver market. But while neither was particularly a money-chaser, they shared a certain philosophy of material pragmatism.

"Gold," Friedland was fond of saying, "is a useful product. Later perhaps we'll convert Summitville into a really neat ski resort."

In the summer of 1983 Gondi and Yorkton headed up the second issue of Galactic stock, by now priced at $3.93. Before the year was up it had traded as high as $13.25. By that time of course the huge Summitville property was in place, having been acquired from the giant Anaconda organization, which had reached a corporate decision to divest itself of its mining properties.

Almost immediately, Wright Engineering of Vancouver had done a preliminary feasibility study that indicated 58 million tons of ore grading an average of 0.02 ounces of gold per ton. Later exploration extended the reserve figure. A huge heap-leaching operation was designed, following close on the heels of the pioneers in the field, Glamis and Pegasus. At the time it entered production, however, Galactic was the largest heap-leaching recovery installation in North America.

Gondi's early entry into the Galactic picture might suggest he was working more from intuition than from his characteristic geologist's appraisal. But the Wright Engineering prefeasibility report was well advanced before the Yorkton issue took place, and was enough to convince even a geologist.

The following summer, 1984, saw an additional issue with Gondi and Yorkton as lead underwriters. This was Galactic's third equity offering and comprised 350,000 units priced at $5, with an additional 500,000 at $5.50, each unit comprising one share of stock and two stock-purchase warrants to purchase additional shares at $5.25 and $5.75 for a period of six months. The ultimate proceeds of the issue exceeded $6 million.

While Gondi's house headed the issue, a feature of the offering was the entry of the U.K. banking firm of Laing and Cruikshank as underwriters of a major portion of the units, for resale to British institutions. The British house had earlier participated in the financing of Canadian gold-mining companies such as Breakwater and International Corona.

Among the senior management appointments Friedland made in that year was vice-president finance, Robert Cook, a former senior vice-president with Cypress Anvil Mining Company, Lal Gondi's old alma mater.

When Summitville attained full-scale production it was producing at its capacity of 125,000 ounces of gold annually, at a cost of something over $150 an ounce. It was not the most economical gold producer in North America, but it was certainly among the largest. Friedland had achieved several significant goals, one of which was to move "from test start to pit operations" in six months. Something of a record in the industry.

Friedland, with Gondi's assistance, had established another record as a pioneer in the offshore funding of relatively junior mining companies (a metier that was burnished to a bright lustre by financial practitioners such as Doug McRae) employing financial instruments such as senior bullion loans that featured low effective rates, and the forward selling of gold actually produced by the borrower as security for the obligation.

Gondi's fine hand is visible in the sort of transaction that was going on as Galactic approached the crucial stage of its pre-production financing. He had by this time added deep-thinking in the commodities markets to his other market preoccupations. With the commencement of the production phase alone, Galactic negotiated a US$25 million line with Bank of America. The eventual total required to put the huge Summitville site into production topped US$40 million.

The incredible speed with which Galactic moved from penny stock to major producing mine (summer of 1982 to April of 1986) and the constant stream of financial issues that fuelled that growth and development (nine or ten separate private placements or public issues, involving stock, units, debentures and bank loans) raise the question of to what extent management had to dilute or give up equity positions in order to finance Galactic's meteoric rise to the production of revenue.

With slightly over 10 million shares currently outstanding Friedland has managed to avoid excessive equity financing in the course of leveraging the company to meet its objectives. He avoided the anomaly encountered by many junior companies when they issue equity repeatedly in order to produce the required capital, only to discover they have surrendered more control than might have been advisable in the process. (The alternative for young mining development companies is to farm out parts of the property for either cash or participation by a working partner, in order to ensure the financing and development of the property.)

"Which alternative is ultimately more costly," says Gondi, "depends on the property. But with Bob the question would have been academic. He would not have given up a part of Summitville—it was too important to him that the project should have been done by Galactic all by itself. Which underlines the fact that his performance within two or three years was phenomenal."

Gondi became a Galactic director and also served on the board of Quartz Mountain, a company closely related to Friedland's Galactic. In fact, Quartz Mountain was an interesting parallel to the Summitville project. Dr. William Bird, Quartz Mountain chairman, originally purchased the Crone Hill and Quartz Mountain properties in southern Oregon from the Anaconda Minerals Company, as Friedland had at Summitville. With the ultimate size of total reserves subject to future delineation, the company quickly proved up as much as 25 million tons of ore grading an average of 0.04 ounces of gold per ton.

According to Bird, Quartz Mountain's long-range strategy is to develop a strong position in low-cost gold properties by the use of "solid financing," which indicates the reason for the appointment of Gondi to the company's board in 1986.

Although the Crone Hill area has been a known gold-mining location for more than one hundred years (organized mining development first took place in the 1930s) Bird's company was the first in its long history to acquire control over all 8,000 acres of the site. This acquisition was costly, and to meet its cost, and the expense of conducting a complete feasibility report on the entire property, substantial equity financing comprising stock and warrants was arranged during 1986 with private investors and financial institutions in North America and Europe.

As with Galactic, success for Quartz Mountain is seen by Bird as being due to superior development and mining activity, backed up by "financial flexibility" of the variety that can be produced when people of Gondi's capability literally have a foot in both camps.

Illustrating the importance of this combined development-financial program, Quartz Mountain's strategic plan for mine development included two major phases requiring substantial capital. The first stage, which brought the company to prefeasibility, included fill-in drilling, metallurgic testing, environmental permitting, and evaluation of other targets, and cost approximately US$1.2 million. This was followed by the second stage, bringing the property to the feasibility stage with a complete on-site heap-leach test plant in addition to drill evaluation of established targets, which cost about US$2 million.

The importance of financing throughout emphasizes Gondi's role on the Board. In late 1986 a private placement was made of the company's stock with warrants at a unit cost of $2.33. Initial proceeds from sale of the issue were sufficient to carry the company through the prefeasibility stage of its program, while the delayed-action effect of the warrant subscription (to purchase additional stock at a price of $2.42) was earmarked for the subsequent feasibility study.

Gondi's appointment to the Quartz Mountain board was not one of those polite gestures that corporations often tender their fiscal agents. "Having served in the field," says Bird, himself a professional geologist, Ph.D. and Professor of Geological Sciences at the University of Colorado, "Lal brings particular sensitivity and understanding to the mining and mine-financing process."

Occasionally, in his financial career, Gondi's footsteps inevitably strayed from the virtuous path of the mining industry. In 1984, he and the Yorkton organization functioned as lead underwriters for NETI Technologies, the Canadian subsidiary of a high-technology organization based in Ann Arbor, Michigan. The public offering of the Canadian company through the Vancouver Stock Exchange was quite obviously made because of the relative economic and regulatory ease available there compared with the SEC's requirements in the U.S. For whatever reasons, the NETI issue, at close to $9 million, was the largest initial public offering ever made up until that time on the Vancouver Stock Exchange.

NETI, an organization committed to computer conferencing and other software systems, began with an unusually strong concept and for a while had its future success substantially discounted by an eager after-market. From its issue price of $4.30, NETI stock experienced a subsequent high in the $9–$10 range before it subsided—largely on the basis of disappointing earnings. Ultimately it became the subject of some disillusionment on the part of the same investors who had demonstrated such overt enthusiasm. The company, hardly to be faulted for the stock's rise and fall since it had not promoted the stock from within, settled down to the more realistic objective of developing its product and marketing-reach in a tough competitive marketplace. From the outset it was led by the highly motivated Dr.

Larry Brilliant, a long-time friend of Robert Friedland.

Also, in 1984, Gondi did another major financing, this time for Goldsil, an interesting gold-mining company run by the equally interesting Donald Busby, an ex-South African stock player who had been a relatively recent arrival in B.C.

Gold fever was rampant that year, with activity mounting in both Quebec's Casa Berardi play and the La Ronge field in northern Saskatchewan, the latter the locus of Busby's Goldsil. Goldsil and two partners had identified a sizable ore body that was part of a much larger 200,000-acre area, the exploration of which required substantial financing.

Another company Gondi has assisted in financing is Vancouver's North American Metal Corporation. Having farmed in on a fifty per cent interest of Chevron Minerals, Ltd. at Dease Lake, B.C., North American Metal found it necessary to raise total financing of $9 million to earn its position, since Chevron had already expended over $12 million in total development.

Gondi, as one of North American Metal's formal fiscal agents, assisted in private placements among senior European financial institutions and the B.C. government. Part of this overall financial plan was activated through a major chartered accountancy firm in the form of a transfer of North American Metal's tax write-offs for a tangible return of over $1 million.

It would be difficult to overestimate Gondi's contribution in all of these major financing challenges. Collectively, they illustrate the breadth of his financial grasp, even while he was still a relative newcomer to investment finance in terms of years.

The greening of Lal Gondi, however, really took place in 1986 when he teamed up with two other partners to buy the stock brokerage firm of Haywood Securities Inc. of Vancouver. "The principal idea behind the new firm," says Gondi, "was to create an organization dealing mostly with the mining industry, but with an orientation mostly toward the benefit of the individual client. The underwriting and trading strengths and our solid research base, as far as I was concerned, would give us the follow-up to the basic recommendations we would come up with, and in general would support that client orientation."

The term "client-oriented" is far from novel in the securities industry. But with Haywood, the unique structuring of the organization around a research and underwriting base is highly unusual for its size and location. This tends to emphasize how serious Gondi is in his claim. Haywood differs widely from the standard VSE house, which normally consists of a few administrative and cage people flanking a platoon of salesmen.

Gondi's vision of the ideal new house materialized. In the first year of operation the clients that followed Haywood's official recommendations saw an appreciation of 62%. And the "research base" was filled admirably by the person of Anthony Garson, formerly gold specialist for a leading New York house's subsidiary in Toronto.

"Lal is basically the financier," says Garson. "As such, he's constantly initiating situations with both an underwriting interest and as investments to recommend to clients. Lal's geological discipline is of the utmost important in that role."

It has been mentioned that for Gondi to act like a chief executive officer in the new firm would have limited his true effectiveness as underwriter and broker.

"They have hired the right people to deepen their management strength," says Robert Hunter. "From the point of view of companies like ours we'd naturally like to see Lal remain a 'straight' broker forever. Everybody in fact in that organization does his own thing, but they're flexible above everything else. I recently referred a young broker to them, simply because they are so flexible. He had been with a national house and completely bored."

There seems to be no disagreement about Lal's function within the Haywood organization. "Lal sticks to what he does best," adds Garson. "And no doubt he always will. He spends most of his time pursuing possible deals, meeting new people and handling his personal clients."

There is a persistent suggestion around the Street that Gondi is somehow a contradictory, complex individual, but those who know him well deny that.

"Lal is so straightforward as to be easily understood, " says Garson. "Both personally and professionally. He's not an analyst in the sense that he makes academic judgments, for example. He uses his technical background to separate out value, but then he applies a sort of personal judgment. This leads to a reluctance to make negative responses, because he's also acting on a diplomatic level. He is extremely busy, yet he'll find time for anyone in the organization who needs him. I've never known him to waste time in any activity, though."

The ultimate question arises. Even small investment houses must have a certain capital investment level to meet the liabilities and obligations they must carry. Since he is senior partner as well as chairman, how in the space of just ten years in the industry did Gondi put together the kind of capital necessary to purchase his position in Haywood?

"There weren't any 'special deals' where I made a fortune overnight," laughs Gondi. "Nor was I born rich. I'm afraid it was just a case of earning it piecemeal, year in, year out."

Actually, it wasn't as prosaic as that. Gondi's capital investment in Haywood at the time the house was purchased was slightly over $.5 million. And in each of the three years previous to that, his annual income as a broker and investor had exceeded $1 million.

Which might suggest one of the reasons why Lal Gondi, super stock broker, came in from the cold world of the mining geologist.

———————

CHAPTER 16

Harry C. Moll

The ultimate wizard

If one visualizes a typical financier as looking like Orson Welles in Citizen Kane, Harry C. Moll certainly does not fit the picture. He is a handsome, genial man who looks as though he should be playing the role of U.S. President in a Hollywood movie. His silver hair and bright blue eyes give him an air of distinction, and the well-cut grey suit and conservative tie add to the overall sense of security the man exudes. There is an aura of the tycoon about him, though, in the cordless telephone buzzing with long-distance calls, in the two eager assistants, and in the crisp stock market buzz-words—orders to "buy," "sell," "hold"—being bandied about.

In spite of the excitement and bustle around him, there is something soothing about Moll. His speech is slow, almost drawling, and his manner composed and warm. There is something courtly and old-fashioned about him, as though he has decided that the hurried and harried look of the typical promoter on Howe Street is not for him. He appears to have all the time in the world and to be happy to chat. Moll's background, like Murray Pezim's and Bruce McDonald's, is small-town, and he emanates a genuine down-home charm.

"I like to talk about new things," he says cheerfully. "I like to learn things. A year ago, for instance, I went to buy my daughter a computer, because she's into computers in school. I went in there to buy a $1300 computer and ended up with one worth $5000." During that transaction Moll learned about computers. Today, Harold C. Moll is the chairman of the board of directors of a company that is involved with a process that will revolutionize computer technology. The process is called "stereolithography," the company is "Lionheart," and the subsidiary that Moll controls is called "3-D Systems."

Harry's manner is offhand but proud when he talks of his latest venture. "Lionheart will be a major corporation—and I mean *major*," he says. "I'm the president and founder of 3-D Systems and it is going to revolutionize the manufacturing world." He is not the only one to think so. Experts and major publications in the field can't stop extolling it.

"There's an old adage," wrote the *Electronic Engineering Times,* "The simpler and more basic the technology used, the better the invention." Stereolithography uses some very simple and basic technologies to perform its magic. "3-D is the hottest deal I've done in my life," maintains Moll. "The stock has a real chance at reaching $100—that's $500 million!"

The process essentially is one which cuts out the tedious, laborious and expensive process of making prototypes. "The process uses ultra-violet light that instantly solidifies liquid plastics, literally 'printing out' cross-sections of an object on the liquid's surface at a computer command," wrote *Forbes* magazine in 1986. This will mean millions of dollars saved, not only for the auto industry but in architectural and industrial design, and even in the cosmetics field.

"You can create a design on your computer and build a model of it in minutes," proclaims the 3-D Systems literature. "Change the design and build a new model. . . . Get finely detailed, accurate plastic models without tooling. Without machining. Without all the normally time-consuming and expensive process of crafting models with today's technology. The time and dollar economies are so great that the Stereolithography system will pay for itself in six months or less." Lest one think this is only hype, Moll adds that similar opinions come from *Business Week, The Wall Street Journal, Electronic News*, and a newsletter on computer graphics.

Harry is justifiably proud of his role in developing this product. "Once they get it engineeringly perfect on the screen all they have to do is press a button and in eighteen minutes they have the finished product," he says, "no matter how complicated or difficult." He adds that large corporations, like General Motors for instance, take up to six months to build a model of a new car. With stereolithography they can do the same in a day —or in a few hours. "That's pretty staggering," he says. But what is even more exciting to him is that as he works on the financial phase he is able to learn at the same time. "I've become better educated because we're putting up the money for the deal," he says with satisfaction.

Harry has not always been involved with high-tech affairs; in Vancouver he is actually better known for his restaurant deals. "I started Sneaky Pete's here in Vancouver," he says, "also Charlie Brown's, Sugar Daddy's, Harry C's. . . ." The list goes on. He is still associated with Hy's in Los Angeles, in Century City. He originally became interested in the restaurant business when "Herb Capozzi had an empty room and we said, 'Why don't you rent it to us and we'll open a little club?' He put up the money for the renovations, which were supposed to be two hundred dollars and ended up a couple of hundred thousand, and the success of Sneaky Pete's was phenomenal." Moll subsequently became a partner in Charlie Brown's, one floor up, then sold out in 1974 to open Harry C.'s and the Beverly Hills Cafe. His last major venture with Hy Aisenstat was in 1978.

Little wonder, then, that he looks as comfortable as he does, sitting at Hy's Encore having lunch. Almost everyone who is anyone stops to have a chat with him and to sing his praises. "He's the best promoter around," says one passer-by enthusiastically. "The greatest," concurs Arthur Abrams, of Davidson Partners.

Moll seems to derive genuine pleasure from these contacts, and from his life, both business and personal. He has the comfortable look of someone who has arrived, on time, without fuss, and without losing his sense of humour. He has no hesitation in acknowledging that not all of his deals have been successful, and ruefully admits that when a deal doesn't fly he loses more money than anyone else, because he is always the largest shareholder in his own deals.

He insists that the secret to success lies in not becoming greedy. "We're not greedy," he says. "Certainly not in terms of the piece of the operation that we take in return for putting up the money and financing the deal. Certainly not as greedy as they are in the U.S." He adds that when his companies put up the money they control the operation *de facto*, but rarely involve themselves with the day-to-day management of the firm. "Hopefully the business plan reads well," he finishes cryptically.

"I'm a long-term player," he says. "I won't get involved in a deal unless I totally believe in it. Our stocks can sit in a range that is unpromoted for months, even years, until we really have something legitimate to talk about." Being a "long-term player" does not imply that he is not interested in selling at a nice profit once a company has succeeded—but deals don't always work out that way.

"We financed a company called Deco Plant Minder for some people in the U.S. for three or four million dollars," he says. "The company just didn't work. We listed the stock here in Vancouver and I was the major shareholder. By the time we delisted the company, within a couple of years, they had gone through all the money. But at the end I had more stock than I started out with— bought at substantially higher prices. If a deal doesn't work, I won't be inducing people to buy the stock to consolidate my position."

He goes on to say that he does intend to sell the Deco Plant Minder company to someone who can take it further than he can. "Someone who can take it from what I sold out for to much higher numbers," as he puts it, hastening to add, "I'm not talking about selling stock on the way up, so that we still control the company but have sold all our free stocks. I would never do that. But I would build a company to the position where the thing could be sold to a larger corporation."

There is another reason for Moll's reluctance to hang on to

companies: He tends to get bored easily and likes to start new things. He likes the thrill and the risk of starting up new companies, not the comparative security of an established business. "I can only be in a deal a year and a half or two years," he confessed, "and if it doesn't work out then I am doing something wrong."

Harry recalls an old saying, "It's not the deals you do, it's the deals you don't do." "If you are right one time out of ten in this market you're in good shape," he says. He estimates he has probably been right somewhere around twenty-five per cent of the time. How does he decide which deals not to get involved with? "First of all the deal has to excite me," he says. "The deal has to be big enough, and the guy that presents it to me has to be a man I have total respect for, because he is the guy that's going to have to run the show."

He agrees with Gus MacPhail, who says the risk-capital business is really a "people business." He adds that a good promoter can make all the difference. "A good promoter is able to create the excitement that goes along with a speculative venture-capital market," he says. "If a bad promoter were to get a deal that had 1% gold, the stock might go up to 50 cents. If Bruce McDonald or Murray Pezim handled the same stock it would go up to $10.00. That's the difference."

Being a good promoter requires credibility in the investment community, though, and Moll says that is the most complicated of all things to acquire. "Credibility is very difficult to establish," he says seriously. "First you have to have a style, you have to be a person people want to hang around or be associated with. The association is important. If we do a deal, or if Murray Pezim does a deal, people want to grab it. All the good promoters are men that people want to be around." Moll adds that a reputation for honesty is also imperative; you have to give the investor a fair shake. "The days when you bought all the stocks cheap and sold them high, those days are gone forever," he smiles.

"We're always up-front," he says flatly. "All our people are on the boards of all our companies. We're responsible for our actions. We have to be, since we are financiers, not managers.

We're a venture-capital group," he explains, "and that's unique to Vancouver. In the old days you could shoot from the hip; now the market is being run by M.B.A.s and C.A.s and Ph.D.s. The venture-capital person who requires money, in the United States especially, has to give away so much that it takes the entrepreneurial spirit out of the whole operation. And that's why management and deal people in the U.S. are looking at the Vancouver market."

Moll may get his feeling for wild-west entrepreneurialism from his small-town background. He was born in Trail, B.C., fifty-one years ago. "My father worked for C.M. & S., Cominco, in Trail for thirty-five years, until he retired," he recalls. "He kept saying 'I never want you to work up there.' I did work up there—for five days—and thank God they laid me off, because I could still be there!"

The young Harry Moll had always been interested in corporations and corporate structure. As a child he thought he would be a lawyer when he grew up. "I wanted to be a lawyer because I was interested in corporate law," he explains. "I used to read books on law, and I knew how to put together companies, corporate structures. I knew about presidents and boards of directors and preferred shares and all of that stuff."

However, Moll never attended law school; he joined the Bank of Montreal in Trail instead. "I went into the finance end right out of high school," he says. He found he had a natural aptitude for finance, and became, at the age of twenty-four, one of the youngest bank managers in Canada. "Later, when the Bank of Nova Scotia got into the consumer-finance business, it went around hiring all the experienced people it could find—and I happened to be one of them," he finishes modestly.

Before he became the whiz kid of finance, the thrill-seeking young man (the child is father of the man, as the cliché goes) had considered the Air Force as a career. He qualified for officer training and found it "glamorous," so he decided to become the "top gun." "Fortunately," says Harry, "after I had been through pre-flight school and flight training, the Air Force wanted me to become a Flying Officer Observer (sort of equivalent to a flight engineer now). To sit in the back seat of a CF

100 rather than in the front seat." He could not visualize himself as anything other than a jet pilot, so he left the Air Force.

Then, as now, Moll wanted to be in the front seat, with the action. In charge. He decided to go back into finance, the only other business he knew. He did management training at Household Finance until the Bank of Nova Scotia lured him away, and then he flew into consumer lending in the heady financial sky of the early sixties. He stayed with banking until 1963, then went into sales. "I was extremely successful," he says without false modesty, "making more than $20,000 a month." He sold steel buildings, and now considers that experience to have been invaluable because it taught him how to sell, a priceless asset for a promoter.

He moved to Vancouver in 1963 and started to dabble in the stock market. "You start as an investor; then you say, 'How long has this been going on?' Pretty soon you are involved in putting deals together, getting burned as you go—and burning—but after the first two experiences I started to do my own deals. I've never worked for anyone since; I've been a partner or a director," he says.

Just investing was not enough for Harry. His interest in corporate affairs had not waned—after all this was the same person who had pored over law books when he was a boy—and he wanted to be in charge, just as he had been when flying. "I wanted to get my teeth into everything, from investing, to taking positions, to investor relations, to running my own companies," he says. He started small; now he has over fifteen large firms in his "stable," as he calls it. "I'm the major shareholder in all of the companies we now have," he says.

Moving to Vancouver was not only a significant turning point in Moll's career, it also marked the end of his high-flying single life. "I moved to Vancouver, met my wife, fell in love, and got into the stock business," he says simply, summing up the whole extravagant year in one short sentence. Harry is obviously still deeply in love with his wife and credits her with being the stabilizing force in his life. "If I get too far over the line, my wife gives me a left hook," he laughs.

Petite and vivacious, with sparkling brown eyes and sandy-blonde hair, Suzy Moll exudes energy, warmth, and solid common sense. "You have to know when to stop," she says firmly of her husband's financial wheeling and dealing. "You need to keep things in perspective." She laughingly says that when Harry gets back from Los Angeles, thoroughly spoiled from being wined, dined and chauffered, she asks him to take out the garbage. This would bring anybody's feet back to earth.

Suzy remembers meeting Harry nearly twenty years ago when she was a contestant in the Miss Canada pageant, as Miss Vancouver. She had gone to Hy's with a pageant official, and there she met Harry Moll, then a dapper thirty and wearing a trenchcoat—one of the handsomest men the young woman had ever seen. She still seems to think he is, but is far too sophisticated to say it, and far too sensible to let him know it too much of the time. She takes quite seriously her job of keeping his feet firmly planted on the ground.

Suzy and Harry Moll's two children also keep them both well grounded. Taylor-Jean, nine, and Mandy, a little Korean girl of five whom they adopted two years ago, don't really care that their father is Numero Uno—or well up there, anyway—at the Vancouver Stock Exchange. They just want to know if he's going to make the school play, or take them swimming. Suzy Moll says her husband cares deeply about his family life. "The day we got Mandy, Harry drove up in a station wagon," she says happily. He explained that her Mercedes would not have been suitable for chauffering two children. Granted, the station wagon was a Mercedes Benz, too, but—"It's the thought that counts," she twinkles irresistibly.

Perhaps because of his family, Moll is not the workaholic one normally meets in the stock market. As a rule, he gets up around 6:30 a.m., makes phone calls for about half an hour, then runs and exercises. He drives his children to school, and is in the office between 9:30 and 10:00. His office work accomplished, he does the rest of his business over luncheon meetings. "I very seldom work in the afternoon," he says, "so I would say that after the luncheon meetings I'm usually finished."

This is not strictly accurate; he does often go to afternoon meetings with other promoters and financiers to talk deals and details. He insists on being home early on Fridays, though. "I play with my kids, swim in the pool, ski—the kids are great skiiers. Then, Monday to Friday I'm barrelling. If I'm not home I'm working," he says; and for Moll, as for other high-profile businessmen, often the most important time is that spent socializing. It is important to be visible when money is your stock-in-trade. "You're working all the time, because it's all one-on-one," he explains. "As soon as you're not seen they start dealing with other people." Moll does not deal with individual investors; he has to sell his stock to brokers with scores of clients. "I don't have the time," he says about this. "So I have to talk to people who have hundreds of clients to tell the story to."

He laughingly adds that while it is important for him to look good too, he has absolutely no eye for colour or design; so Baron Lee, of E.A. Lee, has complete power over him sartorially. "I'm always dressed immaculately, everything coordinated," he says, "but that's no credit to me! I could never figure out what tie went with what, so they write it on the back of my tie." He turns his tie around to prove his point and one of his assistants jokingly comments that if Harry is given a tie for Christmas he comes unglued. Moll glares at him with mock annoyance. "If there's no writing on the back of my tie I won't wear it," he says defiantly. It's a wise man who can admit ignorance about something. "To know that you do not know is best," said the Chinese sage, Lao Tzu, and Harry Moll has no qualms about subscribing to that age-old wisdom.

Unlike many businessmen, Moll knows the advantages of a healthy body and always takes time to exercise. "I'm the only promoter you know that always has his running shoes with him," he says. "I'm up before seven and I run three or four miles, no matter where I am, and then I do my exercises. I do it at home and I do it on the road. People who travel with me either come with me and get in an hour and a half or two hours of exercise, getting back to reality, or they can sit up in the room and do whatever they like. I tell you, you can't keep up the pace that is required to make deals successfully without having that kind of discipline," he adds firmly. "I've got the discipline. I don't smoke; I probably drink too much, gamble too much, play too hard, but regardless of what I did the night before, I'm up in the morning even if I've got to *crawl* around Hyde Park in London—or wherever."

That kind of regimen is rare for people who spend so much time deal-making in those proverbial smoke-filled rooms, or over an elaborate meal with drinks, but Harry is not your ordinary stock promoter. He is not sure precisely what it is that sets him apart from the rest of the herd, and, in fact, he does not really seem to think of himself as different.

His wife says that in her view a large part of Harry's success is due to his attitude—that of a consummate gambler, one who is not afraid of taking risks. "He even owns shares of several race-horses," she says proudly. Moll agrees that he enjoys the thrill of gambling, then, more seriously, he explains that being a promoter is much more than being a person who likes to take chances. It requires a certain innovative, creative quality. What makes the Vancouver Stock Exchange so unique, he says, is the personalities of the brokers. "They're innovative," he points out. He modestly does not include himself in that umbrella comment.

Moll does admit that he has managed to arrive at a stage where he can "pick and choose." When he started out he was not in that fortunate position. He enjoyed being in the restaurant business at first; it was only later that he began to concentrate on finance to the exclusion of all else. His first real success was Cornwall Oil and Gas, which he subsequently sold to Jack Singer, one of the wealthiest men in Canada. "The stock went up to $25," he recalls almost dreamily. And then in 1981 the market turned.

Moll was not much affected by the bottom caving out of the natural resource field, he says, because—unlike many players on the Vancouver Stock Exchange who are as irresistibly drawn toward mining deals as lemmings are to the sea—he does not have a mining background. "We look more to the industrial high-tech market," he says. He adds that he has been very lucky. "We have had very good underwriters—Canarim, Continental, Davidsons, and Brink Hudson—and extremely good European contacts, so if we like a deal we're able to expose it to the proper people that are able to finance it. Hopefully the deal becomes successful." If it does not, Moll has more stock at the end of the deal than he started with and, like the ship's captain of proverb, he goes down with the ship.

Moll has always preferred to do a large part of his business in Europe and in the United States. He particularly likes Europeans, because, he says, they are more sophisticated than North Americans. "I've been to Hong Kong but I've never had any success there," he says of the Pacific Rim. "I find Europeans more willing to take a chance, and more willing to take long-term positions in stocks they believe in." Moll approves of this view, it being in agreement with his own, and adds that Europeans also have a more global view. "They're able to deal in the world market," he says, "in the *global* atmosphere rather than in localized situations.

"Unfortunately, in Vancouver, great as it is—and this is where we do all our deals—well, long-term means the day after tomorrow. It is absolutely unheard of for a promoter or entrepreneur to come from Brazil to Vancouver and interest a Vancouver broker in purchasing a large position in his company, one that the broker will have to hold on to for three to five years. No one in Vancouver really has the capability or foresight to take that kind of an opportunity and put it into reality. Yet a Vancouver promoter can go to London or Zurich and do business with people who will take a major position. I'm talking in the neighbourhood of $50 million to $100 million. They will take a longer-range approach to situations that are beyond the boundaries of the U.K. or Europe. They could be dealing in Texas, they could be dealing in Vancouver—they're used to it."

Nevertheless, Moll is happy working within the Vancouver Stock Exchange and only wishes it would pay its administrators better. "I like the entire approach of the Vancouver Stock Exchange and the Securities Commission," he says. "Their only problem is lack of funds. They need to pay more in order to attract better people who are capable of administering a business this big." This is something he obviously feels strongly about. "I mean, we are talking billions of dollars and we're trying to hire a guy for $60,000 or $70,000 a year to run it. It's ridiculous. And then when they do get good people, as soon as they're trained... well, who's going to work for $60,000 a year when he can go out and make $200,000 or $300,000 in industry? As soon as a good person is there at the Stock Exchange or at the Superintendent of Brokers he gets stolen away."

Moll is at his best under pressure. "It's the nature of the beast," he says ruefully. "I put together the deal; arrange the debt financing, and the public relations or the investor relation to handle the market, so that the stock performs consistently with what the company is doing, and is trading at a multiple probably higher than it should be, but hopefully the company will build in behind it; then I lose interest," he says. "You talk about it for so long and it succeeds. Then you've got to start something else."

Moll maintains that he is not the only one with a short attention span; other successful promoters are the same. He recently ran into Murray Pezim, who told him he was bored to death. "Everything I'm doing is financed—I've got to get into trouble," he told Harry. The "high" can only last so long, says Moll, then "you've got to go and try something else."

It's that living on the edge that excites the daredevil businessman. Moll experienced some thrills during the time he was flying for the Air Force; more recently he took up race-car driving, after Paul Newman's driving partner told him how exciting it was. Now when he's in Monte Carlo he walks around the track so that he'll know every bump and depression on it when he watches the race on television. He thoroughly enjoys driving race cars but insists that he really is a very boring person. One wonders whom he would consider exciting. Evil Knievel, perhaps?

Moll enjoys the perks that success brings, but he says nothing beats the thrill of financial dealing. He obviously enjoys his life, what he has achieved and all the trappings that go with it, but part of him still seems to yearn for the stimulation of starting from scratch. Naturally, at age fifty-one, with a family to support, he would not want to start with nothing, but he does hanker for more and bigger thrills. He says pensively, almost to himself, that he wouldn't mind if 3-D Systems were a huge success, so he could sell out and start over. "I'm not looking to build an empire," he says almost wistfully, "but I'd like to sell one of my companies to General Motors or Xerox or whomever, end up with the cash, have it in term deposits and treasury bills all over the place—then start a deal. I'd like to have it all put together, then do it all over again. But I'd really like to cash out just once. Have it there and say, "O.K., now you really have money; money, rather than $20 million worth of paper." The little boy who read about putting companies together wants to do it all over again, and to do it even better the second time around.

Harry C. has already made his million on the stock market—succeeded in business without really trying. Actually, he has worked very hard, but his aptitude for business made it seem easy. So what is the secret of making a million on the stock market? His blue eyes twinkle, all boyish maunderings forgotten. "Will Rogers said it best," he says. "He said, 'Take all of your holdings, buy good stock. When they go up, sell them. If they don't go up, don't buy them.'"

Well, it's nice work if you can get it—and Harold C. Moll has got it.

———

CHAPTER 17

Bruce McDonald

The Midas touch

Richard Angus Bruce McDonald, Chairman of Noramco Capital, spent much of his youth racketing around the world, learning how to do business on the floors of the stock exchanges in Geneva and Rome. The most obvious traces of that experience are in his dress and manner, the former more elegant than is usual on Howe Street, the latter with a hint of continental charm. Less obvious, but more important is his attitude.

Doug McRae, who also spent time in Europe, maintains the European viewpoint is emphasis on personal integrity and management ability over tangible assets. ("Generally they buy management before they buy property," according to McRae.) It is Bruce McDonald's management style—hands-on, genial, but hard-hitting—and his personal integrity that reflect his European ventures most clearly. The more noticeable elements are what catch the eye: dapper white pochette peeping out of the breast pocket of his well-cut grey tweed jacket; the conservative softly-blended burgundy, fuchsia, and black of his tie, which indicate that McDonald's eye for colour is as keen as his feel for finance. McDonald is not tall, yet he gives the impression of height. He is stocky and powerful, but looks contained. As he smokes Rothmans cigarettes and thoughtfully responds to questions, he has the confident air of a man who has succeeded. "We allow people to make money *with* us," he says. "That means a lot in this business. When we bring in an issue we leave plenty on the table for everybody else." This is significant in a business where the guiding principle is often to run stocks up and then sell. "I'd just as soon the stocks sit there," admits McDonald with a smile. "Oh, we've all fooled around with markets just to see them go up and down, but there has to be a reason. We won't encourage a stock to be higher unless there's been a discovery on the property or the company has made unusual progress in some area. We're not necessarily just stock people; a lot of the things we take on are long-term."

He considers his early experiences on the trading floor to have been the best education and the best introduction to the business world. "It's where a young fellow should start to learn," he says firmly. "It's where you learn the business; that's where I learned everything." He learned how to buy and sell, when to do it, how to tell when a particular stock would fly, and how to price it. "Pricing," he said during an interview with *B.C.Business Magazine*, "Don't forget that pricing is all-important in any kind of trading or underwriting." Pricing is just what he had learned to do.

In addition, growing up on the floor ensured that he would make future contacts. "That's where all my friends are," he explains. "We grew up together in the business. I was very young when I was working in those places—Europe, New York and Toronto; now I can pick up the phone and talk to any of the senior guys there."

McDonald has an even better advantage. He grew up in a mining town and learned the ins and outs of mining long before he hit the Toronto Stock Exchange. Noramco benefits from his experience. Although McDonald and Noramco finance many deals that have nothing to do with mining their major focus remains the discovery of ore bodies, especially gold. "I grew up in the mining business," says McDonald. "Then I watched people, different mining companies, over the years . . . I never claim to have a nose for *finding* anything, but I do have a nose for surrounding myself with the right people."

Those right people include mining engineer Rick Killam, geologist Daniel Innes, now vice-president of exploration, and president Gordon Keevil (uncle of Teck president Norman Keevil, Jr.). "We've got a tremendous staff headed by Gordon Keevil," says McDonald. "I don't make any decisions as far as the mining properties are concerned but I can read reports. I've got enough knowledge to be dangerous." He tries to look sly, and fails. "Dangerous to myself," he adds, deadpan.

"We're not big risk-takers," he continues, more seriously. "A lot of the time we go into properties that were in production before, and change them around," Such properties might have closed down when gold was around $30. "As you know, gold is $450 now," he points out. "Our dollar is right in the garbage can, so to speak, so we can make our capital costs, which are very low right now. Gold is actually over $600 in Canadian funds, and our production costs run around $200. It doesn't take a genius to figure out there's $400 leeway in there. All you have to do is be fortunate enough to come up with the ore bodies."

McDonald has been lucky in coming up with those ore bodies. Golden Knight, the deal with which he shot to prominence, was one. *B.C. Business Magazine* wrote: "McDonald surfaced for the railbirds on Howe Street in late 1985 when all eyes turned to Casa Berardi, a gold play in Quebec that showed all the signs of stretching on forever." Essentially, what happened was that in 1984 McDonald's Golden Knight Resources Inc. acquired from Inco, for $3 million, a forty per cent interest in the Casa Berardi property in northwestern Quebec. The property, which straddles the Ontario-Quebec border, is basically 882 claims in a volcanic belt, with three main zones of ore, and promises to be one of the best gold mines in Canada.

"Inco had been sitting on a property that had eighteen drill holes where they were looking for base metals," explains McDonald. "The drill holes indicated there was a potential gold ore body and the potential looked pretty good. So we agreed to spend three million. Inco hadn't spent that money because it wasn't in their budgeting—for any number of reasons, low nickel prices, pollution problems . . . . For whatever reason, it was not in their budget to spend exploration dollars. I thought the potential was great, and we started spending money on the property, and through the use of flow-through shares came up with an ore body within three or four months."

Teck mining stepped in soon, although it already had a fifty per cent share of McDonald's Golden Hope Resources Inc., the Estrades project nearby. Teck president Norman Keevil, Jr., was quoted in the *Northern Miner* in June of 1986 as saying that Teck would like to increase its equity position in Golden Knight, "but probably not immediately." [By the end of 1986 Teck had taken over the management and financing of Golden Knight from McDonald.] Keevil added that the Estrades discovery was being studied by Teck and reserves were estimated at 2.4 million tons of gold, silver, copper and zinc. Golden Knight so far has upward of ten million tons at 0.22 ounces gold per ton indicated, and this will probably increase as exploration continues.

"The majority of the ore bodies that are found are found by small companies," says Teck president Norm Keevil now, "or by so-called 'junior mining companies' like Bruce McDonald's." He adds that Teck's role is to come in and provide the management and the financing to "bring these into line." Keevil has nothing but praise for McDonald, saying that their deal was made with a handshake and that McDonald did not renege on the deal, although he could have done.

McDonald explains, "My background is in the brokerage business and certainly that is a business where your word is your bond." He in turn thinks very highly of Teck. "We agreed that Teck would be better able to manage that property with Inco than we could," he says, "They were better equipped to do it. So I swapped a lot of my Golden Knight shares for shares in Teck. Teck's done very well with us and we've done very well with them. I wish everybody could go through life like that. Our association with them has been tremendous." He adds that

Teck owns around nine per cent of Noramco Mining.

Noramco Mining, with McDonald in control, operated and managed over thirty-five active mining properties in 1986, spending over $40 million on exploration; that figure was expected to rise to $65 million in 1987. In its company literature Noramco calls itself "a mining finance house that is actively involved in the exploration and development of ore bodies." In the past three years its major finds besides Golden Knight and Golden Hope have been Emerald Lake and Highland Crow, both gold mines. Its basic corporate philosophy is that due to its smaller size Noramco can invest more risk capital in "non-mature" projects with potential than can larger firms.

Risk capital is the reason McDonald came to Vancouver in the first place and the reason he stays there. "Venture capital is understood out here," he once said. "perhaps better than any place in the world—at least in terms of junior mining." McDonald left his life as a broker in Toronto because he was tired of dealing with clients and saw more opportunities out here. "People here could put companies together, operate them," he says. "I felt I could do a better job."

Part of the reason he has done a better job than many is his childhood in Noranda, a mining town in northern Quebec. "My dad worked in the mines and liked to trade in the stock market," he says. "He was quite a character." At age fourteen McDonald won a hockey scholarship to "St. Mike's School" in Toronto, then, at sixteen, he got a summer job at the Toronto Stock Exchange. "I worked there for a few years, and then went to Europe and worked. Geneva... Rome... Bermuda... then New York."

McDonald attributes his success to his flight from poverty. "I don't like being poor," he says. As he lights another cigarette and empties the ashtray he ponders on that for a moment, then adds, "But it's not only that. You want to prove something to your peers, to the people you work with. You want to prove that you can be bigger than they are."

Perhaps because McDonald settled in Toronto after his travels and worked there for several years, he does not share the antipathy many westerners feel toward the eastern establishment. "I have an exceptional relationship with Toronto," he says matter-of-factly. "I get along very well there. Our company keeps an apartment there, and a lot of our companies are listed in Toronto. I believe that Vancouver is by far the best exchange for issues at a junior stage and for venture-capital issues, but I think when they reach maturity you have to take them to Toronto in order to raise the kind of money they need. We certainly couldn't do any 10—15—20 million dollar deals, let alone 85 million, here."

He does concede the two places are very different. "I think probably one of the reasons people in Vancouver don't get along with Toronto is that they want to force these venture-capital companies down easterners' throats and can't understand why easterners don't want to swallow them. Or list them. That isn't what Toronto says its Exchange is about. When the companies reach a mature stage in their progression *then* they should be brought to Toronto." He adds that much of the animosity is a thing of the past. "Continental and Canarim have both bought seats in Toronto," he points out. "So I think the whole problem of animosity is out of the way as long as we realize we're a venture-capital exchange and they're a different kind of exchange, a more mature one. If we all recognize the difference we can all get along."

McDonald tends to get along with everybody, and does not confine his deals to Canada. "We're active in the U.S.," he says. "It doesn't matter to me where we are. Although we like to live in British Columbia, the majority of our money is spent in the East." He adds that although he thinks there is a great future in the Pacific Rim region, the government will have to display more foresight. "We're going to have to get some people with more vision on the west coast if we are to realize that future," he says. "Noramco has not got *one* project in British Columbia. I've talked to Vander Zalm about it and they're all very nice and say 'oh yes, it should be done' and 'they'll talk about it'—but they *don't* talk about it. They're letting B.C.'s second industry fall apart. The exploration that should be done here is not being done because there are a lot better incentives for mining in Ontario and Quebec than there are in British Columbia."

McDonald goes where the opportunities are, and where his technical staff and his talent for finding ore guide him. Then, with the backing of larger companies like Teck and Inco, he rounds out the deal. "First, we put as much money in the ground as possible in any given situation, keeping administrative and other costs shaved to the bone," he says. "Second, we do as much as we can with government-sponsored programs, such as flow-through deals. And finally, we make it a practice to work with the best people available under our own roof and to deal with the best people possible as partners. Can you think of any better partners than Inco and Teck?"

Certainly one could not think of a better partner than Bruce McDonald. The real trick to the whole thing, he says, is not to become greedy. "We're selective in what we do," he says. "We'll finance ten to fifteen small companies this year in things other than mining. Generally they need money for expansion, or because they've become big and have incurred some debt and they need to reduce their debt load because the bank is leaning on them again. You need money to grow, there's just not two ways about it," he says firmly. "We'll put up the money in the meantime and arrange for them to go public on a basis that's good for them, good for the public, and, as long as neither side is greedy, then usually everybody can make money. That's where the key is, to keep greed out of it." He pauses for a moment, then adds, "We're not greedy, we just want to have a fair advantage."

It is obvious from McDonald's pleasant but spartan office that he is not greedy for himself. His desk is cluttered with papers, files, and a computer terminal, but half of the large office is empty, graced only by a Persian carpet and a telephone on the floor. Commenting on the rather hollow feel of his office he says casually that they'll "get it done one of these days." Does he care? "No, I don't," he says cheerfully. "As long as we're working and making money that's all that's important. There will eventually be six of us in here," he adds. "I don't know what I'd do if I had to sit and work in isolation."

Contrary to what many people think, McDonald says he is really quite conservative. "We don't take many chances," he insists. "When we do things we usually bring the public in at the same price we pay. We don't mark things up too much, consequently we've had a good following. We're not tremendous gamblers. If you want to gamble then go and do it in Vegas, not downtown."

Bruce McDonald takes his work seriously, unlike many of his counterparts who also handle large sums of money but consider it just a sophisticated version of Monopoly. "It's not a game," he says emphatically. "It's not a process. It's building a company, and certainly it's nice to see the fruits of that, but to me it's not a game. It's anything but. We put a great deal of effort into everything we do, so we're not perceived in the same light as the ordinary promoter on Howe Street."

Undoubtedly because of this essentially conservative outlook. McDonald has not had too many ups and downs in business; most of his major losses have been connected with his personal life, notably his married one. In the early eighties he found himself starting over with practically nothing, because he had given everything to his ex-wife. He calls this his "divorce period" and says, "The company had a bit of a dip in the eighties, but that was caused more by marital problems than financial."

McDonald has been married three times. His first attempt was a "short affair" when he was very young. "My son was born then, so I guess I must have been slightly involved," he laughs. (That son is now a trader on the floor of the Toronto Stock Exchange. "He started where I did," says McDonald proudly, "but he's better off than I. At least he went to university! I'm not really smart enough to know when I'm in trouble so I plug on.") His second marriage ended with that "divorce period;" now he is happily married, with two small children, a girl and a boy.

McDonald says starting over did not bother him because he is not much concerned with money itself. He knows he can make it any time. "I've always been extremely confident of my ability to make money," he says without emphasis. "I could start over again tomorrow and make money again." He says much of the time he doesn't really know whether he has any money or not. "I have assets," he says, "but it's not money I can go out and spend. It's a percentage of a company that I own. I can't sell it, I can't trade it, can't deal with it—I don't even get to see it. So it doesn't seem to me I have money."

He has not surrounded himself with the toys many successful men like to have: ski cabins, boats, fancy cars (although he has just bought a new Mercedes, which, he confesses, is the first new car he has ever owned). He also has a house in West Vancouver, but he says success has not changed his lifestyle. "The only thing I want the money for is so I can have a low aggravation scale out there."

One of the things that rate high on his aggravation scale is queues, and a recent deal he put together may ensure that he may never have to stand in line again to see another movie. Some time ago Nelson Holdings, a movie company based in London and Los Angeles, asked McDonald to organize a financial deal for them. "They bought a company called Embassy Home Entertainment from Coca-Cola," he explains, "for CDN $110 million."

R.A. Bruce McDonald of West Vancouver, B.C. is now one of the directors of Nelson Holdings International. That company owns all of Galactic, Embassy Home Entertainment (which acquires rights to movies and distributes them on videocassette), and most of Pacific Vending and Autovend Technology. The last two distribute video-cassettes to the public. With all the components of the motion picture industry under one umbrella, it would seem that Nelson has the market cornered. Peter Brown says the deal was the VSE's largest financing. He calls it an "international public relations coup."

That coup was organized by McDonald, who, with his ability to get the right people together, called in Loewen, Ondaatje McCutcheon & Company, a Toronto-based firm known for its creative investment and underwriting deals. A memo from the firm proclaims that Nelson Holdings "is poised to develop into a major North American entertainment company," and all the press clippings agree, from the *New York Times* to *Variety*. McDonald is more restrained. "I'm not in the movie business," he demurs, "I don't even like Los Angeles. I'm in the financing business. It was strictly a financial deal."

McDonald tends to reserve his essential enthusiasm for mining deals. "I have a better understanding of mining than most," he says modestly, and although he does sound pleased about the Nelson business, he verges on the poetic when he speaks of his mining deals and Noramco Mining. "We've had five mines going into production in four years," he says enthusiastically. "Nobody has ever done that before. Nobody." He considers the Noramco Mining financing deal the biggest coup of his career. "We were a private company. We took it public and raised $50 million," he says proudly. "We matched the public's $50 million. Some people were a little suspicious of it, told us it wasn't an institutional stock, it wasn't this and it wasn't that. Actually, it's a very secure, stable company with over $50 million cash right now in live revenues. I'm proud of putting that together." He smiles reminiscently. "It was the first one. Since then we've had lots."

"Lots" is an imprecise way for McDonald to speak, considering his facility with numbers and the manipulation of them. He jokingly says he surrounds himself with all those M.B.A.s, C.A.s and Ph.D.s "because they can count," but when taxed he will admit that he himself knows "how to count pretty well." "Numbers, that's the one thing I could always do in school," he says, flourishing his half-moon glasses. "I used to get good marks in math. I felt I was probably a little bit ahead of the teachers, so consequently I didn't pay much attention in class. They failed me automatically because they thought I was a smartass. I wasn't, I was just bored. Terribly bored." So bored that he did not go back to school after his summer stint at the Toronto Stock Exchange. "I took the Canadian Securities Course when I was sixteen or seventeen, which is much harder than a high-school course, and I got very good marks, so what the hell was I doing wasting my time in school?" he asks rhetorically. McDonald laughingly says that now he wishes he had an M.B.A. —"so I could put the initials behind my name!"

—but a title like "Richard Angus Bruce McDonald, M.B.A." could be rather daunting, something McDonald is not.

Childhood experiences notwithstanding, what is the real difference between a Bruce McDonald and the person on the street who would like to be but isn't? "Maybe they don't want it as much," says McDonald thoughtfully. "That's the only thing I can think of. Oh yeah, a lot of people say they'd love to do this and they'd love to do that, but they don't have the commitment."

McDonald does have the commitment. His day at the office begins at 6:15 in the morning, and he usually stays around until six in the evening. "My evenings and my weekends, my friends and my social life all revolve around my business," he says. "I don't take much out of the business and I put everything back in." His years in the brokerage business are useful to him now; he finds most aspects of the financial world come to him almost instinctively. "The experience I had in the brokerage business, and on the various stock exchanges gives me a tremendous insight," he says, "and reading prospectuses and working through the business as I did, I know how to speak to people in the business. I know what they're thinking and I know what the brokers want."

Perhaps because both he and Murray Pezim started out poor, in contrast with the Peter Browns of this world, the two are often spoken of in the same breath. "Murray Pezim is a bright guy, and surrounds himself with good people too," says McDonald, "but he wants to be different. I fall into the mainstream of things and would rather play along with the establishment—although not necessarily in the same way." The basic difference between the two seems to be that Noramco and Bruce McDonald are actively involved in the exploration business, while Pezim is not. He is more a promoter of properties that have been discovered by someone else and that Pezim feels have potential. In addition, the flamboyant Pezim has often said that it's all a game to him, and money is the way to keep score, while McDonald says he finds it no game at all, but a very serious thing.

"Murray's different from me," he says. "He's tremendous,

but he does things as they were done in the old school. It's a very serious business to us and we have to be perceived as serious businessmen, not just as moving paper. We consult with our underwriters and put a great deal of effort into everything we do." He adds that they have already come up with five ore bodies and will do a quarter of a billion dollars in business this year. Murray Pezim, says McDonald, is always "jousting with the establishment" whereas he prefers to play along with it a bit more. "Not that he's wrong and I'm right." he adds quickly. "It's just that you can't compare apples and oranges."

A lot of the differences may be academic; in their varied careers, neither man has come up with too many lemons. Naturally there have been bad experiences; "I guess you have to have them," says McDonald philisophically. Nevertheless, by and large his conservative credo has shielded him from excessive falls.

McDonald says he is no workaholic, unlike many in his field, definitely not one of the "Thank-God-it's-Monday" school. "I work as much as I have to," he says, but concedes that because he enjoys what he does much of his work time is fun. What a lot of people might consider work he does not. "I'm socializing with people I've done business with for years," he says, usually people with whom he makes deals. Many of those deals are done almost informally over a coffee or lunch, with a handshake.

McDonald travels a great deal, sometimes visiting as many as three cities a day in order to explain to brokers and promoters his latest project. He says he does not like that part much, especially since it means leaving his family behind, but he says taking them along would be simply too disruptive for his two small children. "Doing two or three cities in one day—it's a grind," he says. That grind netted Noramco's Golden Day mining deal nearly $85 million. McDonald laughs off the amount. "It's a road show," he says cheerfully.

He admits rather ruefully that because of all the travelling and the hectic schedule he is now overweight. "But healthy," he hastens to add. "I should have time for exercise," he says, echoing the lament of most busy people. "Before I moved out here I used to go to the Cambridge Club in Toronto every day for an hour. When I moved out here I stopped, because there wasn't a club where I knew everyone. I've put on about twenty-five or thirty pounds, and that's just from sitting on airplanes and travelling and cocktails, drinks over lunch, things like that."

McDonald spends all that time socializing and travelling because he likes to raise all the money he needs for a project. He does not like to be in debt, particularly to the banks, institutions he calls "the worst jerks in the world." He says Noramco is well-financed for that precise reason. "We have close to $200 million on deposit with the banks, and that is a much more comfortable feeling than having to have them interview me about how much money they're going to lend me," he says. "Any animosity the west may have toward the east is due to the fact that the banks won't have any lending decisions made out here," he adds.

Noramco's next objective is to acquire a trust company, "our own financial institution" McDonald calls it. "The banking system here is a joke," he says, "so why be a part of it? We'll keep our $200 million in our *own* bank!" He has nothing but contempt for large banks that would rather lend money to Brazil or Dome Petroleum and "blow it big," instead of lending smaller sums to small businesses that have a real chance of making it. "Morons" he says flatly. "It's just insane. Dome goes to Toronto and nails the banks for $700 million; Brazil goes to them . . . . I haven't heard of anybody in Vancouver that's nailed them. They'd rather lend to Brazil or Dome and blow it in huge chunks of a billion apiece than take a percentage of the money they're going to lend out and lend it to some good little business that people need, that you can see a lot of growth in."

McDonald intends to fill that gap—he already has to some extent—and laughingly says that anything under five million they can leave for him. "Let them continue struggling through their lives making money for large corporations," he says expansively. "*They* can lose money. *We* don't lose money because we're selective. We'll finance ten to fifteen small companies this year in projects other than mining. . . . Maybe it would be better if our banking system were not reviewed, because it leaves a great opportunity for people like me."

Noramco has financed a company called American Telecommunications. The stock began at 30 cents and is now around US$5. "The sales this year are around $50 million," says McDonald, justifiably proud of his acumen. "We financed something just lately, called Prescott Development, that makes bullets; we're buying a trust company; we're bringing public a company called "Rent-Your-Own" that will be good for us, good for the public, good for everybody."

McDonald says helping small companies is one of the things he excels at. "We've done it in the past, we know how to do it," he says. "We know how to take collateral, we know how to get them public. With our own trust company, we'll perform all the functions of a merchant-banking operation."

The miner's son from Quebec learned, literally, from the ground up. His classroom was the mayhem of the stock exchange. And from that incomparable educational background has emerged this man, Richard Angus Bruce McDonald, who has undoubtedly succeeded but who has no intention of stopping. His horizons have no limit.

———————

CHAPTER 18

Chuck Ager and Mauro Berretta

Championship tag-team

C huck Ager is in his usual working pose, lying back in his chair with his stockinged feet perched on the corner of his desk, the phone to his ear. His spirited responses to whatever is being proposed on the other end of the line can be heard down the hall and in the other offices at ABM Mining Group. If there is an air of the Right Stuff about him—more the self-assured bearing of a hotshot fighter pilot shooting the breeze with a fellow flyboy about his latest mission than that of a desk-bound mining engineer—it is no accident. Chuck attributes some of his business acumen today to his training in the United States Air Force.

"Discipline and a sense of the world," he says of what he brought away from that experience.

It was at boot camp in San Antonio, Texas, that Chuck learned that an advantage—or disadvantage—is only what you make of it.

"There must have been five thousand guys my age there. They were from the big cities and the farms and everywhere. What I learned there and through my four-year Air Force career was that a little guy from Burns Lake could actually compete with a big guy from Los Angeles. And I learned that extremely well." So well, in fact, that within two years he held the top rank it was possible to attain without re-enlisting.

And that led to the second lesson: that large organizations put restrictions on people as to how fast they can advance. "I didn't like that. I figured you should be able to progress at your own pace. I learned what not to do with my life."

He believes in playing by the rules; it's just that he'd rather be the one making them. And this he has done with extraordinary single-mindedness and determination. When he and partner Mauro Berretta joined forces in 1978 they established a twelve-year plan which by 1990 would see the combined gold-production levels of all their properties (which they had yet to find) reach 400,000 ounces per year. Now, with three years to go, that target is well within their reach.

The entrepreneurial attitude comes naturally to Chuck Ager. He can trace his family origins to 1627, when his forefathers immigrated to America and settled in upstate New York. "Since that time, as near as I can tell, no one has ever really worked for anybody," he says with obvious pride. "They've all been self-employed in one way or another."

His early forefathers were Baptist preachers and, generation after generation, the Ager family has fought in every war the United States has been involved in: the War of Independence, the War of 1812, the Civil War, the Spanish-American War, the First and Second World Wars, the Korean War and the Vietnam War.

Chuck was born in California in 1944. When he was seven his father retired from ranching and moved the family to Burns Lake, B.C., where he bought a building-supply business. At twelve Chuck was doing odd chores around the store. His natural aptitude for mathematics soon advanced him from snow-shovelling and floor-sweeping to bookkeeping and by the time he was fourteen Chuck was minding the store on his own.

"I would come home from school and my dad would leave," Chuck remembers. "I would run the store from three to six o'clock." As weekends and summers went by Chuck gained valuable experience, so that "By the time I was sixteen years old, I had a very good understanding of money and how it worked, and

I was able to judge people very well. I knew everybody in town and I knew if a guy was a good credit risk or not."

In that northern B.C. small-town environment, where there was no television, Chuck read voraciously, everything from comic books to adventure novels to *National Geographic* magazine.

"The *National Geographic* had these great pictures of all the places in the world," Chuck recalls. " I wanted to see all that stuff, so I did."

He joined the United States Air Force at age seventeen and in his four years in the forces he did indeed see the world.

"I was stationed in Turkey when Kennedy and Kruschev decided to have it out over Cuba and I thought for sure we were going to go to war. Nuclear war. I mean, the real stuff."

He laughs.

"Of course, we didn't. Fortunate for me, I guess, or I might not be here."

On leaving the service in 1965 Chuck went to university in California, graduating with honours in mathematics and physics three years later. Then he returned to Canada to complete his studies at the University of British Columbia, gaining a master's degree and a doctorate in geophysics. He now holds the distinction of being both a professional geophysical engineer in British Columbia and a registered geophysicist in the state of California, an uncommonly high criterion to meet.

Along the way he became acquainted with Mauro Berretta, another geophysical engineer who was doing similar exploration and consulting work for major mining companies. In addition to their friendship, Berretta and Ager shared a growing belief that what they were doing for others they could be doing for themselves.

"We were always looking for base metals—copper, zinc— and deposits of that type are usually very huge and very expensive to exploit," Mauro explains. "You're looking at several hundreds of millions of dollars to exploit them. We felt that with gold deposits being smaller and less capital-intensive, it might be possible for a junior company like our own to finance the exploitation."

They also shared another theory: that there was more gold to be had in the hills of Nevada and California. It was on these assumptions that the partners formalized their efforts in ABM Mining Group in 1978 and established their twelve-year plan.

"That was when we started using the Vancouver Stock Exchange," Chuck relates. "We formed the first company we ever did together, called it Inca Resources. We raised the money on the VSE and went into the United States.

"We searched the entire state of Nevada and found absolutely nothing. But we did end up as a result of that in the state of California and we made a discovery at Rich Gulch." Other major acquisitions like Jamestown and Pinetree followed soon after.

The Jamestown Gold Mine, trading under Sonora Gold Corporation, is located seventy miles east of Sacramento. It represents one of the largest known gold reserves in the U.S.A., with reserves estimated in excess of $1.55 billion dollars. The Pinetree project is being developed by Goldenbell Mining Corporation on the site where Kit Carson discovered gold deposits in 1849. It is just one of four development sites in the area and this property alone is expected to yield 75,000 to 150,000 ounces of gold per year.

"We now have in inventory over 6 million ounces of proven gold acquired since 1978. And our goal is to get it up to 10 million ounces and that would be one of the largest gold reserves in North America under one management group," Chuck says. In Sonora Gold Corporation alone there are total reserved of 3.7 million ounces, which is more that the entire known reserved today of all the mining companies in B.C. With these properties, the long-term goals have become a reality.

There is an element of unreality in the thought of the most famous gold region in North America lying untouched and inactive, waiting for two engineers from Canada to walk in and put their names on it. . . .

Chuck explains.

"Historically, Canadians are used to working in remote areas where an infrastructure is not present. You establish a base

camp with tent-frames and tents within a fixed-wing or heli-
copter commute to, say, Yellowknife. It might be 200 miles
north-northeast of Yellowknife. Then you start to go about your
work of mining exploration.

"When you go to the States you find you don't have to do all
that. You drive up in your car and you get out with your city
clothes on and you start to prospect.

"So, if you're a company trying to develop your first series of
producing mines, you've got to locate yourself in a region that
has geographic potential and also doesn't require the enormous
infrastructure costs that would be required for remote mines,
because you can't raise enough money to do both."

Mining in California had been interrupted by the Second
World War and had just not started up again. During that period tighter environmental restrictions were put into effect,
sufficient to discourage most ideas about mining those areas by
traditional methods. Yet the place to look for deposits is where
major deposits have been found in the past.

"There was a tremendous amount of gold production in the
state starting in about 1849 during the Gold Rush," Chuck continues. "The state produced well over a hundred million ounces
and it was at one time the largest gold-producing state in the
Union. Now, I think, Nevada would claim that honour and California is 'way down the list. But California itself has not had
the advantage of using post-war equipment developments like
big-truck/open pit technology on its gold deposits. This is the
first time, the very first time, that California has been looked
on in the gold-mining sector as a source of large-tonnage, low-
grade gold deposits and we're one of the first groups to do that."

It's as simple as that.

Chuck compares today's low-grade, large-tonnage gold development to the early copper development in British Columbia.

"A good example is Bethlehem Copper. Spud Huestis ran it
in those days. People told him he could never mine copper at
that low a grade and those big tonnages and make any money.
And, of course, he did. It set the basis for the Porphyry Copper
Mine development which went into the sixties and seventies.
There was a solid fifteen years of good development there which

formed a basis for some of your larger corporations in the province today. Noranda. Placer Developments. Teck Corporation. The list goes on."

He points to a phenomenon that has changed attitudes and sparked growth at the Vancouver Stock Exchange in recent years. As copper and molybdenum have settled off in price, a pool of technical and financial skill has been freed up and made available to the smaller, younger companies.

"These people are finding their way into the junior companies for the first time since I've been in the business," he explains. "And it's that combination of high technical skill coupled with ability to raise money on the VSE that has created a solid basis for the development of major mining projects around the world.

"In years past, you see, the people primarily involved in the Vancouver Stock Exchange were non-technical people. The attitude was, 'It's beneath my dignity to be so professionally trained and educated and yet deal with the hucksters in the pits selling shares.' That's changed."

It is now acknowledged that both technical competence and financial skill are needed to be successful. "What we say here," Chuck refers to his own company, "is that the technical skill and the money must be in the same pocket."

ABM exemplifies that downscale, sporty corporate model where the owners are still capable of having a thorough personal understanding of every facet of the company, like Sir Francis Bacon, the last man of complete knowledge. Both partners are geophysical engineers with exceptional financial acumen. But, because of their different temperaments, while Chuck Ager is astounding one with the utter simplicity of it all Mauro Berretta will be pointing out the complexities.

"That's probably why we get along so well," Mauro says with a smile. "What he does best I usually don't like to do, and vice versa. He couldn't stand what I do. Chuck is the trendsetter, the pacesetter. He sets the direction, and supplies the optimism and the get-up-and-go. I like that, too, but only to a point; I look after the paperwork and make sure everything's okay with the regulatory bodies."

Mauro watches the money, making sure the cash flows as it should. Their similar technical background allows them both to make their own technical assessments. He explains, "We established a policy a long time ago of doing everything unanimously. If one isn't sure, we can't do the deal. It's worked well so far."

Chuck skips happily over details like California's environmental controls, land acquisition, and permits. Mauro, on the other hand, enjoys the challenges they represent.

"Yes, California is tough," he concedes. "It's probably one of the toughest states to get permits in. It's not impossible though; we've got them. Everybody thinks that California's just movie stars and palm trees. But you get up in the Sierras and eastern mountains and you find it's very much like B.C.—mountainous, rugged. Logging is the main industry. All those small-town areas are fairly depressed right now because of unemployment. Mining is seen as actually very welcome, as long as you do it right.

"We found, when we went to the States, that you can't just go out and stake claims like you do here because land has been owned for many, many years—generations. The way you acquire land there is by making deals with the owners for the mineral rights and it takes anywhere from one to three years to acquire a package of land. But once you have that, the geological environment is certainly very favorable. California is a beautiful 'province.'"

As to the laws that ensure it stays that way, Mauro comments, "We can live with those restrictions," adding that with about twenty-five million people in California, all the operations are inevitably close to populated areas.

"You can't just dump anywhere. You have to clean up the environment and make sure that it's protected, and we're doing that. It's costing money. Our engineers have come up with some new techniques for disposal of tailings, for example, that is environmentally leak-proof."

Where mined-out pits were traditionally abandoned to fill with water naturally and develop regrowth, current regulations demand the presentation of a revitalization plan before production even begins.

"So, you landscape the benches or edges and you've got lake front property. It's worth more than the gold, probably!" Mauro believes that it is simply good business to be seen as socially and environmentally conscious, especially for a public company. But he is also quick to point out that what they are doing is no different from what is done in other mining operations. "I don't think we're unique in this." It is part of today's corporate culture.

Mauro is in *his* usual working pose, sitting up to his desk, businesslike and formal, smoking as he talks in a quiet, precise manner. He is apparently unmindful of the shouting coming from the next office; that's just his partner on the phone.

Born in Italy in 1942 and raised in Windsor, Ontario, from the time he was twelve, Mauro chose the University of British Columbia for his geophysics studies for the sole purpose of seeing another part of Canada. It was love at first sight.

"That was it," he says of his first view of Vancouver. "There was no way I was going to go back. I realized this was where I wanted to live."

Mauro is one of Vancouver's biggest fans and it's not just because he can get away on his boat at every possible opportunity. "I think the VSE is the lifeblood of the entrepreneurial spirit, at least in western Canada if not in all of Canada. I've spent a lot of time in Toronto and you see nothing, nothing at all in the way of free enterprise spirit there that you see here.

"Oh, yes, they have their success stories back there too, like the empire built by the Reichmanns, but you're looking at multi-billion successes by people who were already wealthy to begin with. I'm talking about people who start up an idea from nothing and build it up to something very substantial. I think Vancouver is the best place in the world for that.

"If the politicians in this province play their cards right, I see no reason why it couldn't become, not just in our opinion but in everybody's opinion, the venture capital of the world. It could be another Hong Kong or another Switzerland. I hope they never change that."

Chuck agrees.

"We're now on the verge of becoming a major financial

centre. We are one now but we're not quite mature. We're still viewed as 'From Vancouver? Ha Ha Ha' in other places. But in the mining sector, for example, the majority of mining exploration work done in the western U.S.A. is funded out of Canada. Most of the funding is done in Vancouver for that. And that's quite a change from the past."

He points to major-funding power plays for eastern operations, like Hemlo, that were done in Vancouver. He sees an increasing number of his California contacts turning up in Vancouver.

"The greatness of this city is that you can take an entrepreneur and introduce him to a financial guy and they can actually go out and do something." Five years ago, according to Chuck, he and Mauro were considered oddballs. Now they are on their way to building a company in the image of Placer Developments or Teck Corporation. Their strategy is to accumulate, not trade in, stock. They buy their share position at the earliest point and keep it ("We still have our position in the first company we ever formed") gradually amassing properties that will start to reach their full potential five or ten years down the road.

This meshes with their world view of gold values.

Chuck: "I think that gold is in for a long-haul use, or some monetarization of it. I'm not saying we're going to go back on the gold standard or anything like that. I'm saying that gold is going to be perceived as a store of value and as a mechanism for weighing currencies somehow. I don't know how. But we've got to have some damn stability out there."

It was never a consideration that ABM should be anything less than one hundred per cent successful. They mapped out their future and established ground rules for the trip. They have tracked every mining deal in Vancouver, and still do, to a point where they have developed an instinct for prediction that, according to Chuck, is right eight times out of ten.

The first rule set up was never to lose sight of where they were heading. Building on that plan, day after day, year after year, a solid foundation and operational agility have resulted.

"We demand that each problem have three solutions and we operate with the first solution. If it won't work we replace it immediately with the second, and find a third one to follow that up. We're never caught off guard wondering what to do next."

Chuck admits they've been on the verge of bankruptcy many times, but "What entrepreneur hasn't?" he asks.

"You're always on the edge," he reasons. "You're pushing to the limits of your organization and you never know when you overstep it.

"But we also have a policy here: no debt. And that's our safeguard. Zero debt."

While remaining tightly focussed on the long term, Chuck advocates staying loose on the short term.

"One of the biggest mistakes is to try to build your schedule six months in advance. You have to be able to leave this afternoon at three o'clock to do something if it's that important. If you're precommitted or can't respond, it will probably mean you'll lose a window of opportunity, which will mean you won't make progress. Nothing happens according to schedule. It never has here! It happens sort of on its own and you respond and help it to continue.

"The key word is control. Most of the things in the business world you can't control. There's a small part you can, and it you can control that sufficiently well, you can achieve. That requires perception of the past and anticipation of the future, but mostly it requires now-ness in your decision making. You've got to be an 'on now' person."

Len Ralph, ABM's in-house securities and exchange regulations expert, remembers his job interview with Chuck Ager. Taking the job opportunity very seriously and conscious of the necessity of making a good impression, Len was slightly nonplussed that his interviewer should have his feet up on the desk, treating the situation so casually.

The details aside, Chuck asked Len if the position interested him. Len replied that he would like to have some time to think it over. "Fine," Chuck replied, "but I'm hiring someone tomorrow, so don't take too long." Len called the next morning and accepted the job.

That sense of spontaneity keeps the work fun and has contributed to a very loyal and highly motivated staff. The partners may suddenly decide a deal is cause to celebrate, and take the entire staff on a harbour cruise. The Christmas party could just as easily be held in Sacramento, with all employees and their spouses flown down for three days to tour one of the projects.

The business is all-consuming in their lives. It is only recently that Chuck and Mauro have felt they could gear down from seven-day work weeks to six-day work weeks. Mauro maintains, however, that the change is more due to the efficiency gained with experience. After you've been at it awhile you can complete the same work in less time.

Both partners have FAX telecopiers in their offices at home and after hours they continue communicating with each other and associates around the world. They try to take advantage of their heavy travel schedules by combining family time with travel.

"We're used to coming from all directions for a weekend," Chuck says. "We're international in our view and so is my family. They'll go anywhere, anytime, on a moment's notice."

When a survey project in Japan several years ago threatened to keep Chuck overseas for several weeks, the whole family went along and formed a crew. After the survey work was finished, they toured Asia and the Far East.

"I think the family of any entrepreneur has to be very flexible. They have to be willing to accept the fact that they're in business as a family unit. My whole family is in business with me; it's nothing short of that. It's a lifestyle. There is no boundary in this business; as long as you're awake, you're in business. That's it, and I think it's great. I think you get far more satisfaction because it's a lifestyle you're pursuing. It's a great motivation for you, as an individual and as a family."

He pauses to flash a huge grin.

"That's how we are. We entrepreneurs are all the same. . . . Crazy, I guess."

CHAPTER 19

Arthur Fisher

The flight of the swan

He was driving a country road somewhere in Western Australia's outback. He was not even looking for gold, mineralization, or even promising terrain. Arthur Fisher was simply on holiday, getting away from Vancouver's rain for a while. But he saw all these old blokes, like fugitives from a retirement home. They were walking around on a rocky outcropping up and down beside the road, testing the ground with metal detectors. It was an area of white spread gold mineralization, Fisher noted. He saw, too, that some of the blokes even seemed to be picking up nuggets. And before you could say, "Good on yer, mate," Fisher forgot about his holiday.

A few enquiries, and Fisher did two things: he obtained detailed plans of the area in Perth—the terrain was somewhat like that of Timmins—and optioned as much land as he could for a deposit of $6,000 on two separate properties. Next he went to Southern Ventures, a prominent Australian mining company, to talk about a partnership deal.

After twenty years' experience in the mining industry, Fisher's instinct suggested that the best course was to develop a joint venture with local talent. This has since proven to have been excellent strategy.

And then Fisher returned to Vancouver, a quiet vacationer who had just drawn a line around a future gold mine as easily as most tourists might play a pinball machine. The mine would be called Black Swan Gold Mines, Ltd.

Within four years Black Swan had announced production at its Gabanintha location in Western Australia (the area of the rocky outcrop), and was carrying out exploratory drilling at an even more promising property, the Merriland site in Queensland. Black Swan stock, listed on the Vancouver Stock Exchange by that time, was trading at $7, having surged in the previous year from a low of 40 cents. It seemed that Arthur Fisher, late of Edinburgh, Cape Town, and Toronto, had made a canny move.

But the experience dredged up from years in those other cities, other mines, went back a long way.

Growing up in Edinburgh, Fisher graduated from a good school (George Heriot's) and decided to go to university. It occurred to him that everyone he knew studied either medicine or engineering.

"No one that I knew of," says Fisher, "was prepared to put me through medical school. On the other hand, Anglo-American Corporation of South Africa had offered to do just that for me." [In the engineering field.]

That was the sort of joint venture, even in those years, that appealed to Fisher's sense of value. In other words, not only did he win a complete scholarship from that mining company (part of the DeBeers organization, and the largest in the world), but on his graduation in 1963, the package was still in operation: Anglo-American packed him off to South Africa and a job. Nor did the partnership end there. Just as in the armed forces, of which he had had a taste in the R.A.F. reserve and where he had taken pilot training for three years while an undergraduate, after five years Fisher was "rotated" back home, put through a business administration course, and then re-routed to South Africa again. Considerably more productive, from the point of view of a career, than removing tonsils. Fisher had to admit that up to now the big-company life was not hard to take.

Fisher, the future Canadian carpetbagger in Australia, was exposed to all aspects of mining in South Africa, the country probably most seasoned in its approach to precious-metal extraction, with a century of deep-mine development. Most of his time was spent in the field in all aspects of production in the gold and diamond mines of Southwest Africa, and he was finally placed in charge of production at labour-intensive mines involving 10,000 people mining an orebody 3,000 feet below surface, producing 10,000 tons of ore per day.

It was an immense experience, not to be quite duplicated anywhere else in the world.

When did it begin to pall?

"It didn't, actually," says Fisher, a six-foot robust figure, his black hair not yet touched with grey, "It was very rewarding in all respects, and very challenging. But there were other factors."

The political situation, for example. With two growing children, consideration had to be given as to where they should grow up. On one occasion, just adjacent to where the Fishers lived, twenty-eight persons were killed in a single riot.

Like a timely omen, Fisher was sent on a Commonwealth Mining Congress that toured Canada in 1974.

"Everything about Canada impressed me tremendously," says Fisher. "Everything. Perhaps most of all, there was this sense of security—of safety—which can never be fully appreciated by one who hasn't seen the reverse. Security of course is taken for granted here, and it simply cannot be in other places in the world, notably South Africa. And another thing that made a deep impression was the air of prosperity in Canada, even though the mid-seventies weren't particularly thriving economically."

Fisher's reaction to Toronto was that it was hot and sticky, and that somewhat dampened his realization that this was the economic and financial heart of the nation. "Vancouver, however, was like the promised land," he adds. "But there wasn't a great deal I could do about that, since I didn't have any way to obtain work in Vancouver."

Miraculously, considering that he had not devoted much time to promoting himself, Fisher was offered a position with a well-known mining consultancy in Toronto, David Robertson and Associates, through the Technical Service Council, the Toronto engineering placement organization.

The offer forced him to engage in some introspection, to consider his real position, quite apart from family and other considerations. He had never before this allowed himself the luxury of questioning what he wanted to do. Although he had been at it for some twelve years, with a huge organization, Fisher now decided that he was not a good company man.

"My father was a small businessman in Edinburgh," says Fisher. "My brothers were entrepreneurs, and I felt akin to that in spirit myself. While I had worked for years for Anglo-American, a mining company among the world's largest, I could honestly say I was not the type to suffer fools gladly, especially those in positions senior to mine."

And the fact was that in South Africa one does not simply become a mining entrepreneur, start one's own gold mine, find an ore body and go public. Not with most of the mineralization 700 feet straight down. That is just one of the reasons why, though the B.C. mining climate may be satirized in some quarters, it seems like an Elysian field to mining men from other places in the world. "When I left South Africa," says Goldsil's Donald Busby, "I concluded that Vancouver was one of the few places —perhaps the only place—in the world to be a mining developer."

Arthur Fisher agrees, but admits that in his case the dislocation and relocation process took longer. When he had passed the philosophical barrier and firmed up the Toronto offer, he spent four months in the U.K. settling affairs and arranging his family's migration. Then it was out of the frying pan and into the fire—from the point of view of climate—in Toronto.

But the period with David Robertson and Associates was highly rewarding for Fisher. His training and experience with the Anglo-American organization had been world-class for that type of mining, but with David Robertson, he was introduced to all kinds of mining operations in literally every part of the world. For the five years from 1975 to 1980, he was a consultant on Saskatchewan potash, uranium for the European Economic Community, asbestos in Quebec and coal mines in the eastern U.S.

"I got a pretty wide view of mining," says Fisher, "particularly throughout North America—from New Mexico to Greenland."

His inclination was more and more toward the Vancouver brand of entrepreneurship, less and less toward the Toronto style of interest in the major mining companies. While mining consulting was in a sense working for himself, whether with the Toronto consultancy or later with his own firm, Arthur T. Fisher & Associates, his principal objective was to create his own mining company—to explore, to find ore and develop it to commercial production—the goal of all legitimate mining entrepreneurs.

Meanwhile, he did the next best thing, acting as consultant for companies such as B.C. Resources Investment Corporation, which replaced Kaiser Resources in the western export-coal business.

When the consultancy finally recognized the need to open a western branch office, they established Fisher in Calgary, not Vancouver. That was an improvement, perhaps, but reflected the Toronto opinion that Calgary was a thriving resource city while Vancouver was a casino town.

Predictably, little of Fisher's work was centred on Calgary anyway, and he roamed widely, doing business in Mexico, the western States, and Vancouver. That was in 1979.

One day, out of the blue, the Technical Service Council manager in Vancouver phoned him.

"Arthur," he asked, "do you know where I could find a vice-president operations for Erickson Gold Mines?"

"Speaking," said Fisher, and started to clean out his desk.

The success of Erickson Gold Mining Corporation of Vancouver between 1980 and 1985 was largely the result of Fisher's superlative operational experience. As vice-president mining, he exercised direct control over the Erickson Gold Mine in the Cassiar area of northern B.C., and supervised the design and construction of the Mount Skukum Gold Mine in the Yukon. The properties, widely separated, were almost twin operations, handling 300 tons per day each at an average head grade of 0.50 ounces of gold per ton.

During this period, Fisher also evaluated target situations identified by the exploration arm of the company, and assessed other properties which the company reviewed from time to time.

"Arthur was largely responsible for bringing in the Mount Skukum project in the Yukon," says Fred Davidson, formerly a colleague in the Erickson organization. "In addition to being a top-notch operations man, he also has a unique ability to raise money (something that isn't widely appreciated) and he's a thoroughgoing salesman."

When Fisher joined Erickson it was not a large organization, its Cassiar gold mine in northwestern B.C.(which was forty-five per cent owned) being its flagship. But by the middle of the decade, Erickson had changed hands. Total Compagnie Francaise, a large oil company, had acquired a sixty per cent control block through a subsidiary, thereby literally putting some much-needed fat on Erickson's bones. The name of the new western Canadian entity became Total Erickson Resources.

Fisher had not remained to see the consummation of the deal. Erickson, which he had joined when the price of gold was $200 an ounce, was now benefiting from bullion prices at four times that level—but Fisher had left for yellower pastures. Already he had seen the colour of Australia's outback, and was back in Vancouver eager to convert his Black Swan into a born-again duckling.

In fact, on returning from his truncated Aussie holiday, Fisher's first stop was Total Erickson, where he made his former management colleagues an offer they didn't pick up. It was a bargain— $250,000 would get them half of two properties, while Swan and Southern Ventures would retain the other half. Erickson declined—Australia, after all, was not Vancouver Island. However, some of the individuals in Erickson's management group, such as Fred Davidson, became substantial shareholders—shareholders, no doubt, who were believers in Arthur Fisher and his judgment rather than in a remote outcropping "down under."

This individual response encouraged Fisher to try a different tack. With a group of close friends he subscribed $150,000, sufficient to budget through most of 1983 in a drilling program, proving up the Gabanintha property in Western Australia.

The following year, in 1984, Black Swan went public on the Vancouver Stock Exchange, raising an additional $400,000. This was enough to retain a fifty-one per cent interest in the two properties, which had now developed to the point where there appeared to be every likelihood that production would be commenced within two or three years.

"I couldn't be more impressed with the Vancouver Stock Exchange," says Fisher. "It's a unique capital-raising institution. There's no other place I'm aware of where a small group of entrepreneurs like ourselves could have launched a company such as this—certainly not South Africa, England—even Toronto."

As a result, Fisher and his group found themselves with an excellent little company, with promising projects and an enthusiastic management group that included Jack Jefferson, a former partner in a venture-capital organization. In addition, Black Swan had issued very little equity to attain its current position.

Within the next year, Black Swan management had added another property, in the Merriland area of Queensland, where the neighbours in the mining industry looked impressive—it was close to the huge Placer Kidston mine, producing over 200,000 ounces of gold per year, and it was also near a Noranda Pacific location.

The Merriland site looked even better than Gabanintha, with grades and the probable tonnage being slowly unveiled with the likelihood of an eventual production potential of 50,000 to 60,000 ounces of gold per annum. The Merriland property, incidentally, was farmed out by Esso under an agreement whereby Black Swan initially earned a fifty per cent interest with the expenditure of $50,000, and from this position could increase its interest to 100% by spending an additional $4 million.

Jack Jefferson had assumed the office of president early in the company's existence; he resigned to make way for Fisher early in 1986. "It was just the right progression," says Fred Davidson. "Jack was an excellent organizational and financial man, with of course legal background as well. And with the company evolving so rapidly, he was the first to suggest that what was needed was Arthur's immense experience in mining operations and his other specialties. Both Jack and Arthur had unique talents that, in turn, advanced the company rapidly."

The Australian financial press had already begun to thump the drum about the "next big gold-rush" in Queensland while the Merriland development was taking place. With verbiage reminiscent of the media in B.C., Nevada, and California, the Australian press was touting areas that had once been the sites of gold producers, but which since had degenerated into ghost towns. In the former gold-rush town of Charters Towers, there is the well preserved "ghost of the last great gold era;" the town has the shells of former banks, hotels and even a stock exchange.

The Charters Towers area is at the centre of a gold renaissance that includes potential producers of 500,000 ounces of gold per annum, led by the largest Australian gold mine, Placer Development's Kidston site, which alone is responsible for 200,000 ounces annually. This is the area in which Swan's Merriland property is located.

Most of the new fever stems from the fact that, while the 1850s, 1890s and the 1930s in this area demonstrated all the manic behaviour of California in those eras, the renaissance now going on does so against a backdrop of $400 gold.

There are other factors, particularly Australian, says Fisher, which brighten the picture even more, and suggest why Black Swan should devote its efforts to this island continent rather than to Nevada or the B.C. Interior.

First and foremost, he adds, with his Scots nature bubbling to the top like gold in a leach tank, there is the low cost structure evident in Australia. Recovery approximates US$100 per ounce in most Australian locations, far below North American costs of production which range all the way up to US$200 an ounce and beyond.

Even before that stage is reached, the costs of exploration in Australia, bringing gold to the "reserve" category, tend to run about CDN$7 per ounce. Establishing reserves in North America may incur costs as high as CDN$50 per ounce. The other major cost factor—capital cost for the processing plant— is also extremely low in Australia, due to well-established technology.

There are other clear advantages in exploring and developing in Australia compared with North America, says Fisher. Australia is noted for its widespread occurrence of surface-oxidized gold deposits, which on average bear a relatively high grade (substantially 0.1—0.15 ounces of gold per ton).

In addition, the combination of the fact that Australia is relatively unexplored compared with similar areas of North America, and the fact that there is a relatively low risk of environmental problems, gives the exploration and development company *carte blanche* to a degree.

And finally, says Fisher, there are two financial factors that are highly advantageous. First, exchange rates are such that the value of the Australian dollar against gold has produced a relatively high gold price that is the equivalent of the previous high for gold (about AUS$700 per ounce). Second, at least at the moment, profit on gold-mining operations is not taxed in Australia.

The increasing solidity that Fisher and his management group have built into Black Swan, until mid 1986 little more than a speculation in Australian exploration, reflects Fisher's world-wide experience in all phases of mining engineering.

"When we began," says Ross Glanville, Black Swan director and secretary, and a former vice-president of Wright Engineers in Vancouver, "Arthur and I had other commitments that precluded our devoting full time to the company. Despite his own corporate and legal responsibilities, Jack Jefferson ran the company as president for more than two years, doing a superlative legal and administrative job. But there came a time when Black

Swan had developed to the point, Jack recognized, where its needs were no longer organizational so much as operational, and what was needed most was a chief executive with senior mining capability. Jack prevailed upon Arthur to assume the presidency."

Fisher succeeded Jefferson as president in April 1986, while Jefferson remained as a director and treasurer of the company. At that time Fisher emphasized the fact that Jefferson's careful guidance as president, particularly in a legal capacity, had insured the company's being brought through incorporation and public status in financially sound condition, while the Australian properties had been just as competently assembled.

Part of the cohesion of the Swan management group, according to Glanville, stems from the character of Fisher both as a person and as a professional.

"Arthur is basically an entrepreneurial personality," says Glanville."He'll tell you he doesn't like big companies, although he obviously acquired much of his expertise in twenty years with a world-class company."

The two factors—the entrepreneurial nature and the professional skill—merge naturally in Fisher's sturdy character.

"He has an easy-going personality," says Glanville, "but he displays confidence, even a sort of aggressive approach to business situations. Arthur embodies several diverse talents. He's an extremely competent engineer and a top-notch financial man. He's large enough to encompass all these things."

Management, particularly Fisher, Jefferson, and Glanville, relate well in a business sense, says Glanville, especially since they are really more than associates.

"We discuss," he says. "We don't always agree on things, but we are friends. Again, Arthur's personality figures largely in the ambience around Swan."

The history of the company is indicative of the character of its senior management. Incorporated in 1983, shortly after Arthur Fisher's holiday in Australia, Black Swan at first directed its efforts to developing the Gabanintha and Grant's Creek properties in Western Australia, largely by private subscription. A small public issue followed in late 1984, with the conclusion of a preliminary drilling program that earned out a fifty-one per cent position in both properties.

From the beginning, the avowed strategy of Black Swan management was the development of Australian properties, employing Australian joint-venture partners ultimately to bring the properties to production. That strategy has continued with the subsequent Merriland and Whitelead acquisitions.

Emphasis was placed on Gabanintha first, since that project was furthest along in development, two distinct drilling programs having continued to encourage management. The dual objectives of speeding development toward production and broadening reserves were felt to have been best served by the inclusion of a seasoned Australian drilling partner—Dominion Gold Mining of Perth, which comprised the former management of Anaconda's Australian operations. (Another example of the notable number of instances where contemporary mining has been strengthened by the abdication of the Anaconda organization from all its mining operations, not only in North America.)

Dominion Gold, in any event, farmed in as to fifty per cent in late 1985, with an agreement to pay Black Swan and Southern Ventures $625,000 each in instalments, commencing in May 1986. As the operating company, Dominion Gold since the beginning of the agreement has expanded the effective claim area tenfold. On the basis of this expansion, indicated ore reserves were increased to a total of 1.6 million tons grading an average of 0.13 ounces of gold per ton, literally rendering Swan not only feasible but a substantial mining property.

Moving toward production at Gabanintha, Fisher and his management group anticipated a construction cost of AUS$10 million to construct a 1,000 ton-per-day operation. This should provide about 40,000 ounces of gold in annual production, 10,000 to the account of Black Swan. On that basis alone, production by the vat-leaching process was expected to produce earnings of 70 cents a share fully diluted for Black Swan, indicating a promising level for the stock (say $7—a level that has

already been reached), especially for such a young junior mining company. Those figures were predicated on an average gold
price of US$400 an ounce.

It was clear that for a narrowly-based company such as Black
Swan, Fisher's strategy of bringing in a substantial and experienced Australian partner was sound, even though it necessitated reducing the company's interest to twenty-five per cent.
Both the influx of capital and the farming out of drilling prove
the point, since Swan was not only small but "a stranger in a
strange land."

Junior mining companies in touch with interesting properties
have only two developmental alternatives: they may issue stock
to finance the necessary development, or they may sell an interest in the property, either for cash or in the form of farm-in
work performed. Although the size of a young company's ore
body is not often a finite quantity, the company's treasury is.
Practice, accordingly, tends to lean toward the use of the property as a marketing device. After all, too often companies have
reached production only to find that too much of their stock has
been dealt away. And what will it profit a company to gain a
mine if it dilutes its control?

But Steven Semeniuk, research director for Odlum Brown
Ltd. in Vancouver, believes that the Merriland prospect in
Queensland represents Fisher's most intriguing gambit in Australia. Bracketed between Noranda's Australian property at Mt.
Leyshon (certain to become at least a 40,000-ounce producer)
and Pajingo, where a company known as Battle Mountain is
readying a 60,000-ounce facility, it is generally felt that the
Merriland site needs only developmental work to take its place
as a substantial producer. Again the question presents itself as
to which is the better route—self-financing or farming out? For
Merriland, financing may not be a problem.

Arthur Fisher as a matter of policy does not shrink from either route. As a mining engineer, he has demonstrated a surprising agility in finance. "Arthur recently arranged a private
placement," says Glanville. "Would you believe Denmark?"

Semeniuk believes that Black Swan is in a comfortable position, considering its status as a small, untried junior, the sort of

company that is usually constantly struggling with financing. With a buoyant cash position and forward commitments well within budgeted limits, Gabanintha's impending production would likely be totally bankable. This, however, may not be necessary.

In a review of developments near mid 1987, Fisher informed shareholders that sufficient equity capital had been raised to bring Gabanintha to production and to carry forward the considerable programs planned for Merriland, Whitelead Dam and Grant's Creek, all without recourse to bank financing. It was a substantial accomplishment for a company that only one year previously had held interest in those properties, viewing them as "interesting geological prospects." Now, two of them were within months of production.

And once that initial production is achieved, reasons Semeniuk, cash flow should level out at CDN$3.5 million, most of which will flow directly to earnings, thanks to the kind Australian tax collector. In turn, that flow of revenue may be used to finance the bringing of the other properties to production.

Still another property has been added to the Swan portfolio recently, this time by farming in on a site owned by Dominion Gold Operations Pty. Ltd. in Queensland. Known as the Brovinia property, this location will see Black Swan expend AUS$50,000 in a development program during 1987. Subsequent to the completion of this program, if the company elects to fund the required property expenditures of AUS$65,000 , it will thereby earn a fifty per cent interest in the property.

For Arthur Fisher, the next phase for Black Swan is quite apparent. With a respectable share price, and the advent of solid cash flow, Fisher expects that his company will be well positioned to take advantage of "larger and increasingly interesting projects in the coming years."

"I think you will see Black Swan as a much larger company in the not too distant future," sums up broker Douglas Miller of Brink Hudson & Lefever in Vancouver.

But there is in some way an air of urgency about the whole

exercise, a sense that somehow the strong gold market driving all this activity may not last. Can this universal belief in the supremacy of gold go on forever?

"Well, gold won't go *up* forever," says Fisher. "Fifteen years ago I was in gold, but I was in everything else as well. Today base metals have nothing to drive them forward. So precious metals are the only game. But the amount of money being spent will surely find a lot of gold—with predictable results."

As Ian McAvity, the Toronto chartist, puts it, everyone seems to be hanging around for the last dance.

But until that happens, Arthur Fisher will continue to react the way he did on that day when he saw old men poking at apparently barren ground.

Since that day in Western Australia several years ago, Fisher has joined a significant movement. The gold rush that has taken place and is still taking place in Australia, says the *London Mining Journal*, is far more pronounced than its counterpart in North America, because of more profound change and more basic stimuli.

In the past, Australian gold mining was undertaken by large companies underground. The significant happening today is the exploitation of surface mineralization by small companies. The success rate of such ventures has been impressive and the outlook is even better. Low grades and modest reserves are acceptable because of contemporary technology and the modest requirements of these junior players—and, of course, because of AUS$700 gold.

Ironically, Arthur Fisher, steeped in the culture of the super-large corporation for twenty years in Europe and South Africa, and more recently the product of Canadian venture capital and entrepreneurship as practised in Vancouver, is the prototype Australian mining developer.

Fisher's company in fact answers the *London Mining Journal*'s description of the Australian success theorem, recently put forth: " . . . able to 'think small' and react quickly to opportunities when they arise because there is no complex management structure or bureaucratic inefficiency to overcome . . . such a venture has low capital cost . . . and external financing requirements are generally modest and funds on this scale are usually raised fairly easily . . . in a nutshell, this is how gold mining is being re-established in Western Australia today."

And it is also how Arthur Fisher's Black Swan took flight.

———

CHAPTER 20

Bob Friedland

Howe Street guru

He arrived in Vancouver early in 1982, a slight but charismatic figure, with penetrating eyes and a shock of hair reminiscent of the sixties that had produced him. Robert Friedland was unknown on Howe Street and entirely without associations or experience in the mining industry.

Similarly, the company he was to launch, Galactic Resources Limited, which went public on the Vancouver Stock Exchange in mid 1982 at 50 cents per share, had little capital, no property and no management. In a word, it was typical of the hundreds of penny hopefuls that had been listed on the VSE throughout the seventy-five years of the latter's existence.

Typical in all respects except one: it had as its founder and president a very unusual entrepreneur who at the age of thirty-four had resolved to create a major mining organization. And within five years, with a huge mountain ore body at Summitville, Colorado, and an infrastructure costing $30 million, Galactic had been established as one of the largest heap-leaching gold producers on the continent.

This bizarre, seemingly effortless, progression is a measure of the dynamic character of Robert Friedland, who had rotated 180 degrees from the ethic of the Flower Child generation, which had involved all his energy and kept him travelling during all of his life since leaving college.

Friedland grew up in Massachusetts, where his father was an eminent architect. He chose to attend Reed College in Oregon, and was graduated with distinction with a degree in political science. This was a typical discipline for those products of the sixties intent on saving—or at least improving—the world. He then launched on a medical career, but soon jettisoned it in favour of a lifestyle that at the time was much more important to him.

"My mother wanted each of us to study medicine," says Friedland. "Both my brother and I have entered the mining industry. Fortunately, my sister coming along third in line graduated in medicine."

His mother had little cause for disappointment, however. Leaving Reed College, Friedland traveled widely for some years, mostly in India and Nepal. One of his first observations was the extremely high incidence of blindness among the people of Nepal. He teamed up with Dr. Larry Brilliant (who later became the founder of NETI Technologies, another VSE *tour de force*) in founding the SEVA organization, which raised millions of dollars for the treatment of Nepal's widespread endemic blindness. SEVA continues today to raise millions annually in North America.

Friedland's self-imposed Far Eastern tour accomplished, he did a complete flip-flop, both geographically and in activity. Half-way around the world, he settled in Switzerland where an uncle was an international trader in commodities and currency. According to Friedland, this extreme reaction from his Far Eastern preoccupations was no doubt the result of the length and intensity of his involvement in the Far East, where he had learned six languages and absorbed much of the Eastern religious philosophies. In other words, it was high time for a change for someone still in his twenties who had much that he wanted to do and to learn.

This fortunate Swiss period in his life, when he began to apprentice in the business (or art) of international metals trading, was invaluable to him later when he was developing innovative financing vehicles in order to bring a major mine to production. And like mining impresario Bruce McDonald of Noramco Capital in Vancouver, who started his adult life as a floor trader on the Toronto Stock Exchange, Friedland's trading instincts, his sense of timing and value, had been sufficiently honed during his Swiss sojourn to benefit him in his later deal-making endeavours.

But he had no interest in a protracted stay in the capital centres. With his exercises in serving humanity and Mammon behind him, Friedland next decided it was time to embark on a career in business. He was after all entering his thirties by this time, and it was time to achieve some large commercial project that would offset his earlier ventures of the mind. Even metals trading was in a way more cerebral than physical. What he sought was a venture on a grand scale.

He chose the trading of timber tracts in the Pacific Northwestern States, just why nobody seems to be quite sure. Perhaps he was influenced by his uncle, whose interests seem to have figured in commodities of all kinds world-wide.

Friedland was a qualified success in the timber business, developing a mini-fortune that made him comfortable financially. But before that happened, an event took place on a quiet Sunday afternoon in Southern Oregon that he says was the most important single happening in his life to that point. Exploring what was known as the Old Warner Gold Mine, Friedland crawled into an ancient, partially collapsed portal—and was permanently bitten by the gold bug, an insidious insect that has driven men to the loss of their reason since the Pharaohs.

"You might say I literally entered the mining industry on my hands and knees," says Friedland. "From that day on, I really knew what I wanted to do—had to do. And in fact, it took a little while, but I remembered the one thing my father ever said to me about a vocation: 'Whatever you decide to do—do it *right*.'"

That simple admonition, as a matter of fact, recurs like a minor theme throughout Galactic's development to production —the acquisition of the best of equipment, hiring the best of consultants, bringing in the best management available. And the elder Friedland's advice was also consistent with the philosophy of concentration that Friedland had made his own in India.

There was, however, no high-flown moral or ethical justification for his entry into the gold-mining business.

"It would be just as logical," says Friedland, "to say that I was sucked into it. The generation of which I was a part—and a very enthusiastic part—mostly believed that commercial activities such as mining, *particularly* mining, were a composite of just about all the bad things in the world: ripping off nature, pollution, exploitation, and damaging the environment. But this sort of consideration, in human terms, pales when you have been confronted with real material poverty on a national scale. Nothing can be more degrading than that. And I had witnessed that spectacle for a good many years."

Nor does Friedland rank himself with those professional market bulls who see gold as representing everything from the ultimate source of wealth to a haven from perennial world insecurity.

"I see gold as a useful product," says Friedland. "I suppose Steve Jobs would describe it as an industry benchmark."

Perhaps the most significant event during Friedland's undergraduate years at Reed had been his meeting and friendship with Stephen Jobs, who later became the co-founder of Apple Computer. The influence of that friendship has remained with Friedland in different ways, most noticeably perhaps in the development of Friedland's own corporate philosophy as he proceeded to build his Galactic organization.

"We expect our products," said Jobs, in a report to Apple shareholders prior to his leaving the organization, "to be industry benchmarks, effectively redefining the field. Our ability to concentrate our resources on a single business has solidified our leadership."

The statement could have applied to Friedland's Galactic, changing words such as "products" and "business" to "precious metals" and "processes". Within five years of his first entering the mining industry, Friedland had added a substantial dimension to the already well-defined heap-leaching process, primarily in the sheer size of its operation.

"The attraction of the system," says Friedland, "lies in the power and the simplicity of the technology."

In addition, Friedland pioneered the offshore sourcing of sizable funds through instruments such as bullion loans made by European merchant bankers. He and financial entrepreneurs like Doug McRae and Chuck Ager set the standards that were to become a regular pattern within the following five years.

Thus armed with his rationale, Friedland, as noted, assaulted the towers of Howe Street. It is interesting to speculate what might have happened had Rupert Bullock, then B.C. Superintendent of Brokers, already installed the policy of having a committee of mining engineers pass qualitative judgment on new VSE mining issues.

Bullock's move came later, the only known instance of a securities regulator seeking to pass advice on to the investing public beyond the standard "full disclosure and let the buyer beware."

"I know it's unprecedented," said Bullock at the time, "but so is this particular stock exchange."

The point is, had that policy been in effect in 1983 when Friedland's Galactic came to market, sans property, sans capital, sans management, sans everything, it is quite likely the young entrepreneur would have been sent packing to Calgary or Spokane. But he was not, and a rapidly growing loyal host of Vancouver investors bought and sustained Galactic's market, even as Friedland set out to justify its strength.

In less than a year a second issue was priced at $3.93, still before the company had a lucrative property. And by 1984, Galactic stock saw a top of $13.25, before selling off in a substantial summer market reaction.

Meanwhile, Friedland had two major chores on his hands—to find an ore body that would do justice to his ambition, and to steep himself in the mining industry he had chosen, in order to make himself capable of handling such an ore body.

Quite unexpectedly Friedland received a phone call in Vancouver from Dr. William Bird, an outstanding geologist in Denver. It appeared the giant American company, Anaconda Minerals Company, having been acquired by ASARCO (American Smelting and Refining, Inc.), was divesting itself of most of its mining properties. One of them was at Summitville, Colorado, a huge low-grade gold-silver deposit possibly amenable to the heap-leaching process, making up in tonnage what it lacked in grade, and, because of the forced-sale nature of the situation, probably a bargain-basement beauty. Could it possibly be just Galactic's cup of tea?

It could, Friedland concluded, and jumped on an airplane. He was determined not to leave Colorado until the deal was tied up, and when he did take his departure he was the possessor of a site that literally blanketed the side of a mountain.

"The thing about Robert," says Bill Bird, "is that he likes to see things finalized before he goes on to something else."

Most people in that situation would have held a preliminary discussion, carefully noted all the options and then gone away to think about it and to consult professional advice. Friedland brought his professional advice with him, he could not see more than one option, and he did not want to delay the decision and risk anything happening to his deal.

He bought the huge Summitville property as the flagship project for Galactic. Friedland confesses that when he signed he had no idea where the millions he was committing were going to come from. (In actual fact he paid ASARCO just under $7 million for a mountainside that looked like a tract of World War I real estate on the Western Front.) Financing, it eventuated, was not a problem once Friedland developed his financial connections in the U.K., in Vancouver, and in San Francisco.

Located in the southwestern corner of Colorado, the town of Summitville was originally the product of an early Colorado gold camp, coming into being about 1870. Beginning as the site of a placer gold discovery, the town flourished when a rich lode deposit was discovered also on South Mountain, the site of the later Anaconda property purchased by Galactic.

Like many other North American gold camps, Summitville had petered out in the early forties, the result of a disastrous combination of $35 gold, dwindling and uneconomic grades, and a preoccupation with World War II by practically everybody. (In fact, it became a priority of war to shut down all marginal gold mines.)

In the years immediately preceding Friedland's blitzkrieg-like descent on Summitville, ASARCO and Anaconda had conducted a huge exploration and development campaign on the property which Bird, with a Ph.D. in geology, was quick to point out was an invaluable asset. Friedland paid a separate $600,000 for all data relating to the Summitville property, and it was probably the greatest bargain he would acquire in his mining lifetime.

"The beauty of this situation," says Friedland, "was that Anaconda knew exactly what they had after the extensive work they had done and they didn't know what to do with it."

What they had of course was a property of only marginal use by conventional mining standards, but a bonanza with the help of modern heap-leaching technology.

It was not that ASARCO and Anaconda were unaware of leaching technology—this after all was 1984, and practitioners like Ed Scholz and Chester Millar had been leaching in the wilderness for the better part of a decade. ASARCO's strategy at the most senior level was not to commit to any major developments of that kind. In fact, they were divesting themselves of almost all mining operations.

So, falling into an almost ready-made situation, Friedland found himself with data that revealed the results of 180,000 feet of drilling and pre-feasibility analysis. Some permitting had even been completed. The data told the Galactic management all they needed to know in terms of grades and tonnage. By the time Galactic's own bankable feasibility study was completed about a year later, those reserves and values had been increased to over 30 million tons grading an average of 0.03 ounces of gold per ton. The probability of further reserve increases was noted as highly likely.

The triumvirate necessary to any successful mining operation (property, management and capital) was rapidly assembled under Friedland's direction, an amazing feat in view of his, until recently, almost complete lack of expertise in the mining industry. Before he acquired his own management team, Friedland had taken on, as his chief geological consultant, Dr. Victor Hollister, virtually the dean of B.C. geologists. Eventually Hollister would be named a Galactic director, but initially Friedland simply wanted to learn from him.

"Vic is my mentor," says Friedland. "Everything I know about this industry I learned from him."

Friedland, however, had enough understanding of what he was doing to build an operating management team without parallel in heap-leaching technology, while he continued to exercise the incredible good judgment on major developments that was to take his junior resource company to major producing status in the course of four years. In addition, as chairman and chief executive officer, he continued to operate as principal fund-raiser for the company.

The first major appointment following the Summitville acquisition was that of Edward Roper as president and chief operating officer. For an individual under forty at that time (1985) Roper had impressive credentials. He had been pit boss at the giant Bethlehem Copper mine in the B.C. Interior. Subsequently, and perhaps more pertinent to his Galactic assignment, Roper had been resident manager of the Zortman and Landusky Mines of Pegasus Gold—one of the few prototype pioneer heap-leaching organizations in North America.

Close on the heels of that appointment Friedland named Robert Cook vice-president finance, the final vital area to be dealt with. Cook had been a senior vice-president with Cyprus Anvil and a specialist in project finance, an art that had become even more relevant to modern mining with the rapid development of projects, their brief life span, and the tendency for contemporary corporations of all kinds to be highly leveraged.

The pattern of Friedland's financial management is equally impressive and would do justice to a seasoned corporate finance team. It is obvious that Robert Cook was vitally involved in the financial planning that took Galactic from junior company to major producer, but Friedland's contribution is just as evident.

The overall strategy was that in the early stages of exploration and development, paralleling the need for a flow of funds, Friedland on three occasions issued common stock with warrants attached, at prices ranging from $5.50 up to $8.75. The value of "warrants attached" issues, particularly for a dynamic company where the stock is in a solid upward trend, is that they provide a delayed-release effect. With VSE issues, warrants are usually priced and dated for a relatively short period of time.

For example, with the issue of July 1985 two million shares were offered at a price of $8.875. Attached to each was a half warrant, two of which entitled the holder to buy a share at $9.50 up until December 24 of that year. The issue netted the company an immediate $17.75 million, plus, on or before December 24, an additional $9.5 million.

During 1985, with the onset of serious capital requirements for plant construction, leaching emplacements, on-site laboratories and other buildings, Friedland made two private placements of subordinated debentures with principals in the U.K., totaling $6.825 million. This was the first inclusion of funded debt on Galactic's balance sheet, but it was probably incurred to hold in check the rapid increase in the amount of stock the company had outstanding.

Finally, while it was recognized that the amount of equity outstanding had seriously eroded the position of major shareholders, the strategic wisdom of that course was vindicated when the major financing for complete mine and infrastructure installation became necessary in order to bring Summitville to production. The debt load, the debt-equity ratio that Galactic had maintained, now made it possible for Friedland to win from the Bank of America in San Francisco a $25 million capital loan, plus an additional working capital line of $6 million.

In April 1986, Galactic brought Summitville into its pre-productive phase with its property fully checked out as to feasibility, its balanced and capable management team operating at peak efficiency, adequate financing in place, right up to the pouring of the first Dore bullion, and with its balance sheet and capitalization in comfortable balance.

With near-perfect planning, Robert Friedland had taken his penny-stock company to the status of one of North America's foremost gold producers, with one of the best management teams in the industry, and in the process had raised well in excess of $100 million in order to realize that objective—all in less than four years!

One of the sidelights not often considered in the Galactic saga is the final, decisive contract that was completed with Bechtel Civil & Minerals Inc., one of the foremost engineering construction organizations in the world. The $21 million contract was for Bechtel to perform all engineering and construction services at the Summitville property necessary to bring it to production. The major elements included a crusher, a conveyor, leach pad circulating system, and recovery plant.

In actual fact this was no mere construction contract. With an organization of the calibre and reputation of Bechtel, the completion of operating-cost and recovery estimates constituted guarantees by Bechtel that would probably have been acted upon by any bank in the world. It undoubtedly was a significant factor in the financial package developed immediately afterward with the Bank of America.

Bechtel's total development plan forecast an average cost factor over the first five years of operation of US$165 an ounce, on the basis of production of 125,000 ounces of gold per annum and daily processing of 17,000 tons of ore.

Beyond question, Robert Friedland has achieved the stature of a senior mining executive, with his superlative ability to negotiate loans with international money-market institutions, his complete grasp of his mine's technical operation, and the proper activation of his top-drawer management team, together with his ceaseless search for new ventures that could carry the company on to even greater heights than those reached at Summitville. Still, it is fascinating to note, there remains in him the youthful, dedicated child of the Kennedy generation who was committed to creating a better world.

Are both these Friedlands real, or is there only one? It has been said he can be ruthlessly tough at a negotiating table, yet he can show even more concern over non-commercial subjects such as the environment.

Perhaps it's all a gigantic game to Friedland. On the future of

Summitville he once said, "Who knows, the mine life may only be five years. This may turn out to be a five-year statement on my part. And if that is so, what do we do with Summitville five years from now? Perhaps it will be a personal summit, capped by creating an elegant environmental sculpture—or perhaps a first-class ski resort."

Friedland may well convert his commercial achievements into landmarks of a different sort. And certainly he would likely be the first mining entrepreneur in history to develop a mine into an artistic or social statement. But that is not to say that Summitville will be his commercial swan song; the essential Friedland has an imperative to produce encores as well.

In fact, Friedland's progression in recent years has been from the drive to create a major mining company to that of developing it into a major corporation that builds mines. There's a difference here of more than emphasis, as his major accompishments of the past year have indicated.

Since Summitville went into production, Friedland's itinerary has been mind-boggling. First he made an extended trip to the Republic of China in late 1985. At that time, Friedland signed a letter of intent with Liu Lu Zhong, president of Xin-Jiang Non Ferrous Metals Corporation, for a joint venture between Galactic and the Chinese company to develop a huge project involving copper, nickel, cobalt, gold, silver, platinum and palladium over a vast area in Western China. Major gold projects may also figure in the joint venture.

Central to the agreement, which under Chinese joint-venture law allows the repatriation of profits by an offshore partner, it is expected that Galactic's heap-leaching expertise will be a major contributing factor.

"It appears," says Tony Garson, manager of research for Haywood Securities in Vancouver, "that the Asian window is open to the West in exchange for western mining technology. Galactic has an opportunity to participate in this interchange."

But the Chinese venture is just one of four huge undertakings by Friedland within one year of Summitville's coming into production in 1986: China, the Ridgeway project in North Carolina, the joint venture with Cornucopia Resources Ltd., and the merger with Quartz Mountain Gold Corporation. In looking at each of them it is well to remember that the total effect presents an enormous good news-bad news picture.

By assuming these four obligations, Friedland first of all lines up a huge potential for gold production: in addition to Summitville's 617,000 ounces of recoverable gold (on the basis of current reserves), the Ridgeway mine would produce 910,000 ounces, and Quartz Mountain somewhere between 400,000 and 1.2 million ounces of gold. Cornucopia, still an unknown quantity, might have recoverable gold in the area of the lower end of Quartz Mountain's estimates.

This huge inventory of recoverable gold, not counting the offshore benefits in China that might result from activity there, would place Galactic in a preeminent position among North American gold producers. But offsetting that is the fact that an immediate and continuing financing program of mammoth proportions would become necessary.

Not that financing large projects is new to Friedland and his senior management, but following the disappointing first production year at Summitville, including throughput and other problems, the inherent dilution and the lag before potential earnings from these new sources could begin to accrue might conceivably produce investor nervousness, according to Garson. The more traditional strategy would likely have been to develop earnings to a higher level and then acquire the new projects in concert with further earnings growth.

In most mining circles slow and steady may win the race, but that has never been Robert Friedland's method. His initiatives seem always to be predicated on the fear that the deal will fade if it isn't done before sundown. He followed such a course with Summitville, with spectacular results that left no question that his instincts had been right.

Ridgeway is an extremely rich opportunity. In May 1986 a wholly-owned subsidiary of British Petroleum North America, Inc., Amselco Minerals Inc., offered, and Galactic accepted, a forty-nine per cent interest in the Ridgeway property in South Carolina, at a cost to Galactic of approximately $36 million. The Ridgeway ore body was estimated at a probable 60 million tons, grading an impressive 0.032 ounces of gold per ton. Even Galactic's half of this project indicated potential gold recovery of half again the total of recoverable gold at Summitville.

But the cost is substantial.

"With Galactic already embarked on a path of financing both the Ridgeway project and the Chinese mining obligations, and potentially Cornucopia and Quartz Mountain," says Garson, "the effects of these financings between now and 1989 are immediately dilutionary to its current earnings."

The Cornucopia venture is in a way more an open option on the part of Galactic than a pooling of forces. The actual joint venture agreed to in April 1987 calls for Galactic to explore and develop deep horizons underlying Cornucopia's Ivanhoe property in Nevada. The president and chief executive officer of Cornucopia, incidentally, is Andrew Milligan, a former senior officer and director of Chester Millar's Glamis.

In return for the issuance to Cornucopia of 420,000 shares of Galactic, approximately $3 million at the time of the agreement, the latter will have several options pertaining to the property in question, sequentially including conducting a deep drilling program, completing a feasibility study, and financing the bringing of a mine to production. In consideration of these options, Galactic will earn fifty per cent of the revenue from the operation of any mine below the 400-foot level.

Analysts, Garson included, are of the opinion that there will be an eventual merger between Galactic and Cornucopia should a successful underground development take place. That possibility, and Cornucopia's proven shallow deposits of 8 million tons grading 0.045 ounces of gold per ton, make the Ivanhoe gambit another extremely interesting move for Galactic.

While up-front financing is not a large item for Galactic in this project, operating costs for a major deep drilling program will be considerable, and the issuance of 420,000 shares of treasury stock was one more dilutionary factor which, given its recent history, Galactic's capital structure could well have done without—at least for the moment.

Quartz Mountain is a very special situation, appreciated by anyone watching gold developments in the western States in recent years. Dr. William Bird, Quartz Mountain chairman, had in fact acquired the Quartz Mountain claims, an extensive group in central Oregon, from Anaconda in exactly the same manner in which Friedland had been able to buy Summitville.

A highly experienced geologist, Bird realized the huge bonus he was deriving from the deal—Anaconda's drilling program, which had largely delineated the extent of the ore body. While a vast program was still necessary, Bird's tactical approach was to drill around and fill in Anaconda's program. Bird and the market both seem confident that a significant ore body will be outlined. The 1987 program includes metallurgic testing and a pilot heap-leach plant.

The newly-merged company can only represent a mutually beneficial development for both Galactic and Quartz Mountain, through the synergistic effect of the whole being greater than the sum of its parts. Under the terms of the agreement, Galactic offered a .45 Galactic share for each Quartz Mountain share. (Mutually accepted "fairness opinions" may result in adjustment to that rate of exchange.)

Here again, the major outlay for Galactic is in treasury stock, but the prospect of bringing in a major mine that could be as much as twice the size of Summitville in its potential will require a huge financing program. Obviously, this was one of Bill Bird's motives in casting his lot with Galactic. (Bird will be named vice-chairman of the new company, which is to be called Galactic Gold Corporation). In the first four months of 1987 Friedland had already completed convertible debenture and common stock financings of more than $57 million.

"Management remains aggressive in relation to new ideas and potential acquisitions," says Tony Garson. "It is through acquisitions and joint ventureships that Galactic's reserve base may continue to expand, which has been the pattern of other successful mining corporations. Potentially, Galactic could be producing 165,000 ounces of gold per year by 1989."

At US$450, that would indicate total revenue of US$74.25 million, a not inconsiderable figure.

And so, half-way through 1987 habitual Friedland-watchers were prepared to wager that the guru who entered the mining industry on hands and knees would continue to perform financial and operational miracles. As wizards do.

————